SLEEPING ON A WIRE

ALSO BY DAVID GROSSMAN

The Yellow Wind
The Smile of the Lamb
See Under: LOVE

SLEEPING ON A WIRE

CONVERSATIONS WITH PALESTINIANS IN ISRAEL

DAVID GROSSMAN

Translated from the Hebrew by Haim Watzman

FARRAR, STRAUS AND GIROUX • NEW YORK

Library of Congress Cataloging-in-Publication Data
Grossman, David.
[Nokhehim nifkadim. English]
Sleeping on a wire: conversations with Palestinians in Israel /
David Grossman; translated from the Hebrew by Haim Watzman.—1st
ed.
p.   cm.
1. Palestinian Arabs—Israel—Social conditions.   2. Palestinian
Arabs—Israel—Interviews.   3. Jewish-Arab relations—1949–
4. Israel—Ethnic relations.   I. Title.
DS113.7.G7613 1993   305.8′0095694—dc20   92-28721 CIP

"Min ha Makom shebo Anu Tzodkim"
from *Shirim* by Yehuda Amichai,
Schocken Books, Tel Aviv, 1977

SLEEPING ON A WIRE

"The Jews don't know enough about us. They don't even want to know that there's another nation here. Who really cares what I feel? Who will want to read your book about us? But it's our fault, too, for not even trying to let you know who we are. We didn't bother. Maybe because we have a feeling that the authorities know everything about us anyway. They're the bosses, you know, the security agents, the state, the Ministry of Education, and it's as if they've already settled everything for us in advance. They've already planned out our future, and all that's left for us is to toe the line. And we really toe it. That's how we've demeaned and wronged ourselves.

"But the Jews have to know what we're really thinking. We've already framed our ambitions, and they contain nothing that can harm the Jews. They can be stated openly and without theatrics: We're not in love with the Jews, not happy, not 'How wonderful, they're here'; but they're here, and we'll have to live *with that. And if we aren't honest with ourselves, we're done for. If we make a big show of it and try to act as if everything's fine, we'll have internalized all of Western politics, and our identity will be lost completely."*

—Mohammed Daroushe, twenty-eight, Iksal

PROLOGUE

One hot night in July 1991, I visited a summer camp in the Lavie Forest. Israeli boys and girls, Jews and Arabs, were standing and debating the state's treatment of its Arab citizens, the Arabs' disregard of Israel's complex predicament, the way the army fights the intifadah. With righteous wrath and youthful charm they hammered home their arguments, worn from overuse. As I watched them, I could not tell by sight who was Jewish and who was Arab. Their features are similar, their clothes and hair styled by the dictates of the same fashions; even their body language is the same, as is the Hebrew they speak. Only the accent is different. I recalled that I had already participated in such an event—when I was their age, more or less, in a Jewish-Arab summer camp in Acre. Then, more than twenty years ago, we might have been distinguished from each other by our dress, language, and degree of contentiousness during a debate, but what has not changed since then is the sharpness of mutual emotion, the powerful need to have this particular individual understand you and confirm your feelings—and the awkwardness and illusion, because at times he is close by, that individual, and then suddenly he is far away, and how can someone so close to me be so wrong about me; how can someone so distant know me so well?

The circle of disputants opened abruptly. A boy of perhaps fourteen, who stood on the outside, was thrust toward me, and a trail of whispers rose and swooped after him. "He's the one who ran away," someone said in an undertone, and the debate instantly died.

"We sat with him all day, three Jews, three Arabs," a boy named Itai explained. "We talked with him, made him think."

The boy, M., listened to what was being said about him. He was a somewhat clumsy, pale type, his movements guarded, his gaze older than his age.

"It hurt me that M. ran away," said Sana,* from Acre. "It was important to me that he stay here, that we change preconceptions together. Because there were two Jewish girls here, right-wing, and they decided to go home . . ."

Murmurs of agreement, Jewish and Arab, and a slight, common sense of pride. I asked M. why he had come to the camp.

"To have a good time. For a vacation," he responded, caught up in himself but apparently not at all put off by the interest he was attracting. "I read that it was a camp for Jews and Arabs, but I didn't realize it was Jews and Arabs together so much. And I—before that, what can I say, being with Arabs really didn't grab me." While he spoke the others were silent, drawn by the confession. "So I came, and right away I saw that it's *really* together. More than I thought. Them and us together all the time. Even at night. And I started feeling uneasy."

*Out of consideration for the reader who does not know Arabic, names and terms from that language are not transliterated "scientifically."

An Arab boy named Basel asked if he had known Arabs before.

"Yes. I was with Arabs once, but not like this. I was with my grandfather's laborers. But with them it was different, and here it became clear to me—I didn't especially like the idea of sleeping together, me and them, in the same tent."

"It didn't bother me to sleep together with Jews," Basel objected.

"I . . ." M. hesitated. "At night I couldn't take it anymore . . . I went behind the tents, until I found a hole in the fence, and I left."

I thought of the way through the forest to the camp—a steep, narrow road between pine trees, the caves, the jagged rocks.

"We warned him not to leave," Itai said. "The forest is full of old wells you could fall into at night."

"It was after nine o'clock," M. continued in a low voice, in awe of himself, as if only as he spoke did he comprehend what had actually happened. "It was pitch black. No one saw me leave. I went through the fence, hunched over, so they wouldn't see, into the forest."

The young people were transfixed by his white face. The strange story stripped them of their youthful cockiness, and for a moment they looked like children. Beyond the small, tight circle, the camp seemed like a far-off memory. Light bulbs weakly illuminated the cots, adolescents walked down the path from the shower; in one of the tents a boy preened in front of a girl, and on the bed right next to them another girl lay on her belly, buried in a book.

"But what exactly were you scared of?" Sana whispered, a lock of hair in her mouth.

"I was scared, you think I know why? That they might rob me. That they'd do something to me . . . I felt really uneasy about it," he said, shrugging his shoulders apologetically. "I mean, about the tent, being the only Jew, and everyone around me an Arab. That we have to be together, for real."

"And did you know where you were going?" asked a voice out of the darkness.

"More or less . . . not exactly. I walked to where I thought there'd be a main road, and I thought I'd wait until morning and find a bus to go home to Jerusalem."

"Did you know the way?"

"I knew I had to go down. I got so mixed up."

"Did you find the road?"

"The police found me by the road."

"They found him in a total daze, crying," whispered a girl behind me.

"How long did you wander like that?"

"I don't know."

"Weren't you scared in the forest?"

"Sure I was scared," M. said, "but I was more scared in the tent."

CHAPTER 1

It was morning in the *midafeh*—the room where guests are received—in the house of Hassan Ali Masalha in Kafr Kara. Passions flared among the men seated on mats; the elder Hassan Masalha was debating with his son. The former was saying, "The Palestinians have only lost and will continue to lose from the intifadah." His son jumped up, mortified at his father's words: "What is economic loss? That's a loss? In the territories they have culture now! *There* they have principles! *There* they have no crime! *There* there are no drugs!" The old man, reclining comfortably on a thin mattress, an embroidered pillow under his forearm, dismissed his son's words with a single wave of his hand. Another elder, Fahmi Fanaka, leaned over to me and whispered, "The Palestinians will have a state, but for us, the train has already passed us by." As I wrote this down, the windows in the large, unfurnished room suddenly shook from a sonic boom. An unfamiliar expression passed over the faces of all those present, skipping like a spark from eye to eye. "It's only an airplane," I said to the man next to me, reassuring him, as we do each other in Jerusalem when there is a loud explosion. "I know," the man replied quietly. "It's probably going to Lebanon." I wanted to ask him another question, but the commotion resumed, the debate between the old father and his angry son, and I forgot the incident.

In Beit Hanina, to the north of Jerusalem, in a small apartment full of burgeoning plants, Adel Mana—who was born in the Galilee village of Majd el-Krum—told me the story of his childhood, and then I remembered.

A long, harsh story. The village resisted the Israeli Army in 1948, and after it was overcome, the army gathered all its inhabitants in the central square. According to Adel Mana, the soldiers shot four of those who had participated in the fighting. Afterward they put several hundred of the villagers on buses and took them to Wadi Ara, where they let them off at some unknown point in the middle of the night and said, Eastward, and whoever returns gets shot. Mana himself was then a one-year-old baby. He wandered with his parents to Nablus, to Jordan, to Syria, and to Lebanon. His first memories are from there, how other members of the family joined them in the refugee camp, how his father would steal into Israel to get money from his grandmother and sisters who had remained in Majd el-Krum, or sometimes to help them press the olives or harvest wheat in the summer.

"At the beginning of '51 we 'made *aliya*,' " he related. "We did what you call 'illegal immigration.' We came in a boat from Sidon to Acre with a few other families from the village. My uncle, Father's brother, was uncertain whether to join us. Of course, he wanted to return to the village, but he was afraid of what they would do to him here. He was also afraid because many were killed when they tried to cross the border. When we set off, he stayed there, in Ein el-Hilweh."

"And then what happened?"

"He married, and he has a family there. We twice submitted

requests to the army to allow him to visit us. They were approved and he came. The last time was in '82. After that they didn't allow it anymore. Now we are almost unable to maintain contact with him. If we can, we send him letters. That's all. If we hear that the air force bombed Lebanon, obviously the first thing we think is, What about him, what about his children?"

It was then, some weeks later, that I caught the glances of the men in the *midafeh*.

In Nazareth I spoke to Lutfi Mashour, editor of the weekly newspaper *As-Sinara*: "My wife is from Bethlehem. She is the spoils I brought home from the Six-Day War, so you see that something good also came out of the occupation. My daughters have a grandfather there, my wife's father. Once the grandfather went to the civil administration to request that they renew his driver's license. He is eighty-five, but his health is excellent and he wants to continue to drive. He came to the administration's headquarters and saw Arabs kneeling down. Not on two knees, only on one. A soldier told him, Kneel like them. Grandfather said, 'I'm already eighty-five years old, and you can shoot me, but I won't kneel down.' The soldier let him be, but said, 'Because of that you'll go to everyone and collect their identity cards.' There were about three hundred people there. Grandfather, eighty-five years old, had to be insulted like that, to have a young soldier use him as an errand boy, and to take the cards from his kneeling brothers. He told the soldier, 'You have power and I'll do it, but why are you forcing them to kneel?' The soldier said, 'How else could I keep an eye on them all?' 'Bring an empty barrel and stand on it.' '*I* should go to all that effort for them?' The soldier laughed.

"This is what my daughters have to hear. These are girls who were born in the State of Israel, and every day they hear a new story from Grandfather, from their uncles, and they're fed up. I should tell you that we have decided to send them overseas to study, because if they stay here, I don't know what will happen to them. They've been through the seven circles of hell since they were small, through insults and curses, through substandard schools, through searches and roadblocks at the airport, and now these stories about their grandfather. I'm telling you that if they stayed here a little longer, we would lose control of them. Had I been in their position, I would have lost control long ago, and I don't know what will happen to them in the future. Don't you know, there's a new generation here. A generation that did not experience our fears, that isn't intimidated by you."

At such moments, almost incidentally, a full, three-dimensional picture took shape as if it were crystallizing in a glass. I really should have recognized it. After all, like everyone else I knew that the Arabs who live in Israel have extensive links with the Palestinians in the territories and in the Arab countries. I knew the historical background, that about 160,000 Arabs remained here after the 1948 war and almost 600,000 of their relatives fled or were expelled. I remembered well the longings of the refugees in the camps for the cities and villages from which they were uprooted, and for their relatives there. But only at the sound of those slight, involuntary sighs, or at the sight of the faces of the men around me draining of blood when an airplane passed overhead, could I for the first time feel it within myself, without putting up any defenses. Those moments were repeated again and again—like the story of the cousin who disappeared in Nablus, arrested by the army for interrogation; for an entire week his whereabouts were unknown. An entire family, in Israel and in Nablus, went mad with worry. And the aunt, in whose house the search was conducted, from whom the entire family's picture albums, all those precious moments, were confiscated. And how you almost die before you find out exactly what names are behind the laconic news on the radio of dead and wounded in "disturbances" in Jenin or in Ramallah, or what goes through your head when the newscaster reports that "all our planes have returned safely."

"My Palestinian brother there," said Hassan Ali Masalah from Kafr Kara, the old man, paunchy and smiling, "is not against my country; he is only against your regime there. He wants to live. They shouldn't kill my brother. They should respect him, and I will respect them. Blood is not water."

"How is it that you Jews don't understand such a thing," a young leader of the intifadah in Barta'a said to me. "You, because of blood ties, are willing to fly to Africa and bring 15,000 Ethiopians in a single day, simply because two thousand years ago they were your relatives. And if they kill a Jew in Brooklyn or in Belgium, all of you immediately shout and cry."

When the realization finally penetrates, through all the functional layers of protection, how much the Palestinians in Israel and in the territories are in many ways a single living body, a single organic tissue, one wonders at the powers of forbearance needed by the Arabs in Israel in order to continue to exercise self-restraint. And one wonders, Do they consider what this restraint implies for themselves, and the significance of their collaboration in Israel's daily routine? How do they excuse the fact that their taxes finance that plane, and the bombs hanging from it, and the soldier in Bethlehem who laughs at Grandfather: "*I* should go to all that effort for them?"

"No, I'm not at all comfortable with the response of Israeli Arabs to the intifadah," said Azmi Bishara, born in Nazareth, chairman of the Philosophy Department at Bir Zeit University in the West Bank. "It is not the same struggle. Certainly not the same price. It's not even a struggle parallel to the struggle

in the territories. Jenin is under curfew, starving, and Nazareth, twenty minutes away, is living normally. But what? We
have *solidarity* with them.

"It makes me feel horrible. It makes me feel sick. Because
I think that somewhere between Palestinian nationalism and
the pitiful opportunism of the Arab mayors there is a path that
can guide us as citizens in the State of Israel. Citizens who
allow ourselves a little more 'solidarity' with the inhabitants of
the territories. So I start behaving a little more like the Israeli
left—what's wrong with that? So I won't be ashamed to march
50,000 Arabs through Tel Aviv. Just like Martin Luther King,
Jr., wasn't ashamed of 50,000 blacks in Washington. I have
no problem with them calling me a nationalist. I'm not a
nationalist. These slogans are not nationalism. They are in
every respect the slogans of good citizens. If the Tempo soft-
drink factory lays off all its Arab workers, I will call on the
Arab population of Israel to boycott it completely! If they don't
want me, why should I drink their Maccabee beer?"

"You mean an internal Arab boycott?"

"Not a boycott as Arabs! Not a boycott as Palestinians! As
Israelis! And as an Israeli I won't be ashamed to have a black
crowd march through Tel Aviv and upset the city. The inhabitants of the territories can't do it, but we can. I should
have and could have organized marches at the beginning of
the intifadah. There was enough anger then for a step like
that. But our leadership died of fear. Our leadership is afraid
that all those nice Jews who are responsible for the 'sector' [he
spits that word out the same way he did "solidarity"] will smile
at us and say in a nice voice, 'You want to be like they are in
the territories? Go on, do something, and then we will treat
you just like we treat them. And remember not to take anything
for granted in our attitude toward you, Israeli Arabs. When it
comes down to it, you are tolerated guests here. And guests
can be shown the door.' "

He is thirty-five years old, black-haired, with a dark face and a thick mustache. At age sixteen he founded the National Committee of Arab High School Students in Israel, the first nationwide organization of Arab youth. In the mornings, instead of going to school, the young Bishara grabbed his satchel and set out on "working tours" of the villages in Wadi Ara and the southern Triangle, organizing high-school students to fight for equality in education. "We closed down the schools a few times, a very militant story. We could decide just like that to shut down a school, no problem. Remember that it wasn't an easy time—in '74 we went around with *kaffiyehs*. That was when Arafat addressed the United Nations and the Egyptian Army crossed the Suez Canal. We had a lot of Palestinian sensibility.

"Today? Today there's a difference between us and the Palestinians in the territories. Our experience is different from theirs. The sensibility is different, too. They can conduct a violent struggle against you. We can't anymore. Not because of the Shin Bet [the internal security service], but because we ourselves are no longer able to see this as a possibility. It is already contrary to the temperament of our population, which has lived with you for decades and is already part of the economy and the way of life and a million other things. The Arabs here are an integral part of your story, even if you haven't fathomed this yet. When the intifadah began, we had to make a quick and clear decision: are we part of it or not part of it? Period. And we discovered that our aspirations branched off at this point from the aspirations of the Palestinians in the territories.

"But in one thing there is no distinction: as far as you're concerned, both we and they are strangers here. Unwanted here. Rejected. And for this reason I say that the old way that Israeli Arabs think about Israel is bankrupt. It can't be allowed to go on. Precisely because of the alienation that you impose on me, precisely because I am frightened, precisely because in your opinion nothing can be taken for granted in your attitude toward us, so I'm also allowed not to have my attitude toward you taken for granted.

"When Martin Luther King put together his movement for equal rights in America in the sixties, he called for total equality, period. Equality that would go as far as positive discrimination in favor of the blacks, in order to correct the injustice of decades. Together with that he had no problem shouting, 'I am proud to be an American,' in other words, as a black man, the country was his, too. The flag was also his. The blacks emphasized that they were no less American than others. Now I ask myself if the American Indians could do such a thing. Can an Indian shout with all his heart, 'I am proud to be an American'?"

"And you, in this metaphor, are the Indian?"

"I think so. From that point of view I am like the Palestinian in the territories. Neither of us is wanted here. Both of us are ignored. And on top of that I'm caught in the perfect paradox—I have to be a loyal citizen of a country that declares itself not to be my country but rather the country of the Jewish people."

Vehement in expression, emotional, a dissenter from birth, his movements untempered, Bishara looks as if a struggle is always going on within him. He lives in Nazareth, in Jerusalem, in Bir Zeit. He likes big cities and divided people. "The most dangerous people are healthy people at one with themselves, people without contradictions—I'm wary of them. I also liked Berlin when it was divided. Now I can't set foot in it. It disappointed me. It became normal."

"And do you feel a link to the land here, to the country?" I asked. "A link to nature? To the view? Is there any place in the country that you especially like?"

He let out a long laugh, a laugh to himself. "You want me to feel something for Karmiel? For Afula? Nothing is as gray as those places. However you look at them. Or Migdal Ha-emek. Would I take a tour of Migdal Ha-emek? You'll find that resistance stronger in me than in Israeli Arabs who have already assimilated the situation and their experience, who have married here, who have children, who go for weekends at the beach. I don't go for weekends at the beach. I don't recognize the beaches in this country. I hate the Israeli beach bum. He reeks of insolence and violence and swagger, and I can't stand it. I feel very foreign among Israelis. It's not just that I have white spots on the map where the Jewish settlements are; I've also got a great emptiness of nature. They always talk about the Palestinians' links with nature and the land. I have no link with nature, not to woods, not to mountains; I don't know the names of the plants and trees as even my Israeli friends do. In Arabic poetry in Israel the names of all the plants appear, the za'atar and the rihan, but I don't know them, can't tell them apart, and I don't care about them. For me nature is, somehow, the Jewish National Fund. All the forests and flora are the JNF. It's all artificial and counterfeit. Can you see me wandering the mountains, hiking for the fun of it, and suddenly the Green Patrol [charged with guarding state lands] comes and asks me what I'm doing here?"

When I met Bishara for the first time, years ago, there was something forbidding in his appearance. I force myself to write this because it is part of the subject as a whole. There's something forbiddingly Arab, I thought—his face is dark, his mustache thick—in the belligerence I attributed to him, all this formed part of the rough outline of the archetypical foreign and frightening Arab. Since then, every time our paths meet, I reflect on that. There is a special joy—joy in the victory of the weak, in the unraveling of any stereotype.

I asked how, in his opinion, Palestinians in the territories relate to the dilemma of the Arabs who live in Israel.

"They look down on us. Yes, yes. Before the intifadah it was the opposite—there was admiration. For a while even phony admiration. Admiration that was meant to inflate the Israeli-Arab experience. Yet I am not proud of anything. What do I have to be so proud of? Of the fact that the Arabs in Israel have not produced anything of significance? No culture, no elite, nothing. Their intellectual life is shocking. What is there for them to be proud of? Of their pursuit of lucrative professions, of money and more money? Of the lack of any intellectual dimension? There is not a single intellectual I can be proud of. Not a philosopher, not a single writer I'm proud of. They're all dwarfs. Look at Emile Habibi, who makes an ideology out of the 'Israeli-Arab experience,' and every time he talks he declares, 'We've stayed here for forty-three years!' What do you mean you've stayed? What's the big deal? But for him staying is a *conspiracy*. Do you understand? [He lowers his voice and whispers.] Some people got together and held meetings and consultations, and after a month of uncertainty they decided to remain in the State of Israel, to keep the flame burning . . . After all, our whole story, of the Arabs in Israel, is no more than the struggle to survive. That's not such a heroic struggle. It was largely a story of cringing, lots of toadying and opportunism, and imitation of the Israelis. And when the Arabs here finally started feeling a little more sure of themselves, they had already turned into Israelis. What Israeli-Arab symbols are there that a man like me can identify with? Nothing. Even when you think that there's an authentic phenomenon like the Islamic Movement, it turns out to be counterfeit. I debated their leader, Sheikh Abdallah Nimr Darwish, in Haifa. An open debate before an audience. I was astounded at how little he understands Islam.

Superficial. He doesn't know it. For him, Islam is only a political tool.

"So where is all the talk about our pride, about our heroism? Listen to a heroic story: Once there was a protest rally in the Communists' Friendship House in Nazareth, and the police surrounded the building. The next day the headline in the Communist newspaper was THE SECOND SIEGE OF BEIRUT! Do you understand? They surrounded the Friendship House in Nazareth! When it comes down to it, the Arabs of Israel, with the exception of the six who fell on Land Day* in 1976, didn't pay much. In other words, it's impossible, it's disgraceful to compare them to the Arabs in the territories. You should see it there; when someone gives a speech, he is the spokesman for an entire history. There are symbols, there's rhetoric, pathos, spark. On our side you hear half a sentence and feel that where we are everything is empty. Our history is cut off."

When he came to our meeting, Bishara was upset. A short while before he had been with his sister in a restaurant in East Jerusalem. His sister is a doctor and lives in Beit Jalla, near Bethlehem. Her Citroën has the blue license plates that show it is from the territories. But there was a little sticker with the word DOCTOR in Hebrew on the windshield. That was enough to get the car torched. "And imagine," he snorted, "there I was helping the guys from the Border Guard put out the fire; it was very embarrassing!"

He was nevertheless able to laugh at the circumstances there, and at himself. So I did not restrain myself from saying to him, "Here they gave you the spark you were looking for." Afterward I asked him whether he was angry at the arsonists.

*An annual day of protest by Palestinian Israelis against Israeli government confiscation of Arab land.

"On the contrary," he said immediately, "I was pleased that they are so good at spotting Israeli cars."

I already knew, after about a month of visits and conversations, that I would almost always get an unexpected response. That the status of the Arab who lives in Israel is so tangled and twisted that I had to stop trying to anticipate, and only listen, to open myself to the complexity, to try to make room for it. Make room for them within us. How does one do that? It is precisely the thing that we, the majority, forbid them with such deft determination.

And here, something like a nervous security guard began running around inside me, reorganizing the broken ranks. It seems to me that the words "make room for them" are what set him off. He is part of me, I've encountered him several times in the past month. Right now he demands to know exactly what I meant—just how much room to make for them? And at whose expense? And is it necessary to open the discussion just now, while the peace talks are in progress? And when the country is trying, with its remaining strength, to absorb a huge wave of immigration? He speaks, and something unpleasant is slowly revealed to me: that when, for example, Azmi Bishara says he wants to march a black crowd through Tel Aviv, something in me recoils. Contorts. And suddenly I am the one facing the test. How real and sincere is my desire for "coexistence" with the Palestinians in Israel? Do I stand wholeheartedly behind the words "make room for them among us"? Do I actually understand the meaning of Jewish-Arab coexistence? And what does it demand of me, as a Jew in Israel? How much room am I really willing to make for "them" in the Jewish state? Have I ever imagined, down to the smallest living detail, a truly democratic, pluralistic, and egalitarian way of life in Israel? These questions race at me, and caught me unprepared—an abstract, perhaps simplistic picture of life with the Arabs was impressed on me from the start, and because of it, apparently, I set out on this journey. I certainly wanted to persuade others it was an imperative, and here, the outer layer of these abstract declarations was quickly torn away, and from within its contents burst forth—demanding, threatening, enticing, shaking the defenses—

Unfolding below the balcony of Tagrid and Abed Yunes's attractive house in the village of Arara are olive groves and fields of wheat. Beyond them is the Wadi Ara road—or, officially, in Hebrew, the Nahal Iron road—and after it low hills, golden in the afternoon sunlight. A burgeoning grapevine stretches over the trellis at the threshold, and inside the house Majd and Sumu—"splendor" and "glory," he two years old, she one—waddle about in their Pampers, whooping at me Hebrew words they have learned—*b'seder, kadima* ("okay," "get going")—and climbing all over Mommy Tagrid. Impossible to have a conversation this way—who will take the children to Grandma? Tagrid will.

"I met Tagrid at her house." Abed recounts their history as we relax on the balcony, looking out over the fields. "I had seen her once before, and I heard good things about her, but introductions—only at her parents' house. I came with a friend who mediated. We went and sat with her father. Her mother, at most, brought refreshments. It was fine. It's a liberal, open family. My family—let's say there's a difference.

"Two days later she went overseas with a delegation, and every week I would visit them, ask what was new with Tagrid, if she had written, if she had called, had expressed any interest.

"When she finally came back, I drove to the airport to greet her. She didn't understand what I was doing there. I thought she would drive back with me, in my car, to the village, but she sent her suitcases with me instead.

"The next morning I let her sleep until eleven and then I called her: How are you, Tagrid? How did you sleep? How was it over there? May I come visit you?

"I came over and we sat alone together. What does alone mean? Every two minutes someone came to take something, to arrange something, and all the doors were open.

"So we began talking. She made inquiries about me in the village, asked if I would permit her to continue her studies. She wanted me to be an electrical engineer, but I didn't want to—being a technician was enough for me. But I promised her she wouldn't have to stop her studies. Even then I saw that her independence was very, very important to her."

"What have you been saying about me?" Tagrid returns, pours juice, brings fruit. Her laughter rings through the house. Her face is sharply outlined and illuminated by a whole range of expressions. Energetic and impetuous. Abed, in contrast, is very careful—part of the hidden tug-of-war of marriage— to keep to a single expression, sober and deliberate. But it is hard to be that way faced with her charm and her bustle, so there is always the shadow of a smile on his lips.

"She didn't stop talking to me about her independence and her freedom, and I promised. Of course." He nods to her, and she to him. "And when I married her, it was a little hard for me. You know, from the very beginning she wanted to do things that I'd never even thought of—'Come on, Abed, let's

have breakfast together.' Breakfast together?! And she would
say, 'Just stand beside me, Abed, be with me.' And I, when
I was still living at home, I would get up in the morning and
my mother would have prepared everything. I would come
home in the middle of the night with friends, at one in the
morning, and wake up Mom: We're hungry, and she would
get up and cook a meal for everyone."

"Those days are gone." Tagrid laughs. "I explained to Abed
what marriage meant for me; it's for emotional support, so that
you have a partner like yourself, right?"

"Okay, little by little I began to understand her. Today it's
enough for me to stand beside her, and that's help for her. I
stand. Talk with her while she cooks. I've gotten used to it,"
he says heavily, as if reciting to himself, "because we're both
working people. We're both teachers. Fairness tells me that
this is my wife, and it won't help me if I'm rude and I say
that I don't want to help. She's tired, too. I don't know how
to cook, but I can help. Straighten things up a little."

I ask, "Change the kids' diapers?"

"No. Not that."

"Why not, really? They're disposable, after all. It's easy."

"No, um, it's not for me. What am I . . . No. Stop it! We
already had an argument about that!"

"I really don't like him to change diapers," she says.

And he: "Bathing them, too. I can't do it alone. Together
—yes. Stand with her—yes."

"And feeding a child? What about that, Abed?" She's pro-
voking him.

"Not that. Only a mother knows how to do that. I lose
patience with the kids after a few minutes."

She: "That's an easy out, Abed."

He: "Even when a woman asks you to help her, she doesn't
want you to do everything. What's a man who does everything?
A man who cooks?"

And she, patiently: "I'm not asking you to change Sumu's diaper. But help me wash the dishes? Why not? That I'm willing to have you do."

"Thanks very much." He brings the exchange to an end and smiles. The crease between his eyes deepens for a minute and goes into shadow.

"In my parents' generation," Tagrid relates, scurrying to the kitchen, pouring coffee, bringing cookies, "the division of male and female roles was not open to question. My mother did not even ask for help. The circumstances dictated she put everything she had into the home. Father worked hard. When he came home, he'd sit down in front of the television, and when he wanted the channel switched he'd tell us to do it. We liked to help him. Mother had no social life. Her relationships were only within the family. Outside the family was forbidden. And no hobbies. No aspirations. No self-fulfillment, other than raising children."

"And what is her attitude toward your way of life?"

"Ever since I've been on my own, Mother has had less and less to say to me. Her advice isn't relevant for me. It's for a different type of woman, a more traditional woman—be acquiescent, always agree with your husband, don't stand your ground. Mother always says, 'It's woman's nature to be weaker and to forgive, and not to argue all the time.' And she always says, 'Don't be so *principled*,' and in that my mother is really no different from many women my age.

"But don't misunderstand me, I have no complaints about her. Mother is a wonderful woman, she gave to us with all her heart. She gave us all of her. If I could only have her natural wisdom. You have to understand Mother within her generation—they lived their lives without my conflicts. There was no consciousness of repression. There was nothing to spur them to rebel, not even to criticism. You'll think it's funny, but I envy them for that, because they received solid values and forms of thought and behavior at home. They were not exposed to other elements that presented them with the opposite, with the temptation. They had security and serenity, and I—" She chuckles. "And don't think that Mother has no gripes about us. Our way of life is perhaps not what she wanted. And she always complained that she had no daughters at home, because we studied and then went to work and married right away and had careers . . . Because just as I miss having a mother who is a friend, she misses having a daughter who is a friend. Things I do hurt her, and I remember that when I wanted to go for my master's degree she yelled at me: Stop! That's enough! You're already twenty-two, get married! What will become of you! And every time I refused someone who came to ask for my hand, she would scream at me."

"She's just saying that so you'll think a lot of guys wanted to marry her," Abed interjects, straight-faced.

"My grandmother once tallied it up for Abed. It came to thirty."

"Maybe they were all bused in together?"

"And what happened in the end?" Tagrid smiles. "I had to battle society, I suffered and argued, and afterward my sisters had it easy. Now I have a sister who's two years younger than me, twenty-seven, and they don't pressure her to marry at all."

I quoted what I'd heard from Rima Othman of Beit Safafa. She said that in London she had met "Arabs that are completely outside." "A boy and girl from the Sabra refugee camp in Lebanon. They originally come from Acre. The girl told me, It's not good that you Israeli Arab women have identified with the intifadah to the point that you're putting off marriage. You have to have a lot of weddings, make a lot of children. They said that if someone from their refugee camp is killed, they immediately hold a wedding on his grave, and the dead person's mother dances."

"As regards the children"—Abed clears his throat—"that is, how many we'll have—we have a dispute about that."

"What dispute?" Tagrid asks. "How many did you want?"

"Not a lot, but as many as possible."

"I'd actually be satisfied with as few as possible."

Abed: "Me too. Six. Okay, five."

"Abed!"

"What are you shouting about? We've already got 50 percent, almost."

"If the next time I have a boy, you're out of luck."

He gags. "But children grow and leave home . . ."

Tagrid turns slowly to him, with all the resplendence of a sunflower. "When I have you, Abed, I don't need the children!"

We all laugh. We even laugh too much. And I laugh, too, as if it all was the warm laziness of the afternoon and honeyed stings between the young man and woman. As if a Jew and two Arabs in Israel can have a friendly laugh over a joke relating to the "demographic threat."

"We have no desire to have more children 'for the homeland' and at the expense of our own lives," Tagrid says. "I'm not selfish, but I think that if I have three children I'll be able to educate them better and bring them up properly; they'll contribute to society much more than nine that won't receive a good education, that we won't be able to support."

"May our holy womb be blessed!" I quote a headline that was printed, until just a few years ago, in the Israeli-Arab press. "Victory will come not on the battlefield but in the delivery rooms!"

Tagrid listens attentively. She meditates. "No. I want very much to have a small family, so I can devote time to things that are important to me. It is important to me to have a career. It is important to me to be a sociologist. It is important to me to work for Israeli-Arab society. If I have a lot of children, I'll be stuck at home. My ambitions will die."

"If I were hearing that for the first time, I'd get mad," Abed sighs. "But I've gotten used to it."

"Admit that it was no surprise to you! Admit that before our wedding we spoke about it explicitly!"

"I talked about that when you weren't here," he says, his face somewhat forlorn.

"You're so fair!"

A few days later I woke up in the village of Iksal, near Nazareth, between Mount Tabor and the Nazareth heights. I wandered the streets—a village of no beauty, cubical cement houses and potholed roads, with electric poles running down the middle. But the yards are thick with apricot and guava trees, palms, figs, and pomegranates. Bare-legged women doused their houses with jugs of water, scrubbed the steps, and beat out rugs. A young woman sent out a clean and polished boy, smoothly combed, and half hid behind her door, leaning on a straw broom, watching him until he was swallowed up by a band of boisterous children. I walked after him, partly for her, partly to test myself—when exactly would the moment come when I no longer remembered her kiss on his cheek and he turned, for me, into *shabab*, a faceless young Arab.

In this very village, a month before, a young woman was murdered. Her brothers and father are suspected of burning her alive because, they claim, she became pregnant by a strange man. When I asked people about her their features slammed shut. "You know our culture," said Leila D. "The Arabs cannot tolerate a disgrace like that . . . they had to kill her . . ." "Still," dared a girl sipping morning coffee with three older women, "they could have taken her to the hospital

in Afula to have an abortion, no?" The three women bowed
their heads, did not respond.

"Had she obeyed the laws of Islam, it would not have happened," I was told by Muhammed Saliman, Iksal's baker and
a member of the Islamic Movement. "According to that law,
if an unmarried girl has sinned, she is to receive eighty lashes
with a whip. If she's married, she is to be stoned until she
dies." Something in my expression, in my secular skepticism,
maddened him; his hands beat down the dough. "But Islam
is very careful. You have to prove the act of adultery or sexual
contact between her and a strange man. You have to bring
four witnesses who saw her in the actual act, four! What do
you think?"

Today there is a machine that makes the *kanafeh*. You mix
flour and water, a little oil and milk, and add salt. The dough
is then poured into a big funnel, from which it drizzles in
filaments onto the circular brown wooden platter that slowly
clangs on its axis. While the baker itemized with odd pleasure
the laws of adultery and the types of stoning, his apprentice,
a deaf-mute boy, gathered up the long golden locks and carried
them carefully in his outstretched arms to the cooling rack.

The baker is about thirty-five years old. His beard is floury,
his T-shirt soiled with egg and oil stains, and his sleeves swollen
with muscles. Pictures of Islamic holy sites, the Kaaba in
Mecca and the al-Aksa mosque in Jerusalem, hang over his
head next to his business license and his VAT certificate. He
has three daughters. "I have never struck my daughters," he
said, and even though I had no doubts about it, he swore twice
in the Prophet's name. The boy behind us filled the braids of
dough with soft cheese, and rolled them up with a quick
movement. "If, God forbid," I asked him, my eyes on the
little *kanafeh* rolling and swelling behind the baker's back,
"one of them commits adultery?" With a sigh he placed his

sturdy arms on the table in front of him and directed his gaze at me. "We'll—put—her—in—a—circle"—he chopped his words—"and everyone will stand around her. And everyone will hold a stone in his hand, and they will stone her to death. That's how it should be. There is no choice. I have pity on her, but whoever makes a mistake," he explained severely, his face producing a deliberate stoniness, an outer crust of faith for me, "has to be treated in accordance with our law. The law is wise; whoever believes in it will go to paradise, and if you do not believe in it, you will go to hell, to the fire. The same with the girl in Iksal, the one who was burnt."

"They burned her," I corrected him.

"Burned, burnt. She died."

"Arab girls are burned daily," Marwa Jibara told me in her house in Teibe. "Not physically burned. When I am burned spiritually, when I hear that they have murdered another young girl like me, I cry out. I cannot be silent. I see what happened in the intifadah. How the women there began to liberate themselves, and then the men got frightened. And at the same time, the occupation authorities helped the religious movements grow, and in the name of religion men again began oppressing women. But they oppress us not because the Koran tells them to but because they choose from the Koran the verses that are convenient for them. Here, my father tells me all sorts of things that maybe in some way he wants to tell me himself, but it's easier for him to say, Our religion, our tradition. He also takes advantage of this pressure. But actually Islam has things that women can exploit for their own good. For example, a woman can give a divorce decree, a *talak*, and not the husband, did you know that?

"So I, when I get married, I want to write in our marriage contract that I am the one that has the right of *talak*. There are already those who have put that in their betrothal contracts. In Teibe alone there are three girls who did.

"Or there are such simple things, like the bride's father always comes and gives her, you know, to her husband. But according to Islam, the father only gives her away if she is under the age of seventeen, and after seventeen she's exempt from that. Despite that, the father always gives away his daughter. What kind of thing is that? Is she some sort of object? Or has she no will of her own and he can market her?"

Twenty-two years old—her eyes are blue and her forehead gleams, her young and affable face bunching up momentarily like a fist, hard and bitter, and her speech is rapid and dense. There is so much to do, to accomplish, to catch up to. "Sometimes I say, if I were Marwa born in France, I would now have at least a master's degree, maybe I'd be preparing for a Ph.D., and my life would be more in order. I would learn more, read more, go to plays, develop. And I—I still don't have my B.A. When I even think about relations with a boy I realize that a relationship would probably demand a lot of energy from me, and I need my energy for places that are more important to me. Or sometimes I think, I'll live without those things. Afterward I think, No . . . impossible. If I don't have the ability to think of myself, how can I have the ability to think of others? It can't be. Without love I stop being human. Without love, what humanity do I have within me? None."

She founded "Jafra," the Palestinian women's movement in Israel, whose motto is "Both social and political change." From the house sitting on the peak of Teibe's hill she pulled strings, made connections. The movement already has a general staff, and there are women's organizations that support her, Jewish and Italian and German women. They have public discussions on the status of women, on sex separation in the schools, on improving the lot of Arab divorcees, and on sex education—which does not exist at all in Arab schools. "Because of that just look, the biological track is always the biggest one at Arab schools, and that's not because everyone suddenly loves biology; it's because they at least explain about the body and about sex. There's no chance of an Arab girl getting sex education in any other way. I used to sit with the older women, I'd listen to them—that's sex education? They talk nonsense, they can't speak openly, every second word is *'eib*, shame, the whole time *'eib*, *'eib*, everything's shameful, everything's bad bad bad. So on the one hand they give us no explanation, and on the other hand they expect us to be, you know, sexy, to attract boys, to get married fast . . ."

When Jibara was six years old her mother died. Almost from that time on she has managed her own life as she sees fit. As a young girl she opened her own store, where she sewed dresses. She paid for a journalism course out of her own pocket so that she would not have to take money from her father. Father Jibara was willing to give her money, but according to Marwa, "I believe that independence begins with financial independence. As long as I keep taking money from my father, I can't talk about equality. Right?"

She told a story:

"When I was in second grade, the teacher told the class—I still hate her for this—'Tomorrow we will celebrate our Independence Day, when the Jews came and liberated our land from the British.' Whenever there was a party I would ask my aunt to bake a cake. She baked me one this time, too. The next morning I took the cake like this, such a pretty cake"—for a solitary moment her voice is in rapture—"and I was about to leave the house, when Father came and smashed and pulverized the cake with his fingers. I didn't understand why he was doing it, and he didn't explain anything. He just destroyed it and left. I cried, I took it to school crying, and I told them that my father had done it and that I didn't know why. I was so naïve.

"Afterward it was Land Day. In Teibe, this man was killed, and I was there and saw him killed. That began to open my eyes. A year later I participated in the first demonstration; only a few people came, because then they were afraid, and I remember walking in the first row, holding the wreath tightly. I was nine years old, and about then I began going everywhere with Father, to the symposiums, the meetings, and the whole time I was the youngest one there, and the only girl.

"At that time I also began to read—by myself, not at school—about Land Day, what days were important to the Palestinians, who were the Palestinians, what was the Palestinian problem, what were we before. I read and devoured and learned everything."

I could see her, a small girl with the ardor that was still apparent in her, and the tenacity, the world opening before her and creating her anew. Because I remembered myself that way, at the age of eight or nine, passionately reading the stories of Sholem Aleichem, stories for children and adults, understanding and not understanding, what is a pogrom, who are the Gentiles, what is exile, vaguely grasping that this was my father's childhood, from which he had been evicted when he was my age; that the people I was reading of had a mysterious link to me, that they were I, but another I. He is very much alive in me, to this day, that child who finished reading *Tevye the Milkman* and accompanied Tevye and his daughters and wife when they were expelled from their home in Anatevka, and who realized suddenly inside, with a wail that broke out and shook him through and through, how hard it was to be a Jew, and more than that understood, for the first time understood and knew, that he himself was Jewish.

"During the Lebanon War I was thirteen, and I began to

go to the hospitals in Israel where the army brought wounded Palestinians from Lebanon. For me it was a chance to talk with real Palestinians, the most Palestinian Palestinians there are. People from the refugee camps. I would go to Tel Hashomer, to Beilinson, stay there three or four days. Sometimes a week. Mostly I would talk to the children there. One boy's entire house had been destroyed, his whole family had been killed, he was the only one to get there, and without a leg. One year and three months old, and every woman he saw he would call Mommy. I spent a long time there; I was thirteen and he would call me Mommy. We even thought of adopting him, my father and I. Then it turned out that his grandfather was alive, and he came and took him.

"So every time I say to myself, Enough. I want to stop it all, I want to live like all the other girls in Teibe, to study and get married to someone in a good financial position, I remember all those pictures, and I have someone who pushes me inside. You have to go on, for all of them, and for yourself, too.

"After the Lebanon War came the intifadah. Those are not just any people in the territories. They are my uncles, because my mother was born in Nablus, and friends, and children that I've known ever since I was born. And here, suddenly, it's our struggle together, so how can I not?"

"So you participated in the intifadah?"

She hesitates for a moment. Her hand is on the smoothness of her neck.

"Okay," she finally says. "It's true."

And she told the story in a single rush of words, almost without breathing.

"Ever since the intifadah began, I felt that I had to be there. On television I saw the Palestinian women demonstrating and facing your soldiers, and I was jealous. I wanted only not to be here. I wanted to take part in the war against the occupier.

Whenever I could I went. I had to see everything, to hear, to talk with the people. I even ended up being in Nablus when your units killed the Black Panthers [one of the armed Palestinian groups], and I went to the mother of the barber in whose shop they hid and she showed me everything, where they came in and the bullet holes. There was an eight-year-old boy there who saw it, and hid under the table when they came in and started shooting; he saw it all and wasn't hit. You can imagine what it is to hear it all straight from people who were there and who took part, and not just to read about it or see it on television.

"Or, for instance, we're always hearing about the murder of collaborators. Once, when I was at my aunt's house in Nablus, at three in the morning someone came by and shouted to turn off all the lights, and the whole street turned off the lights. And the guys went into the Almasri Building and brought out a boy they wanted to interrogate. They were in the building's garage, and my cousin and I peeked out from the window; we heard the voices, and every time they saw us they shouted at us to get back inside. I couldn't sit in silence and not watch it, because when they were interrogating him I said, Hey, good thing they're interrogating, but then the army suddenly came to the alley, and then the interrogators suspected that the boy's parents had called the soldiers, so they took out a dagger and struck the boy. I was horrified when I saw it—they didn't hit him because they'd found him guilty, only because the army had come, you know; they didn't really interrogate him, and they ran away.

"I was there during a curfew. I can't describe it to you. On the one hand, I felt like I was in jail. I felt I was nothing. Zero. That there were people playing with my fate and deciding for me when to go out and when to be imprisoned. But on the other hand, what happened in the house during the curfew! Once there was an eight-day curfew, in the casbah. There was no more milk for the babies. They gave them only water. Afterward the water ran out. People began helping each other. To take care of the babies and the old people. And the hope —it's hard to explain. Now maybe it's changed a little, but when we sat there eating breakfast, the last word at the end of the meal was *inshalla binnisr, inshalla biddawlah,* may we [meet] at the victory, may we [meet] in our country. And when I was invited to a friend's, at the end of the visit I would say, The next time I come to you may it be under Palestinian rule."

Her face metamorphoses across from me; she is transported to Nablus. This is how the people in the refugee camps looked when they told me years ago about the spring in the village from which they had been uprooted, about the orange groves they had lost.

"In my house, in Teibe, when I heard on the radio the names of the fallen, it hurt me, yes, but it was not like actually entering a house and seeing the mother and family of—"

She chokes.

"Excuse me, it's a little emotional for me. When I entered the house of a fallen fighter, it was as if I was entering a mosque. All the pictures of him hanging on the walls all around, and the leaflets, and the letters from all the organizations—all that shows the unity of everyone at this moment, because all share in the grief.

"I would leave and come back to my village in Israel, and here everything is like it always is, life, business, whatever interests the people, and I go on with my life but remain there, watching, and thinking, I don't want to live the way you here live. Even if I'm here, I want to live like they do there. It's true that I don't suffer from hunger like they do. But every time I eat something—okay, not every time, but a lot—I look at the food and think, Now I'm eating. I am full now. I have everything. And there are others that have nothing. And I stop the meal. I was mad at myself, as if I have things that others

lack. Father and I, neither of us has that thing called 'me.'
The me does not exist for us. Father would give his entire
salary to people in Tulkarm so that they could buy food. Now
there isn't anyone who can make up his bank overdraft. But
he can't stop. And I'm the same way."

"And in Nablus," I asked, "did they appreciate what you
did? How did they relate to you?"

"Well, how do you think," she responded with a lilt, her
lips crinkling. "Like an Israeli Arab." She spit out the word
"Israeli." Silence, and an unasked question. Marwa is tense
again. "What kind of label is that, 'Israeli Arab'? I don't know
any group by that name. I'm not Made in Israel. You, for
example, have a sense of belonging to the State of Israel, right?
I don't. That's the difference. I've been living in Israel for
twenty-two years, and I have absolutely no feeling that I am
Israeli! I just have an Israeli ID card. And I won't have any
connection to it as long as Israeli soldiers shoot at my cousins
in Nablus."

"But Israel isn't just soldiers shooting," I interrupt her flood
of speech. "Aren't there other things in Israel you feel a connection to?"

"I can tell you that the children in the territories don't have
any idea what Israelis are. For them, an Israeli is a soldier."

"But you're not from the territories."

"True. But there's a part of me that keeps me from accepting
Israeli society as a whole. Because of it I have to reject
everything."

"Still, try to tell me in what sense you feel Israeli."

She slammed shut. Her head moved from left to right in a
gesture of resolute negation. Silence.

"In what sense I'm Israeli . . . ?" Again a long silence. It
was possible to feel to what extent the struggle for freedom
really enslaves and expropriates parts of her. "There's nothing
I can say . . . Really nothing," she eventually blurted out.

"It's hard for me to find anything Israeli in me." She has worked as a reporter for the popular afternoon newspaper, *Yediot Aharonot*; she works at the Givat Haviva teachers college, where there is an emphasis on Jewish-Arab cooperation; she organized a women's demonstration in Teibe, the first of its kind, in the style of the vigils held by the Israeli protest group Women in Black; she speaks fluent Hebrew. "I'm a stranger in Israel. I'm a stranger in Teibe, too. Still, Teibe is my home. I belong to this place . . . Once I thought I would surely marry someone from the territories and move there. When I was sixteen I swore to myself, I will never marry anyone from here. There are no real men here. Only there. Those who struggle are men. The ones here are . . . never mind . . . but today I am sure that, even if a Palestinian state comes into being, I won't move there, because I've started something here, the struggle for the rights of the Palestinian woman in Israel, which I want to complete. Were I to live in Nablus, or in Palestine when it comes to be, I would be making life easy for me. That is, I would be where it was more convenient for me to be."

"But you felt like a stranger there, too."

"That's true . . . they're remote . . . I even heard that they call us *Arab shamenet*, Arabs who've gotten used to the cream." She snorted bitterly, shrugging her lips. "What do you want me to tell you? That's the way it is for us . . . I don't delude myself—there's no one who really wants us to belong to them. Even when Arafat made his declaration in Algiers, he didn't speak of us. At the peace conference they won't mention us either. So who will take my part?"

Her hands, spread in inquiry, seemed for an instant to be straining at that invisible net that hangs between the Palestinians there and here, the mutual resentment, the jealousy, the accusations they hurl at each other—We remained here, repressed and humiliated, to defend the land that was left in our trust; you ran away, you abandoned the homeland. No, you stayed on to serve the enemy, like a woman who, raped by a man, agrees to be his mistress, while we are preserving, suffering and fighting, the true spark of the nation. But you have turned even the heroic struggle for freedom into a string of murders, you haven't learned a thing since '36. What have *you* learned? Only to talk pretty . . . A bundle of guilt feelings, of charges and counter-charges, a deep sense of betrayal gnaws away at both sides. Betrayal of the land, betrayal of freedom, betrayal of duty to fate—that is, as always, the duty to suffer —betrayal in the very fact that you are different from me; betrayals that no one is guilty of, but still someone must be guilty, because there will always remain some indivisible grain of anger and hurt that is directed against Israel.

I had ascended to the home of Marwa Jibara and her father via the paved roads of Teibe. The sidewalks of the main street are set with olive trees and French streetlights; ostentatious multistory apartment buildings stand there, like housing projects in the nearby Jewish town of Kfar Saba, and in the yard —a tractor or a hay-munching donkey or three goats with their front legs propped up meditatively against a fruit tree. As one mounts ever higher in the direction of the house on the top of the hill, the streets become narrow, gray, heaped with cement, but at Marwa's house, in the little, well-kept yard, there is a wonderful lemon tree, and the house is warm and inviting, buzzing with guests and neighbors and children. People are constantly coming and going.

In the corner of the room is a "sculpture" she has erected, made of tear-gas canisters shot by the police and pieces of wall from houses destroyed by the security forces on "House Day" in Teibe. Ribbons of red, black, and green—the colors of the Palestinian national flag—adorn the pieces of iron and stone. Above her head is a painting of a young man towing landward a boat containing a miniature Mosque of Omar. Around the windows, as around the windows in all the Palestinian houses I visited, is etched—like a kind of ironic frame to the story as a whole—the familiar rectangle of peeled paint, left by the adhesive tape that was used to seal the windows against chemical attack during the Gulf War. Marwa herself is short, yet seems tall; her back is very straight, and her bearing is that of a princess. When one of those present in the room, her father or one of his friends, contradicts her, she cuts through them with a single glance, and I can imagine her, small and brave, striding like a chick, with its feathers standing on end, into the hall in which the Arab political parties convened last year on Land Day. Three hundred men sat there while Marwa Jibara demanded to know why there were no women present. "It was Ramadan then, and the assembly was after the *iftar*, the feast breaking the day's fast. The men had come, you know, to listen and debate. I told them, I want to hear why your women aren't here. I guess you left them behind to wash the dishes and cook for tomorrow. Or is the symposium part only for you and they have to stay at home?"

"And how did they react?"

"Some laughed. One said, 'You know, it occurred to me only yesterday that we didn't invite any women!' He laughed, too. Understand that we are triply oppressed—first political oppression, together with the men; and the men are oppressed, so they oppress us—it's natural, so if we succeed in our political struggle and the general oppression lessens, our oppression within our society will lessen, too. And there's a third oppression, our oppression of ourselves. We still have trouble convincing the Arab woman that she is oppressed.

"It's also because we're all so young. When you look at what we intend to do in Arab society, and then you look at us, there's sort of a discrepancy. There's always got to be a man who will do all those things. Someone strong, with a paunch, who will sit on a chair, and then our plan will pass. Girls on diets, apparently that's harder . . ."

Jafra is not the only women's organization that has become active recently in the Arab community in Israel. Maybe the appearance of these organizations, and the fresh breeze they've brought with them, caused the murder of the young woman from Iksal to send such reverberations through Arab society and to fracture accepted mores, to the point of directing open criticism and demonstrations against this cruel custom. A stranger has difficulty imagining what walls had to be breached by the new women's organizations. In some ways they leaped over hundreds of years in an instant. The bloody law of the tribe on the one side and progressive feminism on the other. A colorful bird fluttering out of an urn carried on the head.

"We've also got the matter of the hymen. To this day a girl is valued by her hymen, and that devastates me. Because there are lots of girls who do what they want with whomever they want, and a few days before the wedding they have a little operation that . . . In other words, they put it back on; they go to a Jewish doctor, of course a Jew, and everything's fine! Here, my neighbor is about to be divorced because she got married; she was a virgin, but there wasn't any blood. Maybe she didn't have a hymen from birth. And now two months after the wedding she's being divorced, and they don't get it into their heads, it's so primitive."

I asked whether Jafra would fight for the right of Arab women to live with women.

Jibara blinked. "You mean—lesbians?"

"Lesbians."

"Look . . . that's very complicated . . . very extreme."

Her young neck turned pink, and she giggled awkwardly. "If she wants to live that way . . . fine, she's free to, I won't dictate her life-style. But before I gain acceptance for something like that, I have to gain acceptance for simpler things that are matters of life or death for us."

Then she told of the *kilukal*. This is actually two words—*kil-ukal*, say and said, or, in simple translation, gossip. It is one of the most efficient weapons in Arab society, a whip to crack over the heads of light-headed young camels heading astray, and over insolent lambs. An efficient weapon that anyone can wield against anyone—but sometimes it may kill. Shutfut, a Jewish-Arab group that battles against murders committed for sullying family honor, estimates that each year about forty women are killed in Israel for this reason. *Kilukal* plays a major role in these murders. Women who have left their villages to study at a university in one of the cities find themselves being watched by an unblinking eye. Educated men and women, seemingly enlightened, cooperate with the stalk-and-kill mechanism that begins with a whisper and ends, sometimes, with a sharp blade.

"We in Jafra are so frightened of it," Jibara says. "With every step we take *kilukal* into account, because we are small, beginners, and want to change and influence, and even the smallest tempest can destroy everything we want to do."

"Is there *kilukal* about you?"

"I don't know. Maybe yes. The most widespread rumor about me is that they arrested me. That I'm in jail. There are people who are astonished to see me—'Oh, we thought you'd been arrested!' "

"And when you walk around the village dressed like this, in a fairly revealing shirt, it doesn't attract comment?"

"No. Because when do they talk about the way a girl dresses? When she's weak. When the only thing she rebels about is how she dresses. When only her difference in dress is her flag. Then they'll talk about her. But when she's independent in every way, they can't say anything about her. After all, I rebelled against everything, not just against the dress code."

Marwa's father, Shaker Jibara, fifty, listens to her the whole time, observing her with pride and some wonder. Marwa got her blue eyes from him, and perhaps, once, his glance was as piercing as hers. He had been a member of the Al-Ard Movement, one of the first political organizations established by Israeli Arabs, and spent time in an Israeli jail; previously he had been a teacher. A small, powerfully built man, adorned with a reddish-brown mustache broadening over his smile.

"First I'd like to set up a men's liberation committee."

Everyone laughs. Marwa does not even smile.

"My father's comment is not frivolous. A lot of things hide behind that sentence. Perhaps Father will please explain himself to us."

"I don't give you all the rights you want, Marwa?"

"Ah! I'd like to ask you, you really didn't feel threatened and you didn't get tense because of the rumors in the village that they were going to arrest me? And isn't it true that you wanted to restrict my activity because of that?"

Shaker Jibara clears his throat, pulls himself up slightly. "I'm proud of your work for the Palestinian people. I'm proud that you work for good causes, but you've got to remember what the limits are and not cross the red li—"

She jumps up from her place: "What is the red line, Father?!"

"The red line—in other words, only to work in an organized, legal way, and also, you know, every community has its morals, and even if I sometimes criticize my tradition, I can't go out in the street and scream against it. I've also got to yield to it, to be rational."

Marwa Jibara falls silent. Her foot drums on the floor.

Her father turns to me: "That's A. B, her temperature is always too high. And I tell her, if you want to continue, bring down your temperature a little. Just 150, not 200."

Marwa, her lips rigid: "Father continues to work in his way

and in accordance with his views, but when it comes to me he won't allow it. He's scared that I'll do what I want, because they might arrest me. He's also heard the *kilukal*, maybe it's even the Shin Bet that's spreading it, to impede our, the new women's, activity."

And she left.

Two weeks later, when we met in Tel Aviv, she came, summery and pretty, as usual boiling over about something, fanning her own flames, wanting me to judge between her and someone who had done her an injustice. She got hold of herself, sighed. "It won't do me any good anyway . . . You see, I give in, too." The young waitress offered her orange juice drenched in a heavy Russian accent, and Jibara checked, "Is it fresh-squeezed?" The young Russian looked at her in confusion. "What do this mean . . . I don't understand the words . . ." Marwa gave her a sideways glance, and a wall of alienation and separation momentarily rose between the two young Israelis. "I don't want from a can," Marwa pronounced between her teeth. The poor waitress melted away.

"My father," she told me at that same meeting, "to this day does not grasp that I am already twenty-two years old and that I am something other, outside him. Outside his body. I don't accept that part about arranging my life for me. I'll fight back. I have to fight him, too. I rebel against him. He acts like every other father in the world. Keeps an eye out for his little daughter, who will never grow up, who needs to be watched. I want to convince him that I've matured. That I've grown up. Sometimes I stand by him and tell him, Look, I'm even taller than you."

I thought of how her father had charged at her when she was a little girl, pulverizing her cake without a word. How violent that deed was, mixing political protest, male aggression, and humiliation of her young womanhood, now so constrained, so clench-fisted.

"But maybe it's a little hard for him, for your father, even if he's progressive and liberal, maybe it's hard for him that you're so extreme and uncompromising."

"If so, that's his problem. Because the way he educated me, it was only natural that I'd turn out this way."

Then she told of her childhood. Of her mother, who had died of cancer when Marwa was six years old. "I have a very strong memory of Mother. Very very strong. I'd run from her to Father because he was more, you know, forgiving. She was what today they would call a 'liberated woman.' Feminist. Many people who knew her, when they see me today, say I'm precisely her. I learned my independence from her without even realizing it. Without her teaching it to me.

"I learned to do everything alone. Even to braid my own hair. At the age of twelve I was already cooking and sewing. A lot of things happen in the world because something is missing, because of the void, and that void also gave me a lot, because I had to fill it all. Today I look back and say, My father really loved her. She was everything to him. So sometimes the thought occurs to me that maybe he, just a little bit, raised me to be like her."

CHAPTER 3

They gathered together: seven members of the Kabha family. All live in the village of Barta'a. Four in Israeli Barta'a and three in the eastern half of the village, in the intifadah.

The village of Barta'a spans the two banks of a wadi, and all its inhabitants belong to a single *hamula*, or clan, the Kabha. The Kabha family line twists and stretches back to the eighteenth century, chronicled as a testimony and memorial on parchment. The clan has lived in its village for many years, far from the main road. They married each other and worked their lands until, one day in 1948, on the Greek island of Rhodes, during one of the meetings of the committees that drafted the cease-fire agreement between Israel and Jordan, someone traced a green line through the valley between the two parts of the village. With a sweep of his hand he sundered families, ties of friendship, land, a fabric of life. The whole, complete village turned into two incomplete ones, and the two amputees faced their separate fates.

For eighteen years they longed for each other. For each side, the amputated limb was no less sensible than the remaining one. Israeli and Jordanian soldiers prevented free passage of civilians, and afterward, when incidents between the armies became more frequent, a border fence was erected in the wadi. Despite this, the separation was not complete. Smugglers crossed the frontier and passed on news and greetings; family celebrations were held on a hill overlooking the other side. A narrow canal was built to bring water from the spring, which remained on the Israeli side, to the center of Jordanian Barta'a, and the women in Israel launched paper boats down the canal with cargoes of letters to their friends. The people would shout the family "bulletin board" to each other over the hills—who had been born, who had died. Mostly they would watch each other curiously, as if they were looking in an enchanted mirror with a life of its own that could show them themselves and their other, possible, fate.

In the Six-Day War the Green Line was punctured. The two halves of the whole tottered toward each other, met in the wadi, clove to each other for several hours, and then each individual returned to his village, bewildered.

"We suddenly saw how different they are," Riad Kabha, the *mukhtar*—village elder—of the Israeli village told me in 1987. "We had already been living with the Israelis for nineteen years. We were more modern than they, emancipated and open. It was hard for us to get used to them. Their internal rhythm was different . . . contact with them was awkward and unpleasant. They had lived the whole time under the oppressive Jordanian regime, and their links with the outside world had been extremely limited. The Jordanian soldiers lived among them and imposed a reign of fear. They were always saying, "Yes, sir," and that affected their entire behavior . . . With them, a married son continues to live with his father.

With us, we already give less weight to a father's advice, and everyone goes out into the world on his own . . ."

I took down his words. I wanted to organize a meeting of the two Barta'as. I did not succeed. Both sides refused. For this reason, after the meetings on the Israeli side I went over to the Jordanian side of the village and spent long hours talking with the young people there. Three of the young "east siders" I met with were riled by what the "west siders" said about them: "*They* suffered more than we did? How many years did they have a military regime in Israel and how many did we? And with us the end still isn't in sight! They talk about oppression? What do they know about oppression? They say we sold lands? Well, there are those who sell land, and there are those who sell their souls."

"Look at it this way," Jawdat Kabha said to me then. "By living here, in the West Bank, I am an international problem. The entire world talks about and mediates for me. No one does that for him. I'm free in spirit, I know that I can say with a clear conscience what I feel about them, about the occupation. He can't do that. He's already completely tangled up with them. He can't even think about it. Better for him not to think."

Four and a half years have passed since then. With much effort I was able to organize a meeting in Israeli Barta'a. The two halves of the village were not excited about getting together this time, either. Yet after delays and evasions, the meeting took place.

The Israelis waited for me at Sufian Kabha's house. A house of magnificent beauty, "the lifework of Father, my two brothers, and me." Actually, many houses on this side of the village look like the projects of a lifetime—huge, rounded, like small seacraft on pillars. The yards are well cared for, containing olive and pomegranate and all kinds of fruit trees. Facing them is eastern Barta'a, poorer to the eye, austere, as if it were stuck to the hill, its unpaved roads kicking up dust and its walls stitched with slogans. Most of its houses are closer to the earth, a kind of architectural steadfastness and devotion—*sumud* in Arabic. We sat and talked in Sufian Kabha's house, waiting for the east siders.

"What did we, the Israelis, experience during the intifadah?" responded Rafat Kabha, twenty-nine, a teacher at an Arab school in Jaffa. "The truth is that on this side we didn't experience anything special. Except for the expansion of our national consciousness. Most of the people here, especially most of the young people, know now that there is a nation. That they belong to that nation, which is struggling for its freedom."

"So now you feel more Palestinian than you did five years ago?"

"Well, before the intifadah I was hesitant about saying out loud that I'm Palestinian. Now I say it openly. Before, if anyone asked me, I would say that I was, you know, an Israeli Arab. Now I'm proud of being Palestinian, because it does not contradict my citizenship," he asserted, "nor Israeli law."

"And how are relations between the two parts of the village now?"

Nasuh Abd Elkader Kabha, thirty-three years old: "Relations are very good! Both now and beforehand, excellent relations!" He clamped his lips shut. He hadn't made a statement but a declaration, one of those declarations that challenge something hanging in the air. He, Nasuh Kabha, was declaring himself spokesman for the cause. "We've always been one family! After all, my uncles live there! Relations have gotten even closer since the intifadah! I really don't know why you're asking."

"Because it seems to me," I said, "that four years ago no one was speaking so warmly of the other side. Neither here nor there."

"No, no. One family!"

"Before the intifadah you were one family, too."

"Now the relations have more—what shall I say?—political significance," Rafat interrupted defiantly. He is broad-shouldered, quiet, mild-mannered, and Nasuh's challenge to me was hard for him to take. "You could say that just as the political situation once pulled us apart, the situation now brings us together. For instance, before the intifadah, a man would be careful about giving his daughter to someone from eastern Barta'a. Now, even though we know that their future is perhaps uncertain, and it is impossible to know what will happen with them, we don't hesitate, because they have pride there."

"And what do you feel when your relatives pay such a high price and you remain passive?"

"We're not passive," Rafat explained temperately. "We give them humanitarian aid and financial aid. We live in Israel, and I'm more or less pleased that I live here. At least I've got some kind of definition; I live within certain borders, in a certain country. And that country has laws. Nothing to be done about it."

"I wasn't asking about your formal status. Your cousin is cooped up by a curfew and you aren't. How does that affect your life?"

"I feel tension, that's clear. Hatred, too. That is," he quickly adds, "localized hatred, hatred only at that particular time. Listen, today, for instance, something happened on their side. It hurt me so much I couldn't eat. You can't have an appetite when you see them peeking out of their windows to see whether there's a soldier near the house. And there were days when the IDF [Israeli Defense Force] went in there and imposed a curfew, and the soldiers walked the streets, and we here were all on our roofs, watching. You see the soldiers going into your aunt's house—my two sisters live there—breaking lamps, closets. I could see a soldier shooting at the loudspeaker on the mosque . . . and when the army goes in there, the feeling of connection actually becomes stronger, all your blood rushes to your head. But I know that I'm subject to the law, and *there's nothing we can do."*

Nasuh: "The intifadah showed me the true face of the Jews. Things I only heard at a distance, and suddenly it was close to me personally. How they go into a house and break things, for the hell of it, and curse, and they include the people from west Barta'a in their curses: dirty Arabs; Arabs, go fuck yourselves—in front of our children, and they even say it in Arabic, to be sure that everyone understands. But what can I do, except help out with money, with food. I'm not willing to give real physical help. I live under the laws of the State of Israel. It hurts me. Listen, on one side are the laws of the country, and on the other the laws of blood!" He falls silent, and suddenly erupts before me again: "But what can I do?! Only envy them, that they are fighting for freedom, and be silent, and tie my own hands, and be furious with myself and silence my inner voice, because there's nothing to do . . ."

Nasuh Kabha is a nature teacher. He studied at a teachers college in Haifa. He has five children. Gaunt and sinewy, he speaks bitterly and very quietly. His emotions are revealed largely by the way he sculpts his words: "I belong to the State of Israel only in the geographical sense. According to an agreement they imposed on me. I am an employee of the Ministry of Education. Receive a salary. Live here. But in the spirit, in the soul, I belong to the Palestinian people. So you tell me how I can educate children in these circumstances. A simple example—I've run into a lot of pupils here who draw, let's say, a Palestinian flag. Now, I've got to tell the pupil that this is forbidden. But the pupil will consider me a traitor. And maybe I'll also feel that I'm a traitor. But if I show any approval of his picture, maybe they'll fire me, or summon me for an investigation. So what do I do? I don't tell him anything. I pretend that I don't notice.

"How is it possible in such a situation to teach young people values, honesty, courage?"

But then the conversation was cut short; I received no answer for the moment. Three young men from eastern Barta'a strode into the room. "Strode" is the wrong word; they swaggered. Three men of twenty or more, apparently from among the intifadah leaders in eastern Barta'a. You could sense how a very slight timidity had suddenly settled over the Arabs from the Israeli side. Not fear, but lowered spirits. After the discussion, when I asked one of the westerners if they still dismissively referred to the easterners as *dafawim*, West Bankers, he took a quick look around him. "You only call them that if you want to die," he said.

The three easterners interrogated me for a few minutes, their eyes trained on me expressionlessly. In the end they consented to talk, calling themselves by false names. I will refer to them below by letters, in accordance with their relative ranks, which were quite evident. First I asked about the changes that had occurred in eastern Barta'a since the outbreak of the intifadah.

A: "Sure, of course there have been changes. Our solidarity and cooperation have developed considerably. And there is also organized resistance to the army. There are youth groups responsible for organizing the struggle against the army. How to defend the village when the army attacks by day, how to defend it at night, and all this in the framework of a contingency plan. Obviously, because of our struggle, we have economic difficulties and social problems, and the organizations work to solve all these problems, and work for solidarity, and they also assist poor and hungry families."

He reached the end of what sounded like a fixed recitation. Afterward he pointed a finger at me. "Write: The '48 are part of us. We share ties of blood and Palestinian identity. The intifadah did not create this link. It only exposed it to some of the people. Most of the people of the '48 had discovered it long before."

I looked at the '48—those Palestinians, like Riad Kabha, Sufian Kabha, Nasuh, and Rafat, who came under Israeli rule after Israel won its independence in 1948—complex people, unraveled people, already tied to Israeli existence by many branching filaments, some of pain, some of hope. Maybe because of this, every time during the conversation that one of the easterners threw out the term "'48" like a lasso to tie them to the pole of their common flag, you could feel something in them twitching, for an instant in discomfort, with a trace of discerning reservation, like the flitting of the pupil in the eye of someone who has been called by the wrong name.

I turned to them and recalled the harsh things I had heard about them during my previous visit here, from their relatives in eastern Barta'a.

"I know the people who told you that," Sufian Kabha responded. "I don't think that whoever said that to you has more national pride than I do. I only know that I've gotten over the whole dilemma of my identity as a Palestinian in Israel. You can't say I'm 'dormant.' On the contrary, I've invested thought in it, perhaps no less than he has. I had to explain to myself circumstances more complicated than his—how to live in an Israeli state and also fight for my people. I don't have a dual identity nor do I have a blurred identity, and I certainly don't have a dormant identity. I've learned to fit my Israeli citizenship and Palestinian identity together, and it is now a single identity, only more complex."

The easterners listened to him attentively. Afterward A

opened: "With regard to the book *The Yellow Wind*—that is, with regard to what you wrote about Barta'a—it wasn't objective. The criticism you heard about our brothers in the west, and also what they supposedly said against us, came from people who now stand against the intifadah or who do not assist it. Such people have no right to determine who has understanding and who doesn't, who has national consciousness and who is a Palestinian."

A spoke Arabic and I, who knew that he and his comrades spoke Hebrew, suggested that we now speak that language. He shot a long glance at me and sputtered contemptuously, "I know only Arabic!"

This was one of the few times during these interviews that people spoke to me in Arabic. The rest of the conversations reported in this book took place in Hebrew, unless otherwise stated. This, of course, is one of the ironies of the situation —when I met Palestinians in the territories they spoke to me in Arabic, made accusations against me in Arabic, hurt and laughed in Arabic. It was very clear where their world and mine were. Things had different names. Even the intonations were those of another language; that internal melody conveys something that words cannot. When I translated what had been said to me from Arabic to Hebrew, it was sometimes fascinating to see the points of contact and similarity between the two sister languages. The Arabic word for "war," for instance, is *harb*, which to my Jewish ears sounded sharp and immediate, yet also ancient, since its root appears in the Hebrew word for sword—and in the Hebrew word for catastrophic destruction, as in *hurban habayit*, the destruction of the Temple in Jerusalem. When things were said to me in Arabic, by Arabs, they always had a more definite, unambiguous, and sharper quality.

Now I was speaking to Israeli Palestinians in my own language, in Hebrew, with its special slang and literary references and protocol, and this was confusing. Even Yiddish creeps in, as when a member of the Islamic Movement tells me that his interest in the Israeli government is purely financial—"It's just gelt, understand? *Gelt!*" The everyday conversation of Palestinian Israelis sparkles with expressions from the Bible and the Talmud, from Bialik and Rabbi Yehuda Halevy and Agnon. Poet Naim Araideh effuses: "Do you know what it means to me to write in Hebrew? Do you know what it's like to write in the language in which the world was created?" When all this is said to me in Hebrew, something gets irretrievably tangled, knotted up in itself.

Language brings out certain nuances of consciousness. It has a temperament and libido of its own. Even one who is unaware of all the mysteries and secrets of the language he uses comes to know instinctively, non-verbally, the huge reservoir of codes that act on different levels and offer ways of addressing reality. One of the marks of the enemy is that he makes use of other names, opposed to mine, in order to describe me and my world. From this point of view, the Palestinians in Israel can certainly *also* be enemies. They no longer, however, have the doubtful privilege of being *only* an enemy. Anyone who has assumed a language the way they have assumed Hebrew has also become subsumed in it.

And when they attack or despise me in Hebrew, there is something confusing and implausible about it. Sometimes the threat is augmented by the similarity of the language, but sometimes the very use of Hebrew moderates the declared alienation. When Sa'id Zeidani promises me that if Israel does not grant him and his children equal rights "I'll try to make your lives bitter," his words make me shiver from the depths of my Hebrew consciousness, which remembers how in Egypt "they made their lives bitter with hard bondage." When, however, Zuhir Yehia explains how Palestinians in Israel must take care not to have any contact with the Shin Bet and concludes with the rabbinical maxim "Beware the authorities," I know that we speak not only the same language but the same code.

I don't know if there have ever been so many non-Jews speaking Hebrew. I've heard an estimation that today more Arabs than American Jews speak Hebrew. One thing is clear—the Arabs and Jews in Israel have a common language, with all that this implies. There was a period—about a thousand years ago—when Arabic was the literary language of Jews all over the Arab empire. Maimonides wrote many of his works in Arabic, among them *The Book of Commandments* and *The Eight Chapters*; Yehuda Ibn Tibun, the greatest translator of Arabic works into Hebrew, testified in the introduction to his translation of an important work of philosophy and mysticism, *Obligations of the Heart*, that most Jewish community leaders in Mesopotamia, Persia, and Palestine spoke Arabic, and that the Bible, the Mishna, and the Talmud all had Arabic commentaries written on them, "because all the people understood that language."

One might suppose that today's Hebrew speakers would better understand how the Arabs experience life in Israel if they knew Arabic and could be sensitive to the worldview and nuances of Arabic and its culture. In a country like Canada, where there is a large French minority, civil servants must be able to speak both English and French. In Israel, where Arabic is an official language, there was a decision in 1988 by the then Minister of Education, Yitzhak Navon, to require all Jewish students to study Arabic at school. That decision has still not been fully implemented—the target date is the year 2000. I am not convinced that these students will be able, by the end of their studies, to read a book, or even a newspaper, in Arabic. They might, however, be able to engage in everyday, practical dialogue with Arabs.

The men of eastern Barta'a speak Arabic clearly.

A: "We want to talk first of all about the subject of the liquidations, which in Israel they totally distort. The constitution of the intifadah states that not every Israeli agent should be murdered. A collaborator will be murdered if that accords with his crime. If his crime caused death, they will kill him. But if it caused only damage and not death, he will not be killed. They will only give him twenty-three lashes and send him on his way. That's all. But you people don't understand that! You should know that with us an action like that has all kinds of stages and procedures! We have an investigatory body. Like your intelligence agency. We have files on suspects. They catch him, interrogate, try to understand him; if he killed, he'll be killed. And there's a committee of seven or eight people who decide what to do with him. They don't just come out of nowhere and cut off his head, what do you think."

Riad Kabha, the *mukhtar* of western Barta'a, listens silently to this explication. When I ask him what he thinks, he shrugs his shoulders, hesitates for a moment, adjusts his glasses, and decides to speak in Hebrew. "Well, these murders are apparently part of the intifadah . . . and you should know that they check out every person very well before they kill him, warn him . . ."

"And do you accept that? Do you see it as something worthy of your support?"

"Look, I also criticize it. I say that it's not good, but if after a long period the person keeps on doing it . . ."

"It's an internal Palestinian matter!" interjected A. "You are forbidden to interfere!"

For a moment I was unsure at whom he had directed his order—only at me, the foreigner?

"Maybe it's possible to say," I asked the Israeli citizens, "that in your case, over the last forty years your thinking patterns and even national character have developed differently from those of the Palestinians in the territories?"

Rafat laughs. "The difference between us and them is mostly that we're under more pressure than they are . . . making a living, loans from the banks, our responsibilities, our overdrafts."

A taunts him, intentionally switching to Hebrew: "You've taken out a mortgage, eh?"

"I don't think that a different national character has been created among us," responds Sufian Kabha, soft-featured, slightly stooped, as if overburdened by troubles. "What happened to us is that, until '67, we were isolated from the sources of the nation, both geographically and culturally, and that delayed the development of our Palestinian national identity. And if you ask why there was no violent resistance to the regime among us, as there is with them, I think that it's because the PLO conceded the Israeli Arabs. The PLO, in the mid-seventies, said that it was developing a diplomatic rather than a military strategy. So it always demanded that the Arabs in Israel, as part of the Jewish state, conduct a purely political struggle. It did not ask them to make an intifadah in Israel. The Israeli Arabs accepted this, because they saw it was in their own best interests."

"And you don't feel that they in fact betrayed you? Gave you up to the Israelis?"

"They did not betray us." He shook his head. "If a Palestinian state is established in the territories, I'll feel that it is being established for my brother in the other Barta'a. If Arafat says that I'm part of Israel, I accept that just as I have to obey the head of an Arab family, as if Father divided his land between his sons. I'm prepared to accept that, even if my brother's portion is better."

I asked the people of the other Barta'a what changes, in their opinion, the intifadah had made in their brothers in Israel.

"Now the '48 know who they are," C asserted, "because there were among the '48 some, not many, who became so much a part of Israel that their consciousness went into hibernation. They got some rights, got a certain education that wanted to make them into citizens, to make them Israelis, and that of course had some effect on a few people who lacked consciousness. Not everyone, you know, has consciousness."

"And did you expect that your relatives in the Israeli Barta'a would behave differently, or provide a different kind of support for your struggle?"

A is the primary speaker. His comrades speak only with his approval. Every gesture and expression of his exudes scorn and arrogance. "It was decided prior to the intifadah that the Arabs of '48 did not belong to the framework of the intifadah. That they would provide only political, moral, and economic assistance."

"That's not an answer," I pointed out. "That's a press release. I'm asking about your feelings."

"I don't think about what he does or doesn't do for me!" A fumed. "When you're under curfew, when the army surrounds you and knocks on the door, do you have time to think about someone else? I save all my thinking power for resisting the occupation! To keep going!"

"But you still made attempts to drag them into the violent struggle."

A calmed himself down and thawed out a smile. "That was only for propaganda purposes. We knew that if we did something in eastern Barta'a, no one would pay any attention to us, because we're far off the road. But if we were to do it in the Israeli Barta'a, everyone would come. Newspapers and television. It was just a ploy. Tactics."

A few days later I met a young Israeli Palestinian, about thirty years old, from Israeli Barta'a, who had not taken part in our conversation. From him I learned a few things that I had no chance of hearing at that encounter. He said that the people of his village were very anxious about the struggle the easterners had begun to conduct on their western land. It included raising PLO flags over houses despite the objections of their owners. One homeowner who dared remove such a flag had been severely beaten. It also included painting anti-Israeli slogans on walls and setting fires in the forests near the village. The leaders of Israeli Barta'a sent a delegation to the other Barta'a and petitioned the intifadah leaders to consider their position. During these talks the people of Israeli Barta'a were subject to a harsh indictment: "We're fighting for you, making a country that you'll be able to live in, too, while you go on with your lives as usual. They're killing us and you give only money, not blood," they told them. Also: "What kind of common fate is it when you live like that with the Israelis who torment us?" But in the end, after receiving instructions from "outside," both boundaries and expectations were defined. Even so, there is still tension, even outbreaks of anger. "This week, for example," the Palestinian Israeli told me, "there was a wedding in the village, and a Palestinian had just been killed in Jenin. The groom's mother wanted music. Some young people from eastern Barta'a came to her and told her that if she put up the loudspeakers they would send four or five masked intifadah fighters to break up the wedding. She gave in." I asked him if my impression was correct that the people of his village were afraid of their brothers in the east. "Of course, there's fear. If you take down one of their flags, it's as if you're against the whole intifadah. There's a lot of violence in them now. They're wilder. Their entire family structure has been destroyed. The adults have no control over them, and the police won't come here every day to save me from them. Even if I brown-nose the police and the authorities, I always have to remember that I live in Barta'a and have to keep up good relations with the easterners."

Riad Kabha from Israeli Barta'a: "During their curfews, there are people on our side who warn them. We're closer to the main road, and if someone sees the army coming along the road, he can give a warning. On the telephone, or by whistling, or . . . [a quick exchange of glances] . . . never mind. The main thing is that we try to notify them. And during the curfew a lot of young people from the other Barta'a who run away from the army come to us, and there are those among us who open their doors to them . . . and we go visit their wounded in the hospitals, and we look after the families of their prisoners, and we put out press statements if they're hurt."

I suddenly had a feeling that I was not all that expendable there. That perhaps, without intending it, I had given the Palestinians living in Israel a rare opportunity to say a few clear things to their brothers in the other Barta'a.

". . . and that's not all," Riad Kabha continued. "The Israel Lands Authority suddenly gave us fifty plots in the Build Your Own Home program for young couples. And we need land like the air we breathe. But what should we do—the Authority chose a tract that belongs to someone from eastern Barta'a, one that the Authority considers abandoned land, that it can hand out as it sees fit. So no one from our side agreed to build there."

Sufian Kabha: "After the army completes its mission [Sufian the Israeli said without noticing, "completes its mission"; A, describing the same kind of action, said, "When the army attacks the village"], you immediately see a caravan of cars and people running from western Barta'a eastward. They're running to see what happened, who was hurt. True, it's a symbolic act, but it shows them that we care about what happens there. That we don't close the door to them. We can't do more than that. What do you want? If I, for instance, were to go there when the army was there, the soldiers would say I was working with the masked fighters. So it's better for me to keep myself safe, and my feelings to myself. I can feel them without actually being there."

"You know the Arabic proverb that the one who counts the blows is not at all like the one who receives them," I said. "Have you in the Israeli Barta'a, during this entire time, done anything, even symbolic, to identify with the hardships and suffering of your relatives? To demonstrate for your children —as an educational act—your common fate?"

Hesitation. They glance at each other. For a while they had refrained from holding wedding celebrations, like their West Bank brothers. Yes, but now the celebrations had resumed. What could they do? Whom will it help if we suffer, too? And we suffered a lot . . . The roadblock at the entrance to the village doesn't distinguish us from them. They humiliate all of us there . . .

Really, I thought, why am I nagging them? After all, I know the answers, which are of human dimensions. What, in any case, did I expect when I asked to meet with the two parts of Barta'a? Did I hope that I would find some kind of common fate in life and death? A heroic covenant of blood?

Maybe I read too many books when I was young. Any hope we have lies in the cautious and troubled prudence of the Palestinians. And anyone who, like me, is the scion of a nation of expert survivors can well understand this shared common sense, as well as its price. They had decided not to participate in the intifadah, and so had been separated by a clear line from the Palestinian struggle (and they—in their internal code—understand better than anyone else the meaning of that separation). They support the struggle financially and morally, and for that reason had been propelled into the margins of Israeli society, losing social advantages and the precarious legitimacy they had gained after much labor. They judiciously looked after their security, and they lost a great deal. There, in the expansive home of Sufian Kabha, over coffee and baklava, when my eyes wandered between the two groups, between the two sets of countenances, that of the exclamation point and that of the elision, it became very clear and concrete to me. Israel may well magnify the feeling of a common fate that Israeli Palestinians feel with their brothers—in the negative, hostile, and tragic sense. The more it represses their brothers, the more Israeli Palestinians will be forced to amplify their own Palestinian nationalism, and the more it will chain them to automatically making themselves into representatives of the other side—something that is not always to their liking. When any of them made a "declaration" to me, it was clear from his expression that he realized how empty his voice sounded. They sat there, cowering a bit, apologetic, guarding both their flanks, soberly observing the nationalist fervor of their other cousins, the militant flush that set them off every few minutes. Facing each other, the two sides looked like two sides of the same rug, and one's heart was actually drawn to the confused, hesitant ones, who implore us to be discerning and generous enough to get them out of here already.

"They gave you a little show," that same Israeli Palestinian, from the same *hamula*, told me when I met him a week later and described the encounter to him. "There's no real connection between the Barta'as. They only unite when there's trouble. But normally—it's like neighbors. If there's a wedding in the other Barta'a, the immediate family goes and that's all. And they don't come to us. We actually tried to organize something, joint soccer games, but there was only one game. At first, our young people were jealous of theirs, who were fighting and being heroes, so they hung up some flags, too, or maybe they didn't [Note: After the massacre on the Temple Mount, PLO flags were flown in eastern Barta'a, but in western Barta'a there were only black flags], or burned Israeli flags, or maybe they didn't. Eighteen of our young people were arrested for a few months. They received harsher sentences than on the other side. But after they saw how much money the lawyer and trial cost their parents, they stopped it. Enough. Barta'a has proven that the Green Line exists."

Toward the end of the meeting I asked the people of Barta'a if when, Allah willing, the peace talks began, they did not want to request that the strange circumstance of divided Barta'a be remedied. Just as an uncaring hand had cut the village apart, it could now, if the opportunity came, reunite it—heal it.

Riad Kabha: "It was our fathers' mistake that they accepted quietly what had been decided about them. We today will not accept another such decision. We will not agree."

"I don't want there to be two Barta'as," A responded, "I want there to be one. Under Palestinian rule."

Sufian Kabha, the Israeli: "I . . . what can I say . . . Look, it would be nice if the Palestinian state grew by about two or three kilometers and I and my land were included in it. I don't care where I am."

"Still," I persisted, "there would be a big change in your life, you'd live under Palestinian rule."

Sufian: "If it helps bring peace . . . fine."

"That's a nice sound bite, but I'm asking you, Sufian, where would you like to live?"

He laughs. "Ask Nasuh first."

Nasuh also smiles to himself. Refuses to answer. Refers me back to Sufian. The other Israelis avoid my gaze.

"I'm asking this because here there's no problem of up-rooting people from one place to another, or of being separated from your land. But the border itself could move, such that your particular problem would be solved. The question is only *where* you would like it solved: under Israeli rule or in some kind of Palestinian entity?"

"Then I want to move there . . ." Sufian concludes faintly.

"You want to be part of the Palestinian state?"

"Look, I still don't know what there will be there, I'm not sure what kind of government will be there . . ."

"A democratic government!" A from eastern Barta'a lashes out. "What else would there be?!"

Silence. Something swift, unnamed, passes through the four Israelis.

Rafat cannot stand the silence. "I'd be very happy if there was a Palestinian state," he said sullenly, "but I'll be even happier when I can live in Israel and be the Palestinian state's ambassador here. Just like American Jews—they live in the U.S. but belong to Israel."

C, the easterner, says, "I don't care. Under Israeli rule or under Abu Amar's [Arafat's] rule. The main thing is to be with my land."

His words surprised me. I asked him to repeat them, and he did so and added, "If there is a Palestinian state, I am ready for them to unite Barta'a even under Israeli rule. The main thing is that we not be divided."

A and B seconded him, and explained, "The main thing is that they not cut apart the lands again." For a moment it sounded like an interesting version of Solomon's justice—the baby itself asked to stay with the strange mother, so as not to be cut in two. On second thought, it was an expression of a characteristic pattern of behavior among Palestinians on both sides of the Green Line—the supreme loyalty is not to country or to nation; loyalty is, first and foremost, to land and family.

A future agreement on the unification of the village—even under Israeli rule—may return the people of eastern Barta'a to the large tracts of their land that remained in Israel and which are now administered by the Israel Lands Authority or even by their Israeli brothers. "Every Arab has two mothers." Nasuh laughed at my astonishment. "First, father's wife, and the second mother is the land. The land tells us where to live."

"If they unite us, then only in Israel," the anonymous resident of the Israeli Barta'a told me. "I can't even conceive of living in a Palestinian state. It will be a new country in which there will certainly be civil war. And there won't be work. And there will be a government of young people, violent and unbending; even their children have changed, they haven't gone to school for four years, everyone is outside the structure; and I still don't know how they will treat us, because we were in Israel. I've already gotten used to living here."

"That's a compliment to Israel," I said.

"That's true," he said.

"You wouldn't have said things like that forty-three years ago, or even twenty years ago," I said.

"Life has a power of its own," he said.

At the end of the meeting with the residents of both Barta'as, when he walked me to my car, Riad Kabha told me a story. I had heard it once before, but this time something was added: "We are here, in this very house, thanks to the guys from eastern Barta'a," he said. "In '72, when the army wanted to put up a fence around the village and make a firing range next to us, in Israeli Barta'a they wanted to meet with the Minister of Defense, to write letters to all the important people, and the people from eastern Barta'a came and said, What do you mean you're going to talk, to go to court?! They came and sat under the bulldozers and didn't let the army by. That's how we liberated that land," he exclaimed, and I could see that he was privately enjoying the very use of those heroic words, so much a part of Palestinian rhetoric: "We liberated that land."

Then he raised his head and looked me in the eye, Riad Kabha, whose hair had gone silver in the four years that had passed, Riad who puts all his time and strength into Givat Haviva, an educational institution that works for coexistence and tolerance between Jews and Arabs, who has spent his whole life running around devotedly, almost hopelessly, between the two rival sides. He looked at me, and his eyes, behind the lenses of his thick glasses, began slowly to smile in resignation and self-irony. "Okay, okay, so *they* liberated the land for us."

CHAPTER 4

"I am Anwar Shadfani, twenty years old, from the village of Iksal."

"I am Suleiman Zuabi, twenty years old, also from Iksal."

"We've been in the same class over the years. I majored in biology."

"I majored in sciences."

"I finished high school in '89, and I've been working ever since in home renovation, agriculture, in the fields, non-skilled work."

"I work in construction. I studied computer science at the Technion, but I dropped out after half a year, because in our sector there's no demand for computer professionals."

"Now I live in my parents' house. We get along well, pretty well—well, not all the time. They argue with me over when I go out, how I come back late at night. I'm always going to Tiberias, Haifa. There are discothèques, places to sit, girls. You can hear music."

"Me, my dream is to make money and then study philosophy. But you can't study philosophy because you won't make any money. On the other hand, philosophy is thinking. That's the freedom you have, that you can think what you want. And in life—okay, you can also think, just don't say everything out loud."

"I'll go to Germany for five years. I applied to Munich, to study theater. That's been my hobby for a long time. An Arab here can say something out loud in the theater. I once heard that someone said, Give me theater and I will give you revolution. When you see an Arab actor standing on the stage, it's an outlet for what you feel. Even if he's playing a Jew, even if he plays an occupying officer, he shows the Jews, underneath his role, what an officer should be."

"But here in Israel only the theater is open to us. We don't make it in anything else."

"For instance, I would like to be a police investigator. An important one, like Columbo, let's say. But to be accepted into something like that I need to get more than 600 points out of 800 on the standardized test, and I can't get that here."

"The standardized test—we go there, and it's all very abrupt for us. New. The method, the kind of thinking, the type of test, the time limits on the questions. Like, how are you supposed to divide your time? Lots of questions and a short time."

"They should have taught us test-taking in school."

"During the test you have to manage a lot of things at once. Like a pilot. Quick thinking. Maybe we have a little of that, but it has to be developed."

"For example, they give you a question in general knowledge: Who is Arik Einstein? You know who Albert Einstein is, but you don't know that Arik is an Israeli singer. Or they ask you in history about the Jews, who you don't know anything about. Everyone knows that those tests fit the Jewish way of thinking, not ours."

"Or logic. They think it's logic, but it's written in such

antique Arabic that no one understands. You need a B.A. in Arabic to understand it! I have an Arab friend who did the test in Hebrew and in Arabic. In Arabic he got a 420, and in Hebrew a 580."

"And today they give more weight to the test than to your high-school exam scores, because they saw that Arabs fail the standardized test more than Jews."

"They just didn't prepare us for that in school."

"I know that there are Jewish schools where they teach drama, where they teach art. We always asked the teachers, but we also asked for computers, and for more classrooms in the school, a gym, sports equipment, English enrichment, and we didn't get anything."

"In the end we collected money among ourselves and we bought a computer and printer."

"And the teachers, there are some of them who've been teaching the same thing for years. That's an educator? He comes at the beginning of the class, opens the book, doesn't look at you. There aren't any new methods. He explains the hard words and that's all. The lesson is over. A teacher who never encourages original thinking."

"Guys who finished ten years ago tell us that today we're studying the same thing they learned then. Sometimes the teacher repeats the same joke for ten years!"

Anwar: "I've got Jewish friends, too. From work. From going out. Though I make friends with Arabs easier."

Suleiman: "Jews—it's hard to change their opinion of us. They don't think straight about us."

"The Jews say about themselves that they're open, but that's a joke. They're always hiding themselves."

"If you want to be friends with a Jewish guy, it takes a long time."

"We say what we think. Sometimes we talk too much. You think a Jewish guy is your friend, you tell him everything, and then he acts like he doesn't know you."

"I express everything I have inside," Anwar Shadfani says. He's a nice-looking boy with a styled haircut and green eyes.

Suleiman: "I lived in the dorms at the Technion. If an Arab and a Jew live in the same room, the Jewish guy will go to the dorm office and ask for it to be changed."

"But we actually want to be friends with them. If I were friends with a Jewish girl, she'd change her mind about Arabs, and I think she'd like me a lot."

"It's easier to convince a girl than a guy . . ."

"But you need time, and she doesn't give you the time, as soon as she hears that you're—"

"But a Jewish girl can love you; the power of love will persuade her."

"In the end it's impossible, however, because the word 'Arab' still means something to her. She says 'Arab' and puts together the Arab from the West Bank and me, and then there's already something bad between us."

"Someone who would just give me the time, I'd convince her in the end."

"Yes, if she just knew him, she'd love him."

"I'd say to her, 'How long will we fight like this?' I'd be willing to marry her, too. If there's love, it's okay. My uncle is married to a Jewish woman. Not an Ashkenazi. A Moroccan. I always actually dreamed of convincing an Ashkenazi. From Tel Aviv. And if I succeed in that—I've really got something."

Anwar: "Sure we're jealous of the Jewish guys who go into the army."

Suleiman: "Every boy dreams of being a soldier."

"To hold an Uzi, for instance. You bet I'd like to. I watch

Stallone films. I want to do that, too. But you know how it
is. Even if they forced me to go, I wouldn't. But I dream.
Imagine myself like that. Rambo."

"If we just did training, that would be okay. But not fight."

"If there is a war between us and Syria, should I have to
shoot at Arabs?"

"But you didn't ask the main thing: What army do I want
to serve in? That's what you should have asked first!"

Suleiman Zuabi: "But we give them a lot of support in our
minds."

Anwar: "If you support them a little too much, you're a
PLO agent and a racist. That's what Jews think of you. You
have to give the Jews a good impression. That's what we're
working on. So they'll like us. Then they'll give us rights. It's
also kind of like theater. Living in a play."

Suleiman: "But I've also got thoughts inside. You can't tell
everyone what you think of him."

"So we hide things."

"I've learned things from Jews. Where there are a lot of
Jews, I can't go overboard in supporting the Palestinians, for
instance. I have to lie a little. But the whole world behaves
like that! Everywhere people act the way I do. In America,
for instance, they don't like black people. But the Secretary
of the Interior there can't come out and say he's against the
blacks. In other words, he lies. You say that's a lie? That's
politics. We're already here, what kind of choice do we have?"

Later that same day, in Iksal, I met Ahmed Musa, seventy-
two, who wears glasses and a robe of pure white. He told of
his life with the Jews. For twenty years he was the village's
mukhtar; afterward he was mayor. Today, retired, he arranges

when necessary a *sulha*, a meeting of reconciliation, between two clans, generally after a member of one has murdered a member of the other. He is full of praise for Israel and can tell many stories from the good old days. "Once, it was in '52, the police chief, Segev, told me to bring six horses to Daburia, because we had visitors there. I went. We waited a little. I saw the old man, Ben-Gurion, coming with the chief and with his whole party. B.G. said, 'In '40 I climbed Mount Tabor on a mule, and today I am riding the noble mare of Ahmed Musa!' Okay. We went up to the monastery there, and B.G. was to eat at 1:30. That was his habit. I brought food from home for him. That's what the police told me, to bring a turkey and a sheep. I told him, Enjoy! He said, No, only if you eat my food. He gave us his sandwiches, and he ate our food.

"The father of Raful, you know, Rafael Eitan, the one who was Army Chief of Staff, he was a very good friend of ours. I remember Raful as boy. Working on the combine. He was harvesting. One day I rode next to him on the seat of the combine. He didn't talk much even as a boy. Afterward, when he was northern area commander, one day there was a police celebration in Nazareth. He saw me there and said, 'Guys, do you get along with Ahmed Musa? Ahmed Musa is a great neighbor!'

"To this day we're okay with the authorities. Ask the Jews. Every time there's a wedding in the village, Jewish people come; you should see how we receive them, how we honor them. When I married off my son I slaughtered forty sheep for them. There were three hundred Jewish guests here. Each one someone important. Even Shimon Peres's brother. Gandhi* brought him to me. And Gandhi—every holiday he

---

*Rehavam Ze'evi, head of the extreme right-wing Moledet Party. When he was in the Palmach, in the late forties, he was very gaunt and wore round, wireless glasses.

would come here with his wife, with the generals; he even brought Moshe-and-a-Half,* the Chief of Staff."

I was impressed at his knowledge of our ministers' and generals' nicknames.

"Know them all! Here there's good relations between the authorities and the people. This village is the best one in the whole area. The intifadah doesn't affect anything, either. There couldn't be any intifadah here. You won't find anyone putting up Palestinian flags or painting slogans. We want our children to go to college. That's the most important thing. You can't drink from a well and throw a stone in it, right?"

I asked him what he would do if Gandhi—who was elected to the Knesset in 1988 on a platform advocating the transfer of Arabs to Arab countries—came to visit him today.

"Welcome him. Our house is open to everyone. That's the Arab custom."

"But he wants to eject Arabs from here."

"I'll receive him. What do I know . . . maybe he talks about transfer because he wants to be in the Knesset? I don't know what happened to him. When I hear statements like that from people who were guests of Arabs, whom the Arabs served, I don't understand where their heads went. But Gandhi, I can't say anything bad about him."

"?"

"No, no. Gandhi is a government minister. I was in his house. I ate his food. I can't talk about him."

He enveloped himself in a robe of silence, and listened to my conversation with his fourteen-year-old grandson, Amjad, and his friend, eleven-year-old Usama.

"The land of Israel," Usama said, "belongs to two nations, but the Jews left here two thousand years ago and returned with the help of the British, so they have no rights here, and

*Moshe Levi, the unusually tall former chief of staff.

it's an Arab land. But they're already here, so we have to find a way to live with them. As for the Russians who are coming, that's a big problem, because the Israelis want to transfer us and bring the Russians in our places, and that's bad, if we don't get equality here like . . ."

His grandfather let out a snort of anger and the boy swallowed his words. We talked for a few more minutes, drank coffee, and before parting I asked the boys what they wanted to be when they grew up.

"I want to be a doctor," said Usama, looking warily at the old man. "To treat Arabs, and Jews, too. I won't make any distinction between them. But I won't treat Jews like Gandhi!" he spit out all at once.

"What are you talking about?!" his grandfather shouted, glancing anxiously at my tape recorder. "Gandhi is a very good friend of ours!"

In his wonderful novel *The Opsimist*, Emile Habibi describes a boy, an Arab in Israel, the protagonist's son, who flees from the army and hides in a cave on the beach. His mother calls for him to come out of the narrow, close cave lest he suffocate there. But he says, "Suffocate? . . . I came to this cave to breathe freely. To breathe freely for once! You smothered my cries in the cradle, and when I grew and listened to you, I heard nothing but whispers. In school you warned me: 'Watch your tongue!' I told you that my teacher was my friend, and you whispered: 'Maybe he is reporting on you!' . . . I called my friends together to declare a strike, and they too told me: 'Watch your tongue!' And in the morning Mother told me: 'You are talking in your sleep. Watch your tongue in your sleep!' I hummed in the bathtub, and Father scolded me: 'Change that melody! The walls have ears, watch your tongue!' Watch your tongue! Watch your tongue! I want just for once not to watch my tongue! I can't breathe! True, the cave is narrow, but it is broader than your lives! True, the cave is blocked, but it is the way out!" [Translated from Anton Shammas's Hebrew translation of the Arabic original]

"A member of a minority group, the Oriental Jew, the Arab, always speaks two languages at least," said writer Sami Michael, an Iraqi-born Jew who until about the age of twenty considered himself—in his culture and values—an Arab. "First, the language you speak with the authorities, with the hostile regime, and the regime was always hostile, from the dawn of history, always intending to harm you, or to take something, or confiscate something, or to take a bribe, or to spy. So you have to be careful. From this come all the conversations that sound empty and simply polite—How are you, how are you feeling, how are things going, may Allah bless your mouth, *alhamdu-lilah*; to a stranger it sounds idiotic and useless, but in the meantime he's giving you a psychological test. To see exactly who you are. To appraise you. Forever, as much as you prove that you're a friend, you'll remain a foreigner. You can join a Bedouin tribe and stay with them for sixty years and they'll still call you 'the foreigner.' That's the first language. They have to use it in order to dissemble, to please, to mislead.

"The second language is the one which they speak among themselves when they're alone, and that needs no explanation.

"The third language is an intermediate one, between those two languages—for instance, when you leave the incubator of your family and go outside, to study or work, then you need to find a language in which you can cope with the teacher or manager who is foreign and perhaps an enemy, but you also have to be yourself.

"Other than that there is, of course, the language that every person has for himself: the internal, individual language. When you're a minority in danger, you sometimes can speak truth only to yourself. You can't trust anyone else. Consider what it's like to live with four languages, four simultaneous ways of thinking. You turn into an actor. That's the perpetual theater."

On my trip back from Iksal, after the meeting with the elderly Ahmed Musa, I meditated on how many of the Arab men and women I had met during these weeks had soft handshakes. I wondered at this dialect of body language, this agreed-upon social sign. Because the soft handshakes had been a surprise. Not weak—soft. Warm. Not the crushing thrust of an Israeli-Jewish hand declaring, "This is the hand of a proud, self-assured Israeli who has nothing to hide, and who, should that be necessary, can grind more than just your fingers into a pulp." No, the hands that I shook were not held out to me in order to say anything about themselves—on the contrary, they were to serve as a kind of passive testing pad for the imprint of my own hand. To take measure of its "voice." I continued to go astray with such questionable thoughts, on the edge of being gross stereotypes, and I tried to remember the hand strength of the Egyptians I had met, and the Lebanese, and there are other nations in the region who still don't put out their hands to us . . . I thought of ploys and camouflage, on how the two partners in Israeli citizenship turn their lying side to each other, and that from such a point of contact no true partnership could possibly grow. How could it grow if Rima Othman, whom I met in Beit Safafa, already knows that she will have to silence her children (who have not yet been born) so that they won't speak Arabic in the presence of Jews, just as her mother silenced her? I considered that the Palestinian minority in Israel—like other minorities in the world—stands out and excels most in the field of theater, and wondered whether there was a special reason. I also recalled the secret languages Jews had developed in their various exiles, with words taken from ancient Hebrew, with the addition of suffixes and declinations from the local language, so that the Jews could speak freely in the presence of those who were not members of the covenant. I also recalled what Primo Levi wrote about the special idiom of the Jews of the Piedmont: "Even a hasty examination points to its dissimulative and underground function, a crafty language meant to be employed when speaking about *goyim* in the presence of *goyim*; or also, to reply boldly with insults and curses that are not to be understood, against the regime of restriction and oppression which they (the *goyim*) had established." It was already autumn, and the cotton plants were turning the fields white, there were wild lilies and herons, and I traveled slowly among them, trying to find my way along the snaking path leading from lie (even if white) to deception, and from that—to what Ghazal Hamid Abu Ria of Sakhnin described to me as "our psychology, that of the oppressed—if they repress 70 percent of your personality, you yourself repress the remaining 30 percent, until in the end, even if they no longer repress you, you continue to repress yourself." The road went on from there, to the question of whether, because of this repression that the Arabs in Israel impose on themselves, it is so easy for Jews not to hear them and not to see them, and if this has not opened the way to Jewish self-deception.

My thoughts kept turning to the old man in the white robe. What right had I to criticize him? From what experience could I judge him, and what hand did I—as part of the Jewish majority—extend to him to prove that he can now be free of his caution and his artifice? After all, it is again, always, the same strong, warning hand.

The Jezreel Valley, which the Arabs call Marj Ibn Amer, stretched out from both sides of the road. These are Iksal's fields, which now belong to the Jewish village of Tel Adashim and which the old man worked in his youth. He passes by them every day and sees others working them now. Everything has changed before his eyes, the view is no longer his, the names are no longer his; his homeland has been translated. I put myself in his place, as a young man standing between the defeat of his nation and the new Israelis, and afterward, as *mukhtar*, between his villagers and the military governor; and now, faced with the intifadah, faced with extremists, faced with the piercing eyes of his grandson, facing the old age that weighs on his shoulders. All the while between the two lines of the gauntlet.

CHAPTER 5

Asem! Aaaaasem!

With all that my lungs can muster. Hands cupped to my mouth: Aaaasem!

The echo bounces back at me from the mountains all around. The pines nod in commiseration. The car, its maw gaping wide, shoots up a jet of thick vapor. Aaaaasem . . .

He said he would meet me at nine under the carob tree. Maybe I got the hour wrong. Maybe I got the carob wrong. The directions I received by telephone said that in the forest there is a road to the village. So I drove into the forest, and now I have been wandering around and losing my way for almost an hour. Somewhere in the heart of this wood there is a village that does not exist, and in the village people I was going to visit because they do not exist. Many are the roads that lead to this invisible village, and my Peugeot, which is no longer young, is jolted and thrown from rivulet to pothole, from rock to hard place.

There must be another way. I collapse on a boulder in the forest and try to gather together the senses scattered by the twists and turns. This could not possibly be the road to the village. Because if people live there, even people who do not exist, there has to be one tolerable road for them to come and go by.

Suddenly a voice calls my name. Who's calling? From where? Is it Asem? Hard to know. The echoes roll in from all sides. Someone heard my cries and he is calling me. Maybe not me? I shout again. Wait a moment, for the echoes to fade out. The man makes a sound. But there can be no real conversation in this seashell of a forest. The words run into each other, I don't even know what direction they're coming from. Again I call out, trying to convey also in the brief name Asem my request that they come rescue me, and my anger at the labyrinth and the bad directions, and I consider, between shout and echo, that even in such a small country as Israel it is enough to step off one's familiar route to be sucked into the absurd.

The other man continues to call me. I have already begun to enjoy the game a bit. Maybe he has, too. Together we were learning to separate the information from its repercussions. I have an opportunity to hear how he hears the overreverberation of my plight, and how our oversized echoes crash and hammer each other so far from either of us. Almost at the same moment we both understand that in order to hear the other, and to succeed in the delicate effort of bringing our positions closer, we must make our shouts much fewer and briefer; then, suddenly, additional voices join in, maybe forest workers laboring on one of the hills between him and me. They see both of us but are themselves unseen. They mediate between us, direct us to each other. I involuntarily recalled the legends I had heard about the people of this village—that they appear suddenly in a house once theirs, that sometimes you open your door unsuspecting and there they sit in the doorway, and when they see you they rise slowly and leave.

After long minutes of mutual echoing, there is a flurry and rustle in the bushes. Someone is running. A boy is running. We meet. He is covered with sweat. He ran two kilometers through the forest to find me. Asem? No, his cousin. He heard me calling, saw the car, and understood I was in distress. And where is Asem? Went to work. Am I a friend of Asem's? What have I come for? Here, let's drive to our place in the village, you'll wait for him there. He'll be home soon. When is soon? Right now. Noontime. One o'clock.

It is now eleven.

Parched in spirit, I slam shut the Peugeot's gaping door. The boy—his name is Jaber—indicates a road, but it is so steep, so full of boulders and holes, that the car cannot withstand it. The motor dies time after time. We choose another way. Three times longer and twisting. We twist with it, we triumph, and in a cloud of dust we finally enter the village of Ein Hud.

A tiny village. Thirty-three houses all told. Built on the mountainside, completely hidden by the trees. One hundred and sixty people live here, present absentees.

What follows is a brief legal explanation, for good hikers.

An absentee, according to Absentee Property Law 5710–1950 (1), is every person who was, after the United Nations partition decision in November 1947, a citizen of an enemy country, or who moved into enemy territory, or who was a citizen of the British mandate and left his or her regular place of residence for a location outside Palestine before September 1, 1948, or who left for a "location in the Land of Israel that was controlled at that time by forces that wished to prevent the establishment of the State of Israel, or which fought it after its establishment." Such a person was considered an absentee from that date, and his or her property and land were transferred to the ownership of the Custodian of Absentee Property.

There are, however, absentees who are, like it or not, present; their land and property were taken, but they themselves live with us, in our country, and the legal and existential category of "present absentees" was created especially for them.

For instance, the Arabs of the Little Triangle—a patch of territory between Jerusalem and Haifa, including the Wadi Ara road connecting the coast with the Jezreel Valley—were annexed to Israel as part of the Rhodes armistice agreements of 1949. Ever since, they have been citizens, but their land and property that remained in Israel after November 1948 had already been confiscated by the state and they themselves became present absentees. The same with Arabs, such as the people of Ein Hud, who abandoned their houses during battles and were not found there on the date that the general census was held. They, too, instantaneously became present absentees. (Every time I write that pair of words I can't help imagining the shiver of delight that must have run through the entrails of the bureaucratic octopus when the term was first ejaculated in clerical ink. Interesting—who coined that combination? Did he act alone, or did an entire company of chalky perukes sit in intense deliberation until this dicotyledon suddenly spawned?)

No one really knows for sure how many present absentees there are in Israel. In 1949 they numbered 81,000 individuals among the approximately 160,000 Arab residents of Israel. They included Muslims, Christians, and Bedouin. Many of them found new places to live, not on their own land, and there they receive the services that the state grants its citizens—that is, they are considered absentee with regard to their property and present with regard to their citizenship.

An enormous amount of property is involved—almost 400 abandoned villages, with their houses and land (more than 3 million dunams, some 750,000 acres); more than 25,000 homes in urban centers, close to 11,000 stores and workshops, as well as movable property, bank deposits, art objects, and stock shares. All these were "absentized" by the law.

But from this low point, from the caste of present absentees, one can descend to even lower levels.

Because Ein Hud here, the village I arrived at, had bad luck in pincers. Not only are its people present absentees, but Ein Hud is one of fifty-one settlements that the State of Israel does not recognize at all.

Their residents have been granted identity cards by the state, but outside this unavoidable act it refuses to recognize them, to provide them with services, to relate to them in any way— except when it is interested in evicting them from their homes. They have been living with us for more than forty years—that is, somewhere around us, on the lowest deck of the ship, in constant fear of being expelled even from the miserable places they hold on to. They build houses without licenses, since no one will grant them one, lurking in invisible villages, where they bring forth unrecognized children who bear, like a genetic birth defect, their present absenteeism.

It was morning and most of the men were at work; mostly women were in the village. For this reason I was not invited to enter any of the houses. In fact, faces turned angry and suspicious in a way I had not encountered in Arab villages up until then. But after a short while a woman brought out a chair for me and suggested I rest in the shadow of her house. Another chair came in its wake, holding a tray of fruit and a small cup of coffee.

A few minutes later all the children gathered around me.

Mustafa came to sit with me. He is a friendly young man, with a carefully trimmed blond beard. He earns his living shuttling the teachers at the local school to the village and back. He brings them in, then returns them. In the four hours between the two trips, he sits and waits. What can he do, he smiles apologetically—it's not worth it for him to go home. You saw the road.

He related that he had had this job for several years. Last year the village council had decided to ask for other bids on the contract and a taxi company in Haifa had won. A week later the owner of the company came and pleaded to be released from his commitment—who was crazy enough to travel that road? Mustafa won the job back.

Then, walking heavily and sitting with a sigh, Ayad came. Twenty-two, epileptic. His entire body shook as he sat with us. A few years ago he had come home from school, it had been a very hot day, and it suddenly began, along the way. He fell down and fainted. He has stayed in the village ever since. Never leaves. Most of the day he sleeps. He has considered taking an accounting course outside the village, but who would take him out and bring him back along that road?

We chatted. I learn that Abu Elheija is a huge *hamula*, with almost 65,000 members in Israel. The name means "father of the wars," a title the founder of the line had won as one of the senior commanders under Salah ad-Din Ayyubi, the Saladin who drove the Crusaders out of Palestine in the twelfth century. The woman brought out more cups of coffee. Time passed. Nothing urgent. Asem would come any minute. In an hour, maybe two. A hot wind blew dust along the goat paths between the houses. Across from me were bountiful fruit trees—pomegranates, grapevines, figs. Next to each house was a flower-filled garden.

At two o'clock Asem Abu Elheija, one of the village leaders, came and recounted: "I was three years old in 1948, when the Israel Defense Forces surrounded our village, the old Ein Hud, and everyone fled. They had no choice but to flee. They feared a slaughter, because before the army reached Ein Hud they heard that there had been some cases in the area, at Tantura, where there was a massacre, so they were scared, too, because they would set out from Ein Hud during the war to attack Jewish convoys and they thought the Jews had come to settle accounts with them, so they fled.

"Our family came here. We hadn't had time to take anything from our homes. Here there was a piece of land that belonged to Grandfather, and his goats and cattle were here. Since there are wells here, he preferred to stay near his goats and cows, on his land, and we lived together with them, in the shepherds' huts. Look over there, at the picture—that's Grandfather, Mohammed Mahmud Abu Elheija."

Grandfather gazes directly at the viewer from over his patriarchal beard. In every house I visited in the village I saw his picture in a place of honor.

"We would look from there down on our Ein Hud, and we didn't want to believe that we would not return. We felt that we would return soon. Grandfather would always go down to his land there, plow it and sow it, so he would not die. He would sow hundreds of dunams, wheat and barley and chick peas, and he would pick the fruit from the trees. The whole area you see here was full of fruit trees.

"In the meantime, other people started living in our place. In '48 they put Oriental Jews into our houses, but they didn't last long. They believe in all kinds of superstitions, and they used to tell how at night they would see eyes looking down at them from the mountains, or stones falling on them from the sky, or all kinds of ghosts, or the land cried to them, or they saw the people of the village returning to take their houses back. So they didn't last, and they left. I myself—what can I tell you—don't believe those stories. When they left, the artists came in; it became an artists' village and they called it Ein Hod.

"At that time the family began to grow. By '64 we had fifteen houses here. They didn't destroy them, but they threatened to all the time. They wanted Grandfather to give up all the land he had below in Ein Hod. They wanted us to give up the land there and buy here. But when we tried to buy, it turned out that it was all a bluff—there's a law of the Jewish National Fund, the JNF, the agency that oversees land purchases, that it's forbidden to sell land to non-Jews. When they saw it was no use, in '64 they confiscated his land for good. They also came and fenced in the land on all sides around us, and then we began to understand that we would never return, that it was impossible to return.

"That didn't satisfy them, the barbed-wire fence. They wanted to make another fence, and they put in those big cypresses, more pressure on us. And among the cypresses I showed you, wherever he had fruit trees, olive trees, figs, he had every kind of tree you could ever want there, they confiscated the land, and ever since no one works that land and no one benefits from it. It's just fallow land.

"We still didn't leave, because when you've already become a refugee, as we did in '48, to become a refugee again from what you founded and built with your own sweat, that was very hard for us to accept. So.

"Ever since we've been closed in by barbed wire, and another fence of cypresses, and around us, on our land, they made a huge park, and a firing range for the soldiers—sometimes I would sit in front of the house and suddenly *pssst*—over my head—and they also put a gate at the end of the road that you have to close and open with a key, the gate to Nir Etsion, the Jewish village built on our land, and in some corner of your heart you ask, What does that mean, you've been put in jail?

"After they fenced us in, they again began pressuring Grandfather to give up the land in the old Ein Hud, and the houses, and in exchange they would give us the land here. Grandfather would not agree to that under any circumstances. Because, he reasoned, there, in Ein Hod, it's my land, and it's registered in my name, so I should give up my land in exchange for my land? Not I.

"In the meantime, the artists were already in our houses. I'm one of those who spent almost all my time there. The truth is, I don't really like what they did to our Ein Hud. They made everything ugly. They changed a lot of the character of the area. But I had a lot of friends there, in the village. Jews. They became so friendly with me that they would come sleep with me here at night, in Ein Hud. I had a friend who lived in my aunt's house—my aunt herself lives here with us. At night I would sit with them there. The truth is, you don't feel good about it. But on the other hand, if something like that happens to you, maybe it's better that your friend lives in the house and not a stranger.

"Even today, go into the houses in Ein Hod, you'll still see a lot of things they found in our houses—pots, pans, plows, urns—that they hold on to to this day, but for decoration."

"In the house I was born in lives a girl, Z. She's my friend [he laughs], even though she's afraid when we meet. I haven't seen her in a long time. I went home with her a few times, and she photographed me in the house, and—okay, I explain it this way, they're scared, too. When they see that our people live near them, come to Ein Hod, they are afraid.

"And despite that I say, That's reality, that's reality! There was a war, the village was lost. Now I've built myself a new village here. All I want is for the government to recognize me, and all I want from the neighbors living in my house is that they support my struggle for recognition.

"But they don't support us. There are some among them who help, contribute, and we have an open invitation to go there, come whenever you want, come into the galleries, but the majority doesn't support it. They claim that they're afraid. If we support your struggle, they'll recognize you as a village and tomorrow you'll start asking for the houses there and make all kinds of demands. On one hand"—he suddenly raises his voice, forgetting the acquired caution of the refugee, which guides his steps—"on one hand, they wanted me to be, you know, their friend, but on the other hand, they say, We'll trample you down, you and your honor and your feelings, and don't open your mouth!"

He halts. Actually clamps his jaws down over the words.

"Nir Etsion," he resumes, "is also situated on our land. My father works there, for them, on land that was his. A man like Father, who had hundreds of dunams, with farming in his blood, has reached a time when he works his own land for $400 a month, after working for them for thirty-five years. And I had an uncle here, he's dead already, he had thousands of dunams. Not hundreds, thousands. All this was his. And he also worked for them as a simple laborer, for pennies. More than that—they would remind him, Mahmud, do you remember who this land belongs to? They'd make fun of him, because they knew it was his land. Every time they told him that, he would say to them, Today it's yours. Get it? Today. But it would eat at him inside.

"Okay, not important . . ." He waved his arm heavily. "The main thing is that recently we've really wanted to improve our relations with the people at Ein Hod. We had meetings with their town council, we invited them to meetings here in the village, and they came, and we really turned over a new leaf with them.

"The first problem is that they made our mosque into a restaurant and discotheque; that's the source of our difficulty with them. But an even greater problem is that they desecrated our cemetery. They destroyed the graves. Now, it could be,

I'm saying it could be, if I didn't know who was buried there, it could be that it wouldn't hurt me. But if you know that that's your uncle's grave, and your grandfather's, your father's and your mother's, and among all those graves an artist came and buried his dog—that's not right.

"So our first condition is that they no longer walk over our cemetery and not make it into a garbage dump. They have garbage bins in the cemetery itself. So at least move the garbage. Up until now they haven't done it. One thing they did in accordance with what we agreed on is that we want them to put up a sign there, temporarily, until we receive permission to fence in the place, to write there MUSLIM CEMETERY, HOLY SITE, LITTERING FORBIDDEN.

"They really did take that initiative. But it was a little hard. They didn't want it to say MUSLIM CEMETERY, HOLY SITE. So we reached a compromise—that temporarily it say DO NOT LITTER ON THIS SITE. We're currently in the middle of the struggle to get that sign. It's being held up in some office. We don't know what's causing the delay."

Architect Giora Ben-Dov lives in Ein Hod with his wife, Mara, a sculptress, and their three children. They bought their house, adjacent to the graveyard, from an American woman who had lived there until 1974. The Ben-Dovs are among the residents of Ein Hod who have supported Ein Hud's struggle to receive recognition and services from the state. Ben-Dov has even drafted a plan that would make the people of Ein Hud rangers in the national park surrounding them, responsible for its upkeep. In 1985 Giora and Mara took part in a large Jewish-Arab demonstration calling for a solution to the problem of Ein Hud. But at that same demonstration they decided to wash their hands of the whole affair. "The minute that the people from Ein Hud started making extreme demands," Giora Ben-Dov said, "the minute their politicians started talking about 'the holy land of Ein Hud,' and Ron Cohen, the Knesset member from the Citizens Rights Movement, said, 'Ein Hud will not fall again,' even those of us who always supported them, even the professional agonizers, went cold and packed up. Listen, I didn't capture the village from them, and I didn't evict old people from their houses with clubs. I came and bought a house, and if we go backward, we'll never finish the conflict, because maybe they're right if we go back to '48, but if we go back to the Crusaders, some Polish graf will come to me and want my house, and there's no end to it. The guys in Ein Hud suddenly began to feel like the representatives of the whole Palestinian problem. No matter that none of them was born here, among us, they've developed such an exile's longing for this place . . ."

I asked, "Why do you care about fencing their cemetery and putting up a sign? What are they endangering with that?"

Ben-Dov: "To the best of my knowledge, the Arabs don't have the concept of the holiness of the dead. With them, after twenty-five years, if the Muslim judge, the *qadi*, gives permission, they come with a tractor and turn the land over, and that's it. But they come and told us, No, we buried an aunt here two years ago. You understand? They started all kinds of attempts to gain a foothold here in our village. Our impression is that they want to gain recognition in the village up there as a first stage in returning to Ein Hod. So, if you give them a toehold here among us, you immediately recognize some, I don't know, injustice, and turn them into poor people who were expelled from their land. That's passing judgment on the entire War of Independence of the Jewish people, and we're already robbing land and exploiting people, and I'm not sure that it really was that way. There was a war. It's over, and now there is a status quo. This status quo involves a measure of separation, and this separation allows each of the sides to develop within its culture, to live a normal life."

"A normal life? Have you seen how they live there?"

"I have no argument with you that their conditions have to be improved. But first they have to renounce their demands to get a single meter here. Any new toehold will challenge our right and our status here. If you give any kind of recognition to what existed before '48, you're actually toppling the foundation on which the whole deal is trying to come together."

"The whole deal, Giora?"

"The *whole* deal, the whole country!"

"We now get water from the water company, via the water of Nir Etsion," Asem Abu Elheija goes on. "At first there was a problem. They didn't want to give water. So until '62 we drank rainwater. Once there was a spring in the area, but the JNF did some work in the area and they buried the spring and it was gone. Sometimes, in the summer, when there was no rain, we had to take water from the Nir Etsion sewer, but actually, then we didn't know it was sewage, we saw water and we drank it.

"As for electricity, we took our own money and put in a solar system—we're the only solar-powered town in the country—but the system is not sufficient. For instance, in this house there are two panels, and that can operate a small, 12-volt television and lights. There's not one electric heater in the entire village and no electric appliances. We bought our village council a television and VCR and computer, but we can't operate them all at the same time. If you turn on the computer, you have to turn off the television, and so on. You're always running from appliance to appliance. There can't be any street lighting at night, either. But it's better than the way it was five years ago, when there wasn't electricity at all. At night we'd light alcohol lamps. A child can't read for long by an alcohol lamp. We've just put in a light at the school. Up until now there was no light at the school and we wanted one. We brought a cellular telephone to the village, so in case of emergency we can call for help. We try to improve things bit by bit."

Asem Abu Elheija reports all this in an even tone, in a quiet voice, not in sorrow and not in accusation. His clothes, hair, and face are still coated with dust from the trip home. A pretty girl and boy, his brother's children, play peek-a-boo with me from behind his back, their cheeks red as peaches and their eyes alive, as if they had not yet set foot in their fate.

"There's no normal access road to this place. Even though we've been pleading with them for years to allow one. We'll do it ourselves. We don't want money from the government or from anyone. We'll go down to the road and ask for contributions. That's how we built the minaret on the mosque. We'll do the road the same way. There are a lot of people willing to contribute. Anyone who has driven here is willing to give. Imagine what it's like in the winter. And think of how it is if someone is suddenly ill or has a heart attack. Or a woman in labor on that road. We already had one case of a baby dying along the way during birth.

"Without a permit we can't pave a road. If you do, they'll come the next day and plow it under, like they did in Elariyan—people paved 700 meters of road and they came and plowed it under. So I don't know what to tell you. We don't even have a sign that says EIN HUD. Every time we make one, they throw it away. So in the end we gave in and didn't put up the sign. If you write us a letter and address it "Ein Hud," they'll return it to you and stamp it ADDRESS UNKNOWN. If you write "Nir Etsion," they'll bring it to us. That's how it is when you live in a house without a permit which they can demolish at any time—you don't belong to anything; we're not included on any of the official maps of the country, only on the maps of the army and the nature reserve. You know, we're terrorists, or animals."

Three days later I returned. I felt something that belongs, perhaps, to that individual private balance between fullness and emptiness, between physicality and absence. A feeling that grew ever stronger. So I returned and met with another member of the village, Mohammed Abu Elheija, who had been born in the displaced Ein Hud. I waited for him in the central square of the artists' village at Ein Hod. Around me were slight plaster figures, like stone silhouettes, headless. The figure of a featureless man sunk to his knees in the ground; one leg and one crutch. I'd seen all of them here before, but ever since I was in Ein Hud, Ein Hod echoes back to me.

"When I was young I didn't know Israel," Mohammed Abu Elheija told me. "True, we're in the center of the country, but I didn't know anything. My village was my country. When I went to Haifa to study at the Arab high school, I was like a boy alone. A boy on the side of the road. One day, in ninth grade—I remember it very well because it hurt—there was a sewage pipe in the school that descended from the third floor, and apparently they flushed up there, and I stood by it, and what did I know about sewage, we used to go in the field, so I put my ear to the pipe to listen, and a group of children there laughed at me. I heard a lot of water . . .

"And what do you think there is today? Here the same degeneracy remains. Here in Ein Hud the school has two rooms. That's the whole school, two rooms! In one room all the children in first, second, third, and fourth grades study, and in the second room are the children in fifth, sixth, seventh, and eighth grades; don't even ask about the quality. What kind of generation can you produce under such conditions? We're always behind in the race. I won't even mention films or theater. My son, thirteen years old, has never been to a movie."

Facts: Only four out of the fifty-one unrecognized villages

in Israel have an elementary school. Only one has a kinder-
garten. In the rest, the children must walk ten to fourteen
kilometers a day to the closest recognized village. Since most
of the villages have no paved access roads, the children have
to walk through forests and over dirt roads, in all kinds of
weather. As a result, children under the age of seven have no
educational framework at all, and girls of all ages are kept from
school by their families, lest they be harassed and the family's
honor tainted. These circumstances ensure that only 20 percent of the children in these villages reach high school. The
illiteracy rate reaches, in some cases, 34 percent. *

We went for a brief walk around the artists' colony. Abu
Elheija related that buried somewhere under the village is a
church from the twelfth century. Salah ad-Din's victorious
armies covered it with earth and built a house over it. I thought
of the mosque and sheikh's grave that had been turned into a
restaurant. I asked him if he knew that the people of Nir Etsion
are the children of the surviving Jews from Gush Etsion, people
who became refugees in the same war that turned his parents
into refugees. "They are refugees," he said distantly, "yes . . .
but I was not the one who made them flee."

He rushed through the streets of Ein Hod. "There are people
who have not come here since '48. My grandfather never
came. To the day he died, in '82, he believed that he would
return for good. For us, the young people, Ein Hod was something theoretical, a place where the old people once were, and
it was there and wasn't there. Only in '76, when I was twenty-
two, did I come here to work for the first time. Renovations.
I renovated old houses. You know what 'old' means. Even
when I went in, I didn't feel any emotion. To this day I don't
feel anything about what was here. Why don't I? I can't tell

---

*Data taken from Majed Elhaj, *Social Education and Change among the Arabs in
Israel* (English) (International Center for Peace in the Middle East, 1991).

you. Here's an example: I never in my life mentioned Ein Hod to my children, never said it was once ours. They never heard it from me. Why? I don't know. Let the analysts analyze it."

He is thirty-seven, father of seven, with a degree as an engineering technician from the Technion, thin and introverted. His speech is even and a bit ironic. We pass his grandfather's house. A two-story stone building. A small staircase. Nice yard. The door bears an odd sign: CHILDREN MAY ENTER ONLY IF ACCOMPANIED BY ADULTS. I peeked out of the corner of my eye at his stony face and considered how much strength it demanded not to tell the story of the old Ein Hud to his children. True, he himself had not been born here, but his father had been evicted. His whole family had been evicted. For a moment I made an attempt to walk through the village of my father's childhood, in another country, with his memories. I tried to be there when the house was taken, when the whole town was taken. And when a strange but apparently friendly woman appears on the balcony of the house that was yours . . .

But he was no longer there to see her. He strode in haste onward, waving his hands in the negative, to erase something. "It's not pleasant for me to be here . . . it's sufficient that I know it from the outside. I'm not curious to see it on the inside. On the contrary, when I have to pass by here, I do it at a distance. I have inside, I guess, something that keeps me away."

It's the Sukkot holiday and the village paths are full of visitors. A young couple asks Abu Elheija where the gallery is, and he explains politely. Afterward he takes me to the village's small amphitheater. On Friday nights he hears the best Israeli pop music coming from here live. I recalled concerts I had heard there, and something twisted in me at the thought of the notes crossing the wadi in joy, up to the ears of the present absentees. Returning to me like an echo, in a slightly different context, came the words of Azmi Bishara: "Once, at night, in the summer, I passed by the watermelon stands in east Jerusalem, by Herod's Gate. I could not believe what was happening there—the eastern city was quiet. Night. Darkness. Only the Israelis danced. Shouted. Went crazy. I could not grasp the contrast. There were no people in the streets, but there were Israelis dancing, and a strong light, and music, and the city was gray, gray."

"Do you know Italo Calvino's book *Invisible Cities?*" Giora Ben-Dov asked as we stood looking out over the beautiful view, the Atlit fortress and the sea reflecting through the small sabra cactuses on his lawn. "It tells of a city where all the people are connected to their relatives by string, and each kind of relation has a string of a different color, for commercial relations, blood relations, etc. Now, the problem there is that too many strings collect in the street and it's impossible to walk, so they go out and build a new city. The same thing happens there. If they go on being stubborn about the ties they have to the cemetery, and we continue being stubborn about our ties to the Patriarchs' grave in Hebron—in the end we'll all suffocate in our own ties, and I say the time has come for us to go to the new city."

The problem, of course, is not the cemetery but the Israeli state's attitude to the lives of the unrecognized. Not only does it not allow them to leave for a "new city"; it also sometimes tries to eject them from their old places. At this writing there is a struggle over the displacement of the unrecognized Bedouin village Ramia, in order to make room for the construction of a neighborhood for new immigrants in Karmiel, a Jewish town in the Galilee. "What will happen, what will happen," Abu Elheija murmurs, and tells of the great overcrowding in his village, where it is forbidden to add even a room, and there are large families, and married children have no space to move and no space to breathe. It reached the point that the village council assembled and planned to divide family houses with walls. Once a month, on Thursday, a helicopter passes overhead and photographs the village, to check whether any walls or rooms have been added. "And if someone from Nir Etsion hears a tractor running in the village, he immediately telephones whomever he has to and they come in an instant." The government established a special patrol, the Gray Patrol, he said, with a helicopter, twenty jeeps, and eighteen inspectors with guns and dogs, and once every two weeks they come to the village and check. (Now I understood why they were suspicious of me when I arrived.) "The state does not recognize us," Abu Elheija says, "but I still hope we'll find our place here. I continue to try to live here as an Arab. To try to tie myself to this administration. Here the government is in the meantime building up hatred that is . . . irreversible. In the end everything depends on the government. If it wants us to reach the state the territories reached, it will decide. Not me."

"And what will happen if they try to evacuate you from there, as they are trying to do with the people of Ramia?"

Abu Elheija turns his eyes away from me. "If they try to evict us again, I won't stay here. I will leave the place to you. Take everything. I'm not willing to live that way. I won't force myself on you. Stay by yourselves."

This, in brief, is the story of the struggle of the present absentees against their fate. They have long been asking the State of Israel to let them, finally, start *to be*. In the 1948 war, Israel's War of Independence, there was cruelty on both sides. The acts committed by the Arabs and the soldiers of Jordan's Arab Legion against the besieged Jews at Gush Etsion were no less horrible than the acts committed by Jewish soldiers against the innocent civilian Arab population. There was a war. People I know spent nights in ambushes alongside paths leading to Arab villages and shot people, women and children, who wanted to return to the houses they had been expelled from. That time has gone. Two and a half years ago I heard a very defense ministerish government official say, at an officers' school graduation ceremony, "We are still fighting for our independence." This means that, according to the way this minister feels, Israeli Jews have still not begun really *to be*. In fact, since I set out on this trip, a feeling gnaws away at me that maybe we have not yet been "liberated." It may well be that as long as we do not end our War of Independence we will never truly be a free nation in our land. "How many more years will you sing the line in your anthem, 'Hatikva,' that goes 'Our hope is not yet lost'?" Lutfi Mashour scoffed. "Stop hoping already and start understanding!" And Abd Ellatif Yunes from the village of Ara told me at the beginning of the summer: "My and your fate is to live together. It would be an error if you ignored me, because whether you want it or not, I'm staying. But I think that Israel would be a better place if a man like me could also feel that he wants to live here, and I don't think Israel can really be a nice place as long as 20 percent of its population lags behind and is not accorded basic human respect."

In the empty parking lot, which is also the garbage pickup point for the Ein Hod artists' colony, which is also the old cemetery of Ein Hud, over a broken plastic sign rolling in the dirt, NO LITTERING ON THIS SITE, Mohammed Abu Elheija says, speaking for the people of his village, "There is no one in our village who still dreams of getting back the old place. What more can we do so that you believe us? A new reality has been created. The new village. If you suggest that we buy or even lease the land on which we live today—even if it is already our property and is registered in our name—we'll accept the proposal. Just make it."

Sometimes a familiar reality—like a familiar text—is handed to us in "translation," revealing to our eyes slender threads we did not see in the "original." For several days I looked at Israel through the eyes of the present absentees, and I knew how much this merciful country of mine, which sends medicine and blankets to every Kurdish refugee and every earthquake survivor in Armenia, how well it also knows how to put on a stone face. From within the denied Ein Hud I could see how that stone mask gets thicker and begins over the years to grow inward, how it molds mind and soul and petrifies the language, until it produces tongue clots like that miserable pair of words.

"At the age of forty everyone has the face he deserves," my grandmother used to say, and we have been here forty-four years. On Bertolt Brecht's wall hung a Japanese woodcut, a mask of evil imagination covered with gold lacquer:

With compassion I gaze
Into the swollen arteries on his forehead
A hint
How tiring it is to be evil.

CHAPTER 6

"When I met Rasan," Irit wrote me, "I, like many Israelis, had preconceptions about Arabs. Before I went to college I didn't know any Arabs at all. In Tel Aviv, where I lived, I didn't have anything to do with them. At least not personally, except as laborers who worked in the neighborhood. Actually, I thought of them as objects. Or more accurately, they didn't exist at all. In my subconscious they were something frightening, threatening, that it wasn't a good idea to have any kind of contact with."

"It was really at college that I encountered the human being within the Jew," Rasan told me at their village house. "All other encounters with Jewish people were racist or exploitative, as far as I could see. At college I discovered something else, other types of people, and I slowly began making my way into that society. At first it was kind of romantic—I discovered some special personalities, I spent most of my time with a group of artists, like a commune, a feeling of being cosmopolitan . . . But outside that bubble my experiences were very difficult. I lived in the dormitories on Mount Scopus. There was the way they kept guard on us, and the way they scattered us, the Arabs, in the far corners of different dorm buildings, so that if there was an attack we'd be hit first—such absurd stories that you can hardly believe them. And there were also the encounters at the bus station with the border guards every time I traveled to the village and back. You don't find anywhere the human Jew who suffered, suffered from racism. Where is he? Is he now transferring it to a different victim, looking for someone else to piss on?"

He is forty-one. A research assistant at the university. One of the 14,000 Arab college graduates in Israel. His beard is short and carefully groomed, his glasses round, and he holds a pipe in his hand. He speaks quietly and with self-assurance, but someone humiliated and wounded lurks in the darkness between his ordered words, and the more he talks the more you see he is one great bruise.

She is thirty-nine, born in Tel Aviv to parents who had come to Israel from Iraq. Today she works in education for Jewish-Arab coexistence through drama. A very pretty ivory-skinned woman with black hair and green eyes. They have three children, two boys and a girl, a nice but modest house at the edge of their village, two dogs, and a litter of newborn kittens. We sit in their yard in the late afternoon. The table holds a bowl of grapes and peeled *sabras*—cactus fruit—straight from the supermarket. The two of them vacillate for a long time before agreeing to talk; he is willing to talk openly, she is apprehensive, for personal reasons, and in the end they agree to talk on condition that their identity be kept confidential. They chose the pseudonyms themselves.

"I suppose I was very naïve when I lived in Tel Aviv," Irit began. "Israel was something holy for me. I was very patriotic. Then suddenly it all became questionable. I met Rasan and

I witnessed things I couldn't believe were happening here. I began to be frightened. I discovered all kinds of things I hadn't known about the Jewish people, my people. The world changed before my eyes. I was afraid for my life and that of my partner. I thought, One day they'll come and bang on the door and take us away, and no one will lift a finger.

"Afterward, very slowly, I began to realize that this was reality for people like Rasan, that there is even a kind of routine to it. A routine of discrimination and ostracism. Even with regard to me. When people hear I'm married to an Arab . . . Here, a year ago I took a course at Bar Ilan University, and when they found out I was married to an Arab everyone got tense. It was a fairly long course, and people got close to one another, but they stayed away from me. One woman told me straight out, 'It's very hard for me with you. You're a very nice and smart girl, and if we had met without this thing of yours, I'm sure we would have become friendly. But it's hard for me to swallow it.'

"Or, for instance, a year before I met Rasan I went overseas. I went through airport security normally: you go, you fly, you return. A year later I traveled with him, and then, all at once—the search through the suitcases. They undressed us. They took my hair dryer completely apart. I told them, Wait a minute, last year I traveled with the same hair dryer and it wasn't dangerous then! I was pregnant. They stripped me down to my underwear. The guard came with an electric instrument. I told her, I'm asking you please, I'm pregnant, don't check me with that instrument. Check me with your hands, do whatever you want. She wouldn't agree. She said, I'll only check you from behind. I said, But I'm pregnant! Do you know anything about the way a woman is built? What difference does it make to a pregnant woman if it's in front or behind? It didn't help. I don't understand, I told her, I'm a student like you, I'm Israeli like you. She looked at me funny and said, I have orders and I carry them out. Those were my first steps as an 'Arab.' "

I asked if her children consider themselves Muslims or Jews.

"The children will define themselves when they decide to do so," she said.

"The children *already* define themselves," Rasan corrected her. "And it happens to them exactly the same way it happened to Irit. People always used to ask me if she feels like a Jew or an Arab, and I never told her anything about it. I didn't ask. But the first time, at our first roadblock, when we left the village and the border guard policeman didn't tell her, 'You're Jewish, get out of the car and wait until I examine your husband,' but treated her the same way he treated me, that's the moment the change in her began. That is, the Jews pushed her to belong to me."

"The roadblocks . . ." She smiled helplessly. "Look, that's already happened hundreds of times, so it doesn't bother me anymore. Isn't it a horrible thing when you become accustomed to the absurd? Whenever they stop us I calm Rasan down. I remind him, You know how they are, there's no way of avoiding it, so let's try to take it easy. I try to calm him down, but it hurts Rasan so much that as soon as I see them in the distance I get all nervous."

Rasan: "The same thing happened with the children. When our son was five years old they stopped us near Kfar Saba. The boy asked, What did the policemen want from us, why did they ask if you're an Arab, why did they take your identity card, why didn't they stop other cars? That way, automatically, and it makes no difference whether I want it or not, whether I teach it to him or not, he's already defined as belonging to the Arabs, but in the negative sense."

"My son was born in Jerusalem," Irit wrote me after our meeting, "and two years after he was born we moved to the village, and that was because in Jerusalem *I* was the one who had to sign the apartment rental lease. We knew that if the landlord knew that Rasan was an Arab he wouldn't rent us the apartment. I'd sign the lease as if I were the only tenant, and then he would move in with me. Living a pretense and a lie put a lot of pressure on us and we felt uncomfortable and frustrated. Then we thought, What about the children? Will they also have to conceal their Arab father? I wasn't willing to live that lie. My children have to know the facts and learn to live with them. In the end, that will be the reality of their lives, and they have to know how to live with it honorably. Here, in the village, unlike in the city, everyone knows that their mother is Jewish. They don't need to hide that fact from anyone. I'd say that they manage it pretty well. Until they were ten years old I'd read them a story in Hebrew each night, and they speak both Hebrew and Arabic as mother tongues. They watch all the Hebrew television programs and are at home with everything that's connected with cultural life in Israel. On the other hand, they study in the village school and live in an Arab society. Not only does no one bother them about it, there's sometimes even a feeling that they are the subjects of positive discrimination. After all, in the consciousness of the village society their mother belongs to the majority group, the ruling group, the elite."

At her house in the village I asked her whether, deep inside, she didn't want her children in the end to cast their lot with "her side."

"They'll make their own choice, just as I did. I never even thought of asking them what they felt about themselves—more Jewish or more Arab. It's not a pertinent question as far as I'm concerned. The main thing is that they be good people, with a good education, with a universal outlook. True, in each person's unconscious there is the identity with which she was born and educated, and it is very hard to free yourself from it. But little by little something is happening. To me also. It's harder and harder for me here. A lot of times I'm shocked by what I see around me. When an Arab child is hurt, no one knows who he is, what his name is, who his parents are. He doesn't exist. He's inconsequential. But when a Jewish child is hurt, they make a whole spectacle of it: they show him on television, give his biography, who his grandfather and grandmother are. Not long ago, two weeks ago, two Arab boys from my village were kidnapped by a Jewish bus driver. Did you hear about it? Two children were kidnapped and beaten, one eleven years old and one thirteen years old, wonderful Israeli kids who speak fluent Hebrew. They know who the assailant is. He wasn't even arrested and there was no investigation. You don't know about it, but such stories reach me every day.

"And I, who was born here, who was part of . . . Oh, I remember, as a girl, when the prisoners of war came back from Syria, I was so shocked. How could there possibly be a nation that could do such things? And to think that my country, in its own prisons and interrogation rooms, does the same thing . . . It's hard for me to cope with that. I don't know how other Israelis deal with it and remain silent. Maybe it doesn't matter to them because it doesn't touch them. Maybe they actually think it's good. I'm not prepared to accept it, but on the other hand I don't know what I can do." She speaks with great composure, without raising her voice. "I remember that once, on Land Day, we sat here weeding our lawn, and I asked Rasan what we should do. Demonstrate? Be more violent? And Rasan said that he is not a violent person, is not able to pick up a stone and throw it. He's not the only one I've heard that from: We're citizens, the country has laws, what can we do?"

"Still," I commented, "you're ignoring the fact that over the years there has been improvement. Only twenty-five years ago there was a military government here, and today there's more openness and consciousness of the problem, and the Arabs in Israel can express their opinions and demand their rights—"

"That's precisely the illusion!" Rasan interrupted me angrily. "That's a fiction. And anyway, what we're doing here is, if you'll excuse me, masturbation! Because what good will it do me if I tell you that I'm discriminated against? That I feel bad living in my own country? Will that improve my life? After all, the system is built so that it allows some exceptional people, like me for example, to advance, and it exploits those exceptions to say, 'Hey, look how this man expresses himself, and we don't cut off his head.' But practically, check it out and you'll see how the system blocks me in all directions."

"The absurd thing is that the discrimination is especially sharp in our situation," Irit said. "The law says that an Israeli couple can get a mortgage from the Ministry of Housing if both of them are citizens and one served in the army. Okay. We meet all the criteria. We're Israelis, I served in the army, we have the right to a mortgage. But they got around it and said, 'Aha! Since you're building a house in an Arab village, you get only what the residents of that region get!' "

"Look how much democracy here is an illusion," Rasan added. "The ultra-Orthodox are also a minority here, a smaller minority than the Arabs, a minority that has declared itself non-Zionist, and look how they dictate your life for you. Look how much money they get. But in 1990, when there was the big political crisis here, and Peres thought of making a coalition with the Arabs, everyone had a fit. 'How can you do that? With non-Zionist Arabs!' As if the ultra-Orthodox are Zionists! As if they serve in the army! We're *a priori* outside the game. Politics, the media, and the economy."

"I understand," I asked him, "that you would like the manifest Jewish character of the state to disappear?"

"A country with a majority of Jewish residents—I have no

problem living with that. Even if the country tries by all sorts of legal means to preserve the Jewish majority, I have no problem, on condition that it be determined with the agreement of the minority."

"Describe such a situation to me."

"Israel can be a country with a Jewish *majority* but shouldn't define itself as a Jewish state. When its symbols include me as well, I'll have something to say and even more to give to such a country."

"You didn't explain what you mean by 'legal means . . . determined with the agreement of the minority.'"

Rasan sucked on his pipe for a long moment. "If Israel says, I want to be a normal, democratic state with a separation of church and state, where every person will have the right of self-fulfillment, then we can sit down and agree that the president and prime minister always be Jewish, according to the constitution. And we'll also write a constitution that will ensure the citizen's fundamental rights, his basic freedoms. (And that's one of the reasons, by the way, that you have no constitution.) There will be a constitution. There will be a Jewish majority. But its laws will protect my rights as well. They'll allow me, not some Jewish official in the education ministry, to decide what my son learns in school. Under those conditions it wouldn't bother me that the majority is Jewish."

"It doesn't bother me that the flag is blue and white," Lutfi Mashour, editor of *As-Sinara*, told me with regard to the same issue. "It's not important to me and I don't care if they call it Israel or Shmisrael or the Jewish state. The decorations don't bother me, the essence of it bothers me. Am I equal to you or aren't I? In practice, do I or don't I have rights? I've even given up on getting a Law of Return for Arabs. I've already made my peace with the fact that the Jews have a place to return to and that the Palestinians can't return here. I hope that the Palestinian state that will be established will be "Jew-

ish" in this sense. But all that is secondary. The main thing
is your attitude to me as a human being. You bring in a huge
wave of immigration—very nice. But a year from now the
Jewish immigrant will be a master. We'll remain the slaves.
So I say, Fine, let it be a Jewish state. But give us the same
opportunities you have! Let it be as in India—a Muslim as
the head of state. You can make agreements like that!" He
thought for a minute and began to chuckle. "It's true, if you
were to tell me now that the president's chair is open to
Arabs—I'd kill you! Because who would we put there today?
What Arab can be such a leader? I prefer living another thousand years without an Arab president to putting any of the
people I know into that position!"

Open parentheses:

"The president's chair is open to Arabs." In Israel will there
ever be a reality in which that sentence comes true? There are
those for whom the idea is a nightmare, and the very writing
of the words, in Hebrew, rubs their nerves raw. But maybe
there are others for whom such a thought—even if it is not
practical for now—may massage a pulled muscle in their consciousness and create a surprising sense of relief—"Why not,
after all?" Really, why not? Why shouldn't Israel have an Arab
Minister of Justice, an Arab State Controller, an Arab as director of the water company or the telephone company, as
director of the social-security system, all of them Arab citizens
of Israel? Or a Minister of Agriculture and a Minister of Finance and head of the water supply, and director general of
the Histadrut Labor Federation and editor of *Ha'aretz* and
heads of the boards of directors of national companies and
chairmen of Knesset committees? Why not? There, in Irit and
Rasan's yard, I knew how little all of us, Jews and Arabs, allow
our imaginations free rein with regard to the possible joint
future. It's as if the paralysis and lack of willpower that control
us with regard to our relations in the present restrict our gaze,

so that there is no power to hope, and within this empty space our traumatic past still rises endlessly, perpetuating and preserving the pattern of our relations.

And an Arab newspaper editor as a member of the sensitive Editors Committee, which serves as liaison between the press and the army censor? Yes. And an Arab El Al pilot? Certainly. An Arab general to head the Civil Defense Force? Of course. And an Arab police chief? Yes . . . but here I feel a little hesitation. Have I reached the boundary of my own private racism? Or the boundary of the dream at the present stage?

So even before we are privileged to see, let's say, an Arab commander of the Rear Defense Command, there are simpler and more vital endeavors that have still not been realized, facts that are hard to face. Twice as many Arab babies die soon after birth as Jewish babies. And 92 percent of Arab wage earners are on the bottom half of the social scale. There has not yet been an Arab member of an Israeli cabinet; the highest political position an Arab has reached is Deputy Minister of Health. In 1989, out of the 1,310 senior positions in the government ministries and their associated bodies, only seventeen were Arabs. Among the 200 boards of directors of government-owned companies, with more than 4,000 politically and economically influential members, there is only one Arab director. Of the doctors employed by the Histadrut's huge health fund, only 2 percent are Arabs. This year every second Arab in Israel lived under the poverty line. Six out of ten Arab children (as opposed to one out of ten Jewish children) live in poverty.

How much luck does an Arab child—as talented as he may be—need to live "just" the life he deserves? To not waste his mind and abilities under the high-jump bar? Are all these exaggerated hopes? Dreams? Visions of a storyteller?

Then what about an Arab member of the Knesset's Foreign Affairs and Defense Committee? No, not yet. What about an

Arab deputy prime minister, who will fill in for the prime minister whenever necessary? Yes . . . why not? An Arab commander of an air force squadron? What about it? Just theoretically, when there's peace? Ah, I need to think, to mull that one over . . .

During such moments of doubt I could understand that there was also something misleading about the immediate connection made between me and the Palestinians I met in the occupied territories before the intifadah. In one, obvious sense they and I had a common interest—to disconnect ourselves from each other. In other words, the aspiration to separate united us. But here, perhaps, in Israel, we, Jews and Arabs, must overcome the residues left by enmity and suspicion in order to come together under one definition, as Israelis, in the framework of a single general civil identity, and this "compression" demands of the two "partners" a huge emotional effort, no less difficult, perhaps, than the withdrawal from territory.

"You speak of national identity," Irit sighed when we spoke of the difficulty of "compression" and on the internal concession it demands. "I can tell you about much more private problems, about my family in Tel Aviv, for instance, about my father, who cut off all contact with me, entirely, yes, the minute he realized that I was going out with an Arab. I haven't seen or spoken to him for fifteen years. And that's my father, who was so attached to me, as only a father can be attached to his youngest daughter. In the army they used to laugh at me, at all the things he used to buy me, always the best and the most expensive—and now he doesn't know his grandchildren, he doesn't know me. He's losing something and I'm losing something. Once we received a videotape of a family wedding and my children saw my father, and my younger son said, 'Wow, Grandpa looks so young, he's really good-looking.' The worst part was a few years ago, when my sister was dying of cancer; just before she died she spoke with my father and asked him to forgive me, to take me back. He went into hysterics. He wasn't willing to consider it. She died, and I didn't go to the funeral or to the *shiva*. My father said, 'Okay, I'm sitting *shiva* on both my daughters together.' Do you understand? He sat *shiva* for me, like for Chava, who married a goy in *Fiddler on the Roof*."

She goes silent for a minute, getting control of herself. Then: "I have a close relative, very close, who married a Christian. She lives with him in Switzerland. But when she goes home, the whole family receives her with so much love. They fight over who will host her, they make pilgrimages to come bid her goodbye. That sharpened the matter for me, that our problem is not religious. It's political. A European or Swiss is not on the same level as an Arab. The opposite—she actually became a model of success, a Swiss!"

I asked how she felt in the village during the Gulf War.

"All of us here were horribly frightened of the gas, the first night was a real nightmare, my son cried because he thought that the mask wasn't sealed properly, and he didn't eat for two days, and I had the additional burden of being far from my family, from all my relatives in Tel Aviv. Imagine how I felt. I hurt so much for my Tel Aviv. I cried when I thought of my city destroyed. And there was no one around me in my situation. No one with whom I could share that anguish. After each alert I would call my sister in Ramat Gan to ask where the missile fell. Twice the call was disconnected, and Rasan shouted, why are you asking her questions like that on the telephone? Don't you realize that you live in an Arab village? Don't you know that they're listening to us?"

"Did you encounter people here celebrating Israel's distress?"

"First of all, and most important, they didn't dance on the rooftops, like the Jews said. In my village, and in other villages I know, they didn't dance! Almost everyone here has Jewish friends, and we live right next to Jewish settlements, we're all in the same boat. True, there were Arabs who told me, You don't care when Palestinians are killed, now you'll learn how hard it is. That I understand. Real celebration of distress—I didn't see any."

Rasan: "If you ask the Arabs in Israel if they want to see Israel destroyed, my bet is that you won't find 10 percent that want that. People already accept Israel. They accept that the country exists but want it to change its character. So that a man like me, a citizen, can say, It's mine. But if the government's policy doesn't go in this direction, our demand in the future will be for some kind of autonomy here, or some kind of recognition as a minority. And it looks to me like that's where we're heading. After all, Israel doesn't intend to change in the coming decade, and I won't undergo auto-castration, suddenly turn into a kind of Zionist Arab, a good little Jew."

"It's interesting," I said to Irit, "that during our entire conversation your disappointment and hostility is directed only at the Jewish side. Don't you have any criticism of the Arab society in Israel?"

"The Jewish side is the strong and controlling side," she said. "It's easier for me to understand the Arabs. They're so pressured by Israeli society, you have no conception. Only someone who lives here can understand it. And I, at least, have an advantage over other Arabs—I have another identity I can hide behind whenever I choose. You understand. My fluent Hebrew and the whole Jewish side of my identity allow me, really, to go from one side to the other whenever I want.

Others don't have that privilege. Yes, the feeling of being an Arab among Jews is so hard that when there's the possibility of fleeing, it's a good feeling."

I asked what made them feel Israeli.

"There are moments," Rasan said, "when, despite all the harassment and the way the situation closes in on you, you still believe in something. You look for the corner in which there's a bit of light, to tell you that it's still worth trying. At least for the little bubble you live in and bring up your children in and for your friends around you—it's still worth making an effort. Then, on the other hand, you run into cases when you start asking questions. What does my activity here mean? What is the significance of all my efforts for that human robot who stops me at the roadblock? What does my citizenship mean? Income tax and VAT? Stopping at a red light? Eating food produced by Israeli companies like Osem and Telma? Studying in the Israeli educational system, one I did not choose? After all, really, if I'm honest with myself, my citizenship here means no more than having an identity card which isn't worth the paper it's written on. Tell me what collective elements are here that I as a man can feel any connection to. Why can you, theoretically, be the director of the government television station when I could never be? What, I can't be just as professional as you? I'm not as reliable as you are? That is, for me being Israeli is what *keeps* me from self-realization! It is a system that prevents me from deciding my fate! I live my entire life in an existential system of foreignness. Do you understand what it is for a man like me to be *a priori* outside the cultural, political, and economic game? Even the Israeli left, which I know wants to make things better for me—when there's a demonstration in Teibe, the left stands there and the right faces off with them—what does the left do? Their leader tells them, I'd better fucking hear you singing 'Hatikva' louder than they do! So with all their might they sing the line from the national anthem: 'A Jewish soul yearns'! So I'm always 'out' in these battles! When I go to Tel Aviv—the heart of your Israeliness, right?—I feel foreign there. Suspicious. Ask my wife. I get nervous and tense. I go there only when I have to."

"And is there a place you feel more comfortable? How do you feel in Ramallah?"

"In Ramallah I feel foreign, too!" he burst out.

"So what's left?"

They fell silent. Looked at each other.

"Nature," Rasan said in the end. "Only nature. We go on a lot of trips. To the north, to the Galilee or to the Negev, to the craters. I cultivate my private relationship with nature." He smiled bitterly. "There it's still a little free of meaning."

"Still," I insisted, "there's a whole country here, such a complex and multidimensional whole. People, opinions, art . . ."

"I don't see any of that art anymore. I—"

"There's some reason that you're staying here. You are people with free professions, you could manage elsewhere also, and you've chosen to live here."

They laughed, unsettled. "We're leaving," she said.

"Planning to leave," Rasan corrected her.

"It's actually because of pressure from the children," she said. "They don't want to be here."

"For a few years, no more," he added. "The kids are sick of the tension here, of this whole struggle."

She: "The truth is that I'm actually the one who wants to leave more. More than Rasan. I look around and I know that I'm no longer at peace with the fact that I live here. I'll join a Hebrew book club—what's so surprising about that? You asked before how it is that I have no criticism of Arab society. Of course I do, after all I live here and see horrible things here, too: see a petrified society, see educated people who find it easy to criticize but don't do anything to change it, and an educational system in which the teachers stand in front of the class and curse the children. 'You're failures, you're asses and blockheads.' To this day teachers hit students, my son was hit more than once. I have lots of complaints. Maybe I don't dare criticize them in public because I'm a foreign implant, I'll always be a foreign body to them, but I expect more of Jewish society, in all areas. It could be that I'll see discrimination in the U.S., too. It exists in every society. Maybe I'll feel that it's not my home there. But I have many more expectations from my home than from other places, and here I've already seen too much, and I can't go on."

Siham Daoud, poet, a delicate young woman of thirty, from Haifa:

"During the war, I heard that there were Arabs who were happy that Saddam was firing Scuds at Israel. I, I have so many friends and people I care about, both Jewish and Arab, so joy never passed through my head, not even for a second. On the contrary. I remember, during the war, a missile fell here near my house. I was horribly afraid. All the neighbors left, the Jews and the Arabs who live in the housing project here. I went down and the guy across the way was sitting in his garden. He had to stay home because he was on emergency duty, he's a nurse at the hospital. An Arab, right? He sat like this, as if all the world's problems were on his shoulders, and said to me, 'I'm very, very worried.'

"I asked him what he was worried about, and he says he is worried because for two days he hasn't sent a thing. No Scuds.

"When I read about it in the papers I didn't get upset. But when it happened to me? Do you understand? Here a man was *sitting, a missile had fallen a kilometer from him, and instead of worrying about himself, instead of—okay, don't worry for the Jews, worry for the Arabs here! We're all in the same boat . . . and he's worried why for two days he hasn't sent anything!*

"I was speechless.

"That same day I had moved in with my friend, a Jewish woman. And most of the days of the war, I was with her. The whole thing, that because of his missiles I couldn't stay at home, really made me mad, and I remember that once I lost my cool; it was the day that there were some four false alarms, and each time we went into the sealed room and came out, my friend and I and two more friends, all of us together, and then at one point I took off the gas mask and said—you know how I cursed him!—Son of a bitch! [She laughs.] And I never curse, so everyone broke out laughing, because it was clear who I was saying son of a bitch about."

Question: *"During the alerts did you sit in the sealed room?"*

S.A. *(a woman of about twenty, who asked to remain anonymous):* *"Yes."*

"Were you afraid?"

"I was very afraid. My sealed room could have told you how afraid I was. I sealed it outside, I sealed it inside, twice, and between the plastic and the glass I also sealed it with silicone, and I sat with the gas mask on, and I was so scared, and I was happy he was shooting the missiles."

"You mean you were happy that they were firing missiles at you?"

"Let's say, not real happiness, just . . . yes, despite it all, I was happy that you, too, a little . . . because a lot of times, when I saw the world's reactions, their support of Israel, when you destroyed our houses in the occupied territories and you imprisoned my family there during the curfew and shot us with

bullets containing all kinds of materials and all kinds of gas, that whole time, twenty-four years already, no one in the world did anything to stop it, and I cried when I saw how cheap our blood, the Palestinians' blood, is . . ."

Zuhir Yehia, forty, Kafr Kara:

"During the Saddam period my thoughts were divided. I was cut in two. Should I invite friends from Tel Aviv? Invite them here? Because if I invite them it's an invitation for them to run away from the responsibility that the Jewish people imposed on them. In the end I invited them; they came to visit, but not to stay."

I asked what he thought about those who left Tel Aviv during the war.

"As an Arab, were the positions reversed, I think that I wouldn't run away and I wouldn't leave."

"In '48 most of the Arabs fled."

"They didn't flee. They were forced to flee. The Arab countries tempted them to come, promised they would return. We've learned a lesson since then. We won't move anymore. The Jews left Tel Aviv out of fear. Maybe correctly, I don't know. Maybe they don't have the nerves for this tension. Arabs already have stronger nerves. We've had a lot of disasters here. Maybe we're more spoiled than the people in the territories, but less than the Jews. You've already gotten used to things being nice."

CHAPTER 7

In the month of May 1991, at an air force base in the center of the country, some 13,000 Ethiopian Jews arrived in Israel in the space of twenty-four hours. Their dark, bare feet felt their way down the plane's metal stairway. Their first glance around was cautious, bashful—not a look that dares to demand possession of its new surroundings. All was suffused with silence. The nobility of the newcomers invested also those who had come to greet them. We saw an entire culture uprooted before our eyes from its habitation come to resurrect itself in Israel. Lofty *Kaisim*, Ethiopian Jewry's religious leadership, swung the *chira*, made of hair from a horse's tail, the emblem of eminence. And almond and olive boys, and little queens of Sheba, and teenagers who don't, really don't, have that bold American look of our own adolescents. And wrinkled, angular, coal-black old men and women, their eyes living embers. A scorched Judaism that strayed for 2,500 years in the snarls of history, rose and declined; and what remained from all these metamorphoses was, perhaps, the thing that we search for in that eternal question Who is a Jew? Because maybe it is precisely they who, in their indigence and their longings, bring to us the unadulterated answer, the Jewish ore itself.

Forty airplanes came and went, for an entire day and a night. On one of the flights, before landing, they were spoken to by a member of their community, Eliezer Rahamim, who came to live in Israel twenty years ago and who had flown to Ethiopia to bring his kinsmen to Israel. "Our dream of 2,500 years is being realized," he told them as the plane circled over Jerusalem. "This we have prayed and longed for, and now we have won the right to achieve it; all thanks to the government of Israel, because, blessed be God, we have a country, and we have a home."

On the night after that same emotional Sabbath, when I saw the immigrants who had just come sitting in a Jerusalem hotel and watching the evening news on television, I asked myself if, when I say "I am Israeli," this definition from now on includes them as well, these new and different ones?

This question obviously did not concern only the technical, formal act of granting Israeli identity cards and citizenship to the newcomers. It related to a kind of effort of the spirit and of consciousness, to a kind of mental extension of that invisible cloak that, by its coverage, defines whom we include and whom we exclude from our nation. Every citizen stretches such a cloak unconsciously over his country (if he has a spiritual attachment to it). At times I examine the boundaries of my private cloak. In my internal experience, does it cover Neturei Karta and the rest of the anti-Zionist ultra-Orthodox groups? Does it still take under its (the chauvinistic brood hen's) wings the hundreds of thousands of Israelis who have preferred for many years to live in other countries? And what about their children, whose concrete links with Israel are even fewer?

In the face of the tidal wave of Ethiopian immigrants, or of the new immigrants from Russia that I meet each day in the large immigrant absorption center near my house, I feel the effort of will, not a simple one, to "make a little room" under the common cloak. Not that there is any lack of room under this abstract cloak, but there is certainly something around me and in me that will be changing in the coming years. New tastes and aromas are now being stirred in abundance into the Israeli stew, and they will change it profoundly. Also, in the new stew my portion will be smaller; my aspirations and my values will encounter—and perhaps collide with—a different world. Despite this, I am happy at the change, curious about it, and ready to endure for its sake the pain of mutual adjustment. In some ways it is a spiritual pain, equal perhaps to the not unpleasant physical growing pains of adolescence.

And there is a question.

"No, I don't want to be hypocritical. When I say that I'm Israeli, I don't include in it that woman from Kafr Kassem or that man from Jaljulia."

Writer Sami Michael:

"When Israeli Arab movements rise and say "We are Zionists," I consider them hypocritical and dishonest. Because this is a Jewish state. That's the way I feel. That's not what I want, but that's the way I *feel*. It may be that I should, somewhere, broaden the 'umbrella' of this definition, but I'm talking now not about rational judgment but about emotional judgment. They instilled in my mind, my heart, that this is a *Jewish* state, and for better or worse I feel that this umbrella covers only the Jews. Not the Arabs. I remember my first jolt with regard to this identity. When I came from Iraq at the end of 1949 and enlisted in the Israeli Army, we had shooting practice, and instead of saying, 'The enemy is coming at you,' they said, 'The Arabs are coming at you!' What? What did that mean? I was shocked—after all, I was an Arab, too! In Iraq it was understood that I was a Jewish Arab! So little by little, through dozens of such incidents that happened to me

here, the Arab apparently left the cover of that umbrella—
'He is the enemy.' Understand that I don't see him as an enemy
when he is under the umbrella, but I see that anyone who
argues that the umbrella includes him too is confused, asinine,
and dishonest. I have not seen that any of them—except for
a few very special people, like Anton Shammas—consciously
want, with all their hearts, to be under the umbrella."

"Still," I reminded him, "there are clear trends toward the
Israelization of the Arab minority."

"Of course! There are such trends! That's the steamroller
of daily life, forcing it on them, as they force it on themselves.
Listen to a story. I was with my wife in Cairo, and we were
walking across Al-Tahrir Square, and suddenly we heard Hebrew being spoken at a shout, fearlessly! It was strange for us
to meet Israeli youngsters speaking Hebrew provocatively and
proudly in the very heart of an Arab country. We approached
them and we saw that they were Israeli Arabs! They were sitting
there on the fence showing off their Israeliness. Hebrew wasn't
then for them the language of the Jewish people but the language of Israelis. I addressed them in Arabic, and they answered me in Hebrew! Do you understand? They were in the
heart of Cairo, where it's crowded, filthy, poor, what they call
Third World, and what it awakens in them—something characteristic of Arabs in general—is the idea that Israel is not only
Satan; it is strength. It is a power. Development. And they
brag about it!"

It is nighttime, and I am in Sami Michael's house in
Ma'alot, at the edge of town, looking out over the mountains
of the upper Galilee. I asked him to explain something he had
said previously.

"It really was that way! To the Jewish generation that raised
me in Iraq, it was clear, as it was to me, that I was an Arab.
With regard to values, with regard to culture—I was an *Arab*!
In addition to that, I was Jewish, just as a French Jew is French

and a Turkish Jew, Turkish. That is the origin and the crux of the whole matter. I was a Jewish-Arab-Iraqi, and I couldn't identify with Iraq's aspirations, with Islam, with the official anti-Jewish policy, with the anti-Semitism that grew during the Second World War. I, with my whole struggle against those trends, came to Israel.

"My first refuge was when I settled in Jaffa. Jaffa was then a kind of ghetto of Bulgarian immigrants and Arabs. I had a room in the house of an Arab family, and I felt good there. It felt like my natural place. Afterward, in Haifa, I also lived with the Arab population, in Wadi Nisnas, and after that I worked on the Communist Party's Arab newspaper, *Al-Itihad*, to the point where the Arabs often forgot that I was Jewish and they'd talk to me about 'those Jews,' just as my mother-in-law used to forget that I was Sephardi and would talk about them in front of me. So I know these things from the inside. When it comes to the whole web of relations between the two peoples, I know it as a Jew, as an Israeli, and also as a man who until the age of twenty saw himself as an Arab, who was suckled on Arab culture, and whose first friends in Israel were Arabs.

"The Arabs, in the early days of the state, did not call us Sephardim. They called us 'Ibn Arab.' That's an honor, 'the son of the Arabs.' But remember what happened afterward. Who was the state's representative among the Arabs? Who was the implement used to impose the military regime, persecutions, and arrests? It was the Jews from the Arab countries, mostly Iraqi and Egyptian Jews. The policeman. And the Shin Bet agent, the interrogator, and the jailer. That created hostility to the Sephardim among the Arabs, hostility they have trouble freeing themselves of. The negative, daily, traumatic contact was with them. The teacher sent to them by the state to teach them Arabic with a grammar different from theirs, and who failed them in that different grammar—and maybe he himself didn't even know how to write a letter in Arabic, the teacher who taught them Zionist history and Arabic literature. Then the border guard, which is almost completely made up of Jews from Arab countries, and the military governors; there was always an attitude of disdain and hatred of the Arab population."

"Sometimes," I said, "you can hear Sephardim making fun of the Ashkenazim, especially the ones from the peace movements, telling them, 'You don't know how to talk to the Arabs. You don't understand the Arab mentality.' "

"I'm afraid," he responded, "that that's a form of racism. As if the Arabs are a certain breed of dog or mouse and you have to talk in their special language. What makes the difference here is not *how* to talk to the Arab, because he's an intelligent person and however you talk to him he'll understand it. The important question is *what* you really say to him. What your declared policy is, and what you carry out in the field. That's not a communication problem. Even if you're the best Arabist in the world, it won't make you a man of peace.

"But the big problem is that in the 'what' we deceive each other, with deceitful words and intentions, so it is a dialogue of deaf people. Sometimes when I see meetings of Israelis and Arabs, I could burst out laughing. They say the same word and mean something entirely different! The word 'peace,' for example. The simplest of words. For the average Arab, from the Gaza Strip or the West Bank, 'peace' means that this country will be destroyed, will disappear along with all its institutions, with all its tradition, with all it brought here, and then there will be real peace. That all the refugees will return to their houses, that their land will be returned, that there will be an Arab majority here again, and then there will be either a PLO state or one based on the Koran.

"The average Israeli Arab—if there really is such a person —his hope is a kind of thing whose realization is hard to conceive. A kind of mad dream of waking up in the morning with the same High Court of Justice, the same efficient police force, the same nice buildings, the same democracy, and the same social-security system—but what? Without Jews. That would be paradise. It means that I, the Israeli Arab, will be a first-class citizen here, with all the values that exist in the country today but without the Jews. Not, God forbid, that they should be thrown into the sea—I am, after all, an advanced humanist liberal—but that some nice spaceship will swoop down and take them away, and each of them will return of his own free will to his place in the world, and we'll meet every fifty years or so on a hike, to share memories."

"No . . . no! I'm sorry!" fumed Dr. Majed Elhaj, whom I met the next day in Shfaram. "Maybe that represents what an average *Jewish* person secretly wants deep down inside—to wake up one morning and not find Arabs here. I think that the Arabs here, over time, have learned to distinguish between dreams and reality. The Israeli Arab is a realist. Otherwise he might slip into some other orientation to the state. But it's no secret that there are a lot of conditions in Israel that encourage extremism rather than the adoption of an attitude of coexistence. Despite that, I'd define the Arab minority as the quietest minority in the *world*, relative to its solidarity and political awareness. I think"—Elhaj smiled at me, or maybe to himself—"that it's really an ideal minority."

"But there's one thing that the Israeli Arab has not and will not come to terms with," Sami Michael continued, "and that's that he is a minority. 'True,' he would say, 'I'm a minority here, on this little island, but look behind you and you'll see a whole *ocean* of Arabs.' Because in international terms, the Arab world is a great power—economically, numerically, in the number of countries, the number of votes at the U.N. And the Israeli Arabs still have a living memory of the way things were fifty years ago. 'We turned into a minority only because of a temporary malfunction. We look to the future.

We, with our birth rate, will again be a majority here. And you, the Jews, are in crisis, both economic and moral. You are failing. The day will come, and with one good battle it will all change.' That's still in the back of their minds. 'So why,' the same Arab asks, 'should I wear the suit you've sewn for me, the suit of a minority? I'll just wait.' "

What a combination, I thought—a majority that doesn't feel like a majority and a minority that doesn't feel like a minority.

Sami Michael: "And don't think that they aren't scared of that future! Because either Israel will exist forever and they'll always remain second-class citizens, or Mohammed will come with his scimitar and I, the Israeli Arab, will have to flee from the houses I've built and from the money I've made under Israeli rule, and all those people from the refugee camps will flow in here, to my house, to my store, and I'll have to pay the price of all those years of plenty I had here. Because you should know that the Arabs outside hate those who are inside. For instance, until 1964, when it was necessary to establish pan-Arab solidarity, Syrian Communists would refuse to meet Arab Communists from Israel. I remember that very well— when they met they would spit in the face of the Israelis. I saw it in Prague: 'You are traitors! You stay there! You benefit from the Zionists and serve Zionism! You don't take up weapons, you don't fight, and you even work for the enemy army and police, and there are Arab teachers and Arab court clerks, and you open profitable restaurants that the Jews come stuff themselves in, and what are you doing sitting in the Knesset? To promote the big lie of Zionist democracy? You are already Zionists yourselves!' That's what they told them. I heard it."

I asked whether, in his opinion, there could ever be among the Arabs of the Middle East true acceptance, the kind that is internalized deep in the unconscious, of the existence of Israel in the region.

"It's doubtful. Let me tell you something: If today some Arab tells you he accepts that in Madrid and Spain there is a Christian, European state, don't believe him. When I was in school in Iraq the teachers taught me about Spain. How my heart ached that I, an Arab, had been defeated in Spain! I didn't even know that we, the Jews, had also been in Spain. They didn't teach me that, neither my parents nor my teachers. To this day every Arab feels the pain of the loss of Andalusia, and when was that—seven hundred years ago? Is that an answer?"

He's over sixty. When he was born in Iraq his name was Samir Mared, and his books deal with the duality, or the split personality, of Jews and Arabs trying to live together, in Iraq and in Israel. He is a man of imposing, dignified appearance, with a long, dark face. Very private, austere. His voice is deep, muted, and each of his words is suffused with his Iraqi pronunciation, accentuating the kinship of the languages. As he speaks, he continually displays the speech of "the other," and then his eyes suddenly return to life, and a dialogue is woven between his long hands.

"Listen, we have a big problem here. I've already been breaking my head over it for years. For me, the intifadah did not change the major thing that awaits us. With regard to what's happening in the West Bank, the solution is already on the horizon. Whether we want it or not, whether we bend our backs or walk erect, the solution is there. The Palestinian state will come in the end. Remaining then will be the difficult and complex and most dangerous question of the Israeli Arabs. And no one is really conscious of that, not Peace Now, or the Jewish liberals in Israel, or the intellectuals who are willing to meet any Arab in Paris but not here. These people do not know the Arabs' secret longings. They don't know the differences between the language they speak with a stranger and their internal language. That is the greatest problem we have here, and I, as a Jew, how will I solve it?"

"?"

"My dream goes like this: There will be a Palestinian state. That's already an established fact. And I'd leave them the damn settlements we have there. Let those settlements stay there, if they don't slaughter them. I'll give them all Israeli passports. They'll have the right to vote for the municipal authorities there, but they won't vote for the Palestinian parliament. The same way I dream that the Arabs here in Israel will vote for their municipal authorities, but with a Palestinian passport! Let them finally have a flag of their own, for God's sake, they'll belong to something; let them vote for the parliament there, and if they want, let them serve in the Palestinian Army."

"Do you foresee a situation in which someone from Horfish or Tarshiha, your neighbors here, will serve in the Palestinian Army?"

"Oh, they won't go." He chuckles, not contemptuously, but out of appreciation of the survivor's cleverness. "Trust them not to go to the army. But I think it will be like this: There will be a Palestinian state, and we'll have relations with it, a kind of federation and strong ties, because, despite everything I told you up until now, the Jewish Israeli and Palestinian Arab are the two most similar nations in this region, and the most different from the others. In their energy, their vitality, in having the mentality of immigrants, the Palestinians are all immigrants as well, like us, and I can't describe to you how different a Palestinian villager is from an Egyptian villager or a Syrian or Iraqi villager. Worlds apart. Here, let me tell you a story about an Egyptian and a Palestinian.

"Before they built the Aswan Dam, the Nile would bring with each flooding the alluvium that fertilized the ground. When the dam was erected they held back the water, the alluvium did not come and the land became less fertile. The government began supplying the *fellahin*, the peasants, and the agricultural cooperatives with fertilizers, for next to no money. Heaps of fertilizer, thousands of sacks of fertilizer, are still rotting in the warehouses today, and the farmer descends with his donkey and two baskets, goes kilometers to seek out the Nile, and takes a little mud to spread on his land. Now I'll give you another picture: After the Six-Day War I worked in the Ministry of Agriculture, and they gave me an assignment to do a survey of water sources in the West Bank, of the wells. This was two or three weeks after the battles. Disabled tanks were still scattered all over. So in some desolate village, a hellhole with no paved road, I saw a well with a put-put sprinkler or, rather, with a pipe coming out of it and a sprinkler at work at the end. I was astounded—a mirage! A sprinkler! I asked the *fellah* where he had gotten a sprinkler. Oho! He knows Abu Yosef, a Jew, and Abu Yosef knows Abu Yehuda, a long chain of names, and he brought him a pipe and fixed him up a modern sprinkler. That's the difference."

"You, the Israelis, are more similar to the Palestinians," a young Egyptian, Mohammed Ayin, once wisecracked to me near the pyramids. "You and they are just the same—short-tempered, worked-up, insecure. One minute you feel like big heroes, and the next like the most miserable wretches in the world. You're always sure someone's trying to cheat you. And you are greedy. You love money. What you won't do for money and power! We're not like that. We won't lift a finger for anything. That's why we look the way we do." He laughed, waving his hand over the desert shimmering in the heat.

I'd add—apologizing for the generalization—a few more similarities between Jewish Israelis and Palestinians. There is an attraction to the imaginary and illusion, a delight in words and mesmerization by them, and an exaggerated confidence in their strength. There's also excitability, and a talent for stirring up emotions to the point of impairing the sense of balance reality requires. Then there's our type of humor, somewhat bitter. And self-irony. And curiosity and vigilance. A kind of strange attraction to self-destruction. Diligence. Great suspicion of foreigners. Excessive pride, and self-pity, and an eagerness to be insulted, and an inclination to self-hatred. And great ambition, I would emphasize, with regard to the Palestinians *outside* Israel's borders—*Yahud al-Arab*, "the Jews of the Arab world," as the Arabs call the Palestinians, a label that evinces acute envy of the hundreds of thousands of Palestinians who have made their way into the social, economic, cultural, and political elite of the Arab countries, where they play the same role that the Jews did in the lands of their exile—a catalyzing, galvanizing, generative, and not much loved force. This ambition is by now hard to detect among the Palestinians living in Israel—neither the drive to excel nor the strength that motivates so many of the world's minorities to stand out and force their way upward into the majority's elite. As if they are still walking gingerly under a low roof—the fiddler's new roof.

"And don't forget that our elites are hard to penetrate," Sami Michael notes. "*Very* hard to penetrate. I learned that the hard way when I came here in 1949. We are willing to open up only in a superficial way. It's interesting that the farther down you go on the ladder there's more and more cooperation. For instance, in the underworld—gamblers, drugs, prostitution. There's real cooperation there. Racism—to contradict conventional wisdom—is farther up. The members of their elite are dying to gain entry to ours. They're itching to be part of us. But they're not interested in meeting your common Buhbut and Boskila. They want to meet the parallel stratum in Israeli society. And the Israelis are unwilling."

"But maybe your comment brings us to the question of Israel's integration into the Middle East. If Israel is at all interested in that."

He laughed. "Look, Israel wants to be part of Europe, and the leading force in Israel in all fields, in economics, politics, sport, culture, like it or not, is the Western-minded. What's that line? 'My heart is in the East . . .'? Where do you see my heart in the East?! My heart remains entirely in the West! No one here wants to be part of the East. And what complicates the whole business is that the East itself is pulling westward."

"In the East," I said, "you actually meet many Arabs—in the Egyptian intelligentsia, for instance—who have developed their own way of taking a lot from the West but without giving up Arab culture. They don't indiscriminately internalize all the West offers."

"Don't forget that they didn't come from Europe and settle in the Middle East! They were born in the East and have lived there for five thousand years. So maybe they're not ready for huge leaps, as we are. But step by step they are turning to the West, and the ones who are remaining authentically Eastern in Arab countries today are primarily the Islamic movements—Hamas, the Muslim Brothers, Al-Azhar University."*

"So, in your opinion, Arab culture as you know it cannot serve as an attractive challenge to Israel?"

"Absolutely not. Because it itself is seeking a different way today. Look at this search for roots that has begun among the Oriental Jews here. In my opinion it is meaningless. Those

*Hamas is an Arabic acronym for the Islamic Resistance Movement and is tied to Islamic fundamentalist groups in the Arab world. Their purpose is to establish religious regimes throughout the Arab world. The Islamic Brotherhood is the oldest modern fundamentalist Islamic movement, established in Egypt before World War II; it now has branches all over the Arab world. Al-Azhar is a prestigious Islamic university in Cairo, established in the Middle Ages.

roots have grown obsolete even in the Arab countries. No one misses them any longer. On the other hand, take a country like Iraq or Syria. The minute they buy weapons from Europe, a plane and a missile and a French or German or Russian tank, they are buying an aspiration to be more efficient, like the West. Accurate like the West. Purposeful like them. You can't chant an Arab folk song for five hours and race around on a modern tractor. That was good in the period of the plow and the camel. Today?"

It was already almost midnight, and jackals yowled outside the house in Ma'alot. They keened so loudly that it seemed as if they were in the room with us. It turned out that they were not far off—they were standing by the wall of the house, munching on the vegetables in the garden, emitting their heartrending, beguiling, and repellent cries.

"What are we going to do here?" Sami Michael sighed. "I really bang my head over it. My ideal would be to reach some kind of joint state, but I don't think that either we or they are ripe for that. And we'd be a minority very quickly—their natural increase has always been larger than ours. Ten years from now, fifty years from now, they'll be the majority and they'll make the decisions. And I, if I've got to be a minority, I'd rather not live in this region. I'm willing to be a minority in the U.S., in Australia. But not in this region, so intolerant of minorities. Look at the Kurds in Iraq, the Shiites in southern Iraq, the Christians in Lebanon, in Sudan, and in Egypt—I wouldn't want to be like them. Not that I'm a big fan of Zionist ideology, I never was, but I'm Zionist enough in that regard, in that I don't want to be a minority in Israel. I'm not willing."

I asked Dr. Ami Elad-Buskila, a scholar and translator of Arabic literature, to comment on Sami Michael's analysis of Arabic culture.

"Arabic culture contains horrible things and wonderful things," he said. "You can't reject it entirely. Anyone who rejects and castrates an entire culture will pay the price. To this day in Israel there is a tendency to make Arabic culture foreign and hateful to the general population, and this creates an anomaly. After all, a majority of Israel's population is a child of that culture. The Israeli Arabs, together with the Oriental Jews, are a decisive majority of Israeli citizens, and hostility to the culture they are rooted in will one day create a cultural and social earthquake.

"I agree completely with some of the things Sami Michael said. But his opinions are correct with regard to what happened in Arabic culture until the end of the 1950s. If we consider literature—it has taken a giant step since then. In the wake of events in Arab society—changes of regime, changes of ideology, changes in the status of women, changes with regard to individualism—there is also a huge transformation in literature, especially in the Arabic short story and novel.

"I've just finished translating a novel by Abd Alhakim Kassem, *The Seven Days of Man*, published in 1969. It's true that if a modern Westerner reads it, against the background of Proust and Hamsun, he'll say, 'Hey, this book isn't very sophisticated. It's very nice, deals with the clash between modernization and tradition, but from my point of view it's *passé*.' But I, perhaps because of my personal background, the fact that my family came from Morocco, from a similar world, because I spent my childhood in Jaffa with Arabs, I feel that this novel gives me—I won't say an escape—but definitely something to hold on to and to remain in, to take refuge in from the world that is sometimes too intense, achievement-oriented, technological, and threatening for me.

"Here in Israel there's a narrowness to the horizons of knowledge among the local enlightened class. For the Jewish-Israeli intelligentsia, pluralism in literature, for instance, means being open to literature from France, Russia, Germany, South America. But pluralism should also be an enjoyment of Tamil poetry and of Kleist, and also, for instance, of the Sudanese writer Elteib Saleh. Maybe someone who lives in Norway can easily ignore Arabic culture. We have no choice. And this culture really does have something to offer. But what does the average educated Israeli know about stream of consciousness in Arabic literature, about its absurdism and fantasy? About the elements of Sufi mysticism? About the reverberations of the existentialism of Kierkegaard and Sartre in Arabic philosophy? How many literature programs have you heard on Israeli radio about Egyptian, Syrian, or even Persian and Indian writers? How many people are even capable of reading Arabic literature? We think it worthwhile to learn French, English, even Spanish, Italian, and German, but not Arabic. How many people on the Israeli left know Arabic? How many of them are able to conduct a real dialogue with an Arab?"

Poet Saul Tchernikovsky sang of Otrok, an exile from his country who rules, happy and wealthy, "over the land of Avhazim." His brother, who remained in the homeland, sent a messenger to him—Or, the poet with the violin, who calls on Otrok to return to his country. The wayward Otrok refuses to return. "He forgot his land on his ivory bed." He also refuses to be tempted by the song of longing to the forgotten native land sung to him by Or. Then Or the poet returns his harp to its case and takes from his pocket a bunch of yemshan, an herb that contains within the aroma of the south Russian homeland, and throws it in Otrok's face.

> Gray distances . . . the day has just lit . . .
> The horses' hooves are cautious . . .
> Otrok comes, the bunched herb in his hand,
> Smells and smells again—freedom
> And tears stream down his cheeks.

On the road that leads from Teibe to Jajulia, in the southern Triangle, I was suddenly filled with a yemshan happiness. A joy at this bare-topped, constricted countryside. On the side of one of the roads, one from which no village could be seen, neither Jewish nor Arab, I stopped and began to wander between the olive trees and boulders and unplowed fields. The sky and a few crooked branches spread over me, and I had a strange urge to peel this land of its names and designations and descriptions and dates, Israel, Palestine, Zion, 1897, 1929, 1936, 1948, 1967, 1987, the Jewish state, the Promised Land, the Holy Land, the Land of Splendor, the Zionist Entity, Palestine. I kept peeling—with a slight twinge of the heart—the paved roads and wide boulevards, the green lawns of the kibbutzim, the parking lots and traffic lights and road signs, the luxurious neighborhoods that look as if they had been written by a copywriter, the water parks and fountains and swimming pools, the synagogues, the mosques, and the churches, the envy-inducing mansions in the villages, the shopping centers and American shopping malls in Tel Aviv and Jerusalem, the Jewish National Fund forests, the green European illusion we have conjured up here to cover the cracks in the skin of an angry and resentful land, a thin, desiccated membrane with one small lake and a thirsty river. A country, Tchernikovsky wrote, in which "one must soften every inch of land, battle every boulder." And Salim Jubran responded, "As a mother loves her malformed child, so I love you, my homeland." There, between two anonymous hills, the forgotten primeval visions returned so clearly to me, that special shade of Israel, brown and rocky, the biblical, pre-Zionist land that the Zionist fathers longed for and beautified in their dreams and poetry, and which they afterward confined and repainted with their deeds.

It was here, in an area crowded with Arab villages, in a place where Zionism has a kind of bare spot in the map of its consciousness, a triangular birthmark, where the tense bowstrings of the definition of Israeliness momentarily slacken in confusion, that I could again sense the simple and mysterious love of the land—that is, of the land itself, prior to any name or title—of this strip of the planet that fate has burdened us with, with its colors and aromas and land and trees and changing seasons. Who knows whether he really loves his land, or if he is doomed to love it because he is made in its mold.

Once or twice during this summer it happened that I glanced at my Arab interlocutors as they stretched their hands out to the view, or rubbed a fragrant sage leaf, the local yemshan, and held it out to me to smell. In doing this, something was conveyed between us—a gift, and a pain with no outlet, and confusion, of the type that can be caused only by another whose life is a kind of alternate possibility to yours.

CHAPTER 8

"You see the wall there, by the bank?" Mohammed Kiwan swings his swivel chair around and points. "There they wrote, in big letters, 'Death to the Arabs.' And next to it, 'A good Arab is a dead Arab.' And that in the heart of the fair city of Hadera, straight across from my office window. Fine, so the day they wrote it I call the Hadera municipality and tell them, Hey, guys, right across from my nice little office they're hanging me! So please, come clean it up. Ten days passed and they didn't come to wash it off. The graffiti pricks me in the back. When did they come? When we brought the press into it; within a day the mayor had ordered the graffiti cleaned up."

He is an attorney, lives in Um Elfahm, works in Hadera. At the beginning of the 1960s he had been a teacher—"an educator," he corrects me—and was fired because of his political activity. At the time Kiwan was active in the Nasserist nationalist movement Al-Ard. In 1965, after Al-Ard was outlawed, he was among the founders of Sons of the Village, a radical Palestinian movement whose aim was to fight for an improvement in the status of the Arabs in Israel. "We called it Abna el-Balad, because *balad* means both 'village' and 'homeland.' It's the unfortunate villager as opposed to the snobbish rich. It's the common man, Voltaire's Candide. I always look for that man. Among you and among us. I'd like to get to the Candides among you, too. But your communications media are blocked to us. How many times have they interviewed an Arab on a television talk show? Despite the fact that we're nearly 20 percent of the population and talk, God knows, just like you. Where's equality of opportunity? We're always shouting, but no one hears. They don't allow us to reach you. Here, two months ago I saw this guy Jojo from Ashdod on television, the one on the beach. What a wise and simple man! What common sense and humanity! I wrote him an open letter, for the newspaper, and called to him: 'I, Mohammed, am searching for Jojo from Ashdod.' The paper, of course, would not print it. So I'm still looking for those Jojos."

"It's not that complicated," I told him. "Let's drive down to see him."

It wasn't all that simple, either. Jojo Abutbul lives in Ashdod, Mohammed Kiwan in Um Elfahm. Who should go to whom? "Tell him we'll meet halfway," Kiwan suggested. "What do you mean halfway?" Abutbul grumbled. "I've got to be in my restaurant on the beach every day, tell him to come here." I mediated, shuttle diplomacy by telephone, one day, another day, until Kiwan finally gave in; after all, he wanted to talk to Jojo, and if Jojo won't come to Mohammed, Mohammed will go to the beach.

On a hot summer's day, at Jojo's café-restaurant, The West Coast, under the palm branches spread over the roof, the two sat facing each other. The restaurant loudspeakers played American music, the beach slumbered beyond. Jojo took a pack of cigarettes out of his pocket. Mohammed took out his pack. They lit their own, relaxed, and Jojo, the host, began.

"When we lived in Morocco, my mother had an Arab housemaid. She nursed me. That is, I grew up with her. I drank her milk. Let's say that when you go to sleep your life is a kind of box that you have to deposit with someone for safekeeping. That's an allegory. My mother would have had no problem handing that box, my life, over to her Arab neighbor. What I mean is that even when it was really a matter of life itself, the trust was so great that it was possible to place my life in her hands.

"So I—I don't have any preconceptions about you. An Arab is a human being. An Arab has a soul. I once talked about the pain. Fifteen get killed in the territories and they put it in small print in the newspaper. A Jew gets killed in an attack and it's on the front page! Why do they make distinctions when it comes to pain? If today I take my cigarette and put it out on Mohammed's hand, and take a cigarette and put it out on my hand, you'll measure the same force and feel exactly the same pain. Emotion. Love. Concern. Your son. These are things that weren't given to us by the Likud or the Labor Party. Not by Judaism or Islam. I lost a son. I know what pain is. And that woman in Ramallah or Nablus, and don't think I'm justifying in any way their stone-throwing, but he's dead. She feels the same pain I felt when my son drowned in the sea. Pain can't be divided; its force can't be measured, because of its relation to a particular person.

"So I ask you, Mohammed, where do we want to get to? Are you satisfied with your plate, your bed, your house, or are you satisfied only with my plate, my bed, my wife, and my children? On the other hand, when a Jewish guy tells me he wants security here, you know? Security has no bounds! You can put a ground-to-air missile on every square meter. Will that give you security? Tomorrow some Ahmed won't come and knife you? So where's my security and where's Mohammed's security? So that's what we have to talk about today, me and you—what are we willing to give each other? And I'm certain that if the two of us sit down and talk, we can finish off all the problems in two minutes."

Mohammed listened quietly, nodding all the while. When Jojo finished talking, he said, "First I want to tell you that I'm glad I came to meet you. We don't know each other. I saw you one time on television and I had the impression that you are a person with healthy natural instincts and a love of life, and I felt that this person is really looking for a way to live together. I'm happy that the minute we met you said that we can solve all the problems straight off in two minutes. So the only question is, What work will that leave you, Grossman?"

We laughed, and drank our first cup of coffee. The beach was still empty—only a few new immigrants from Russia cooking in the sun.

"Before we solve all the problems in two minutes," I said, "maybe we could clarify the most basic concepts, so that we'll know if we're talking about the same thing. What do you, Mohammed, call this country, the one Jojo calls Israel?"

"As far as I'm concerned," Mohammed said, "it's always Palestine. I don't care if Jojo calls it Israel. Jojo has the right to live here as an individual and as a nation, and my right as a Palestinian is to live in Palestine, as an individual and as a nation, with the right of self-determination for the Palestinian people. That's the basic principle, and I'm convinced Jojo will agree with me."

"I agree 100 percent," Jojo confirmed, "but you accept that this is also the Jewish state, right?"

"As far as I'm concerned, Israel can call itself whatever it wants." Mohammed smiled. "If it's just a semantic problem, I don't care. But if it means—like now—that it's a Jewish state with all the privileges and laws that discriminate in favor of the Jews, then other questions arise that I don't agree with."

Jojo stiffened. "Let's get this straight. I, as a Jew, have no country other than Israel. I have to have one country that will be mine. I, Jojo Abutbul, was born Jewish. I did not decide that. I didn't have a store where I could take from whatever shelf I wanted. I was born Jewish. I deserve a place somewhere in the world to live the way I want, yes or no?"

"Ah . . . with regard to that question, you formulated it in a very difficult way."

"I did not!" Jojo cried. "That's a question from the gut, not from the head!"

"Look, Jojo," Mohammed said, getting a little more serious. "Before you came from Morocco, I was here."

"I'm not kicking you out!"

"One second, give me a second. This pretty, sparkling Ashdod of yours, just for your information, even after the country was established in 1948, there were still Arabs here and in Ashkelon, and Israel expelled them in accordance with the infamous Plan D.* Now you're alive and you exist, and you have this country, and I'm not challenging your right to a country, but according to what you say, 'I'm here, I don't have anywhere else to go,' ditto as regards the Palestinians—they have nowhere else to go—"

"I agree with you," Jojo cut him off. "But just a minute! I can help you with something that I don't know if you know. I say that having the Law of Return only for Jews—that's racist! I'm not hiding that! But I ask you, Mohammed, you have the option of getting up tomorrow and moving to Jordan, Egypt, Syria, Lebanon—all those are Arab countries. But here I'm saying to you, in addition to all twenty-two of those countries, I'm saying to you, here I'm going to build another country for

*Plan D was the first strategic plan of the IDF in 1948 to occupy towns and villages populated by Arabs, in lands assigned by the UN partition to the Jewish state.

you, completely Palestinian, in Gaza and the West Bank. Wait a minute! You don't have to take your things and move there. Understand! As far as I'm concerned, you are a citizen of the State of Israel, with all your rights! But by this act that I'm making, do you accept that Israel is *my* country? You can live in it, but under my conditions, my government, my laws. And if I should want to live in your country, it will be under your laws and your government and your conditions. Can you live with that?"

"You and I, Jojo, when we're aware of those discriminatory, racist laws, and we both fight for their repeal by the legislature . . ."

Jojo: "You're not answering me! Say yes or no!"

Mohammed breathes deeply: "If you don't recognize my right to full equality here, I won't recognize your right."

"No, no, you don't understand." Jojo smiles uncomfortably. "I'm saying this: you and I want a divorce. You've been married to me for forty-three years. I love you, you're my soul, everything. I don't want to live with you! Let's get divorced. What do you want as a dowry?"

"I'm not asking for a dowry. We really married against our wills. Not out of love. But today we're sailing on this sea in the same boat."

"And I own the sea."

"I don't agree that you own the sea!"

"But I'm the strong one! If I want, I can come today as Prime Minister Jojo and make a law—Whoever doesn't accept Israeli citizenship in the Jewish state—the *Jewish* state!—gets put in a car and taken away. Can you do anything to stop me? Nothing. Cry, scream until tomorrow!"

It's only Mohammed's mouth that is smiling at Jojo now. "First, Jojo, my friend, inside, in my heart, I don't feel that you are in control and that you have power. I don't feel that

I'm inferior to you. True, you now have strength and power, but I am among those who believe that power changes hands. I'm a minority under you, but you are a minority under me, in the Arab Middle East. I have no feelings of inferiority with regard to you. I was born here. I have the strongest possible links with this homeland. I don't feel that I'm a guest of yours. I sometimes feel, if I may be presumptuous, that you are a guest of mine, and that I accept you because I want to be realistic. That is, the Jewish people's starting point, that they're doing me a favor when they let me live in Um Elfahm, is mistaken. Look, in Um Elfahm we had 140,000 dunams of land before Israel was established, and then the Knesset came and made all kinds of laws and confiscated from Israel's Arab citizens 1,200,000 dunams all at once. Today two kibbutzim and a moshav sit on Um Elfahm's land. On our land! Another thing, 92 percent of Israel's land is state land. If this country really recognizes me as part of it, then I should have a pro-portional part of that 92 percent of the country. Do you un-derstand why I'm shouting? Because when you tell me that you're doing me a favor by accepting me here, you have to look at things from my point of view, and then you'll begin to understand what kinds of huge concessions Palestinians are making today when they offer two states side by side. But if after the Palestinian state comes into being you come and rescind the discriminatory laws, if with regard to the Law of Return, for instance—"

"But here I'm not arguing with you," Jojo stops him. "The Law of Return has to apply to everyone."

Mohammed raises a finger. "In other words, you agree that the Arabs who were expelled from Ashdod can come back to live in Ashdod?"

"Yes! They can buy a house the way I do! I'm not giving them any privileges!"

Mohammed: "Allow me! You're saying that this country, this future country of ours, will agree that every man in the world who wants to live in it can?"

Jojo: "Suits me!"

"Even if some miserable Kurd from Iraq or Turkey wants to live with you in Ashdod?"

"I've got no problem with that. If, if, *if*. If he promises to serve in my army, to be loyal to the *Jewish* state and not betray it. To fight together with me against whoever wants to take this country from the both of us, even to fight against Syria with me!"

"But it should be clear to you," Kiwan says, "that if there's total equality here, the country won't have its Jewish character anymore."

"Why won't it?" Jojo asks in horror. "It has to have! There'll be maximum equality, as much as possible! But subject to this being a *Jewish* country!"

"Then it's not real equality! Then the Jews have extra rights because of their Jewish birth! Then it's no longer Mohammed's country!"

"Just like in Syria there are extra rights for Arabs, as opposed to Jews!"

"Look, if you come at me with something like that"— Mohammed raised his thick, hoarse voice for the first time— "let me tell you that my counter demand is just as purely racist—have the Palestinian state include all parts of Israel in which there are Palestinians! Give me the Galilee and the Triangle!"

"I'm ready to! I'm ready to give them to you, if—*if* you give me Nablus and Hebron, where I once lived!"

"Hey!"

"Why 'hey'? Why not? Don't you see you're talking out of both sides of your mouth? Do Jews live in Hebron today? They do! Abraham lived there two thousand years ago? He did!

Listen to me, Mohammed." Jojo sat back in his chair, lit two cigarettes in his mouth, pulled on both, and passed one over to Mohammed. "For years you butchered and exiled us, and for years we've butchered and exiled you. What I'm saying is this: we have two possibilities. Either we can talk nice and act bad, or talk bad and act nice. In other words, I, according to the way I see things, I prefer to get the dirt out of my mouth. Let's sit in a room and argue for twenty hours; I'll tell you you're garbage, you're crap, and you tell me the same thing, but in the end you and I get up with a clean heart, and we have no more demands, and we've divided up all the property between us, but for always! Finished!"

"I agree with you on that. But understand one thing, that the minute we repeal all the privileges Jews get here, this country will stop being a Jewish country and will become the country of the people who live in it."

"People, what people?" Jojo slaps his forehead with an open palm. "Is England a country of its people? Is Syria a country of its people? England is the country of the English, and Syria is the country of the Syrians. And you, if you live in Israel, will live in the country of the Israelis, as an Arab minority in the country of the Jews!"

Their faces are now close to each other. Their hands, waving excitedly, hit one another, and at times intertwine for a moment. Both are solidly built, with black hair and tough faces. Both look older than they are. Mohammed is about fifty, balding a bit, more careful with his words. Every so often he throws out a bit of legal jargon at Jojo in a lawyerly tone, looking at him over his glasses, putting on a tolerant and didactic expression. It drives Jojo crazy.

Jojo, thirty-eight, is in a blue undershirt and shorts. His sunglasses remain glued to his forehead even when he jumps up in indignation. He has lived on the beach since he was four years old—"Everything I know about life is from the sea."

In his youth he was a violent criminal, terrorizing this beach until he won himself a place and was pacified. Ever since his appearance on television, politicians from all parties have been courting him, and he, "even though I've been Likud from my mother's womb," meets with them all, listens, gives advice—lively, heart-winning, knowing well that they all think that through him they have gained a direct linkup to "the people's voice." His face has infinite expressions, and he talks in a very loud voice, at a shout, taking control of the conversation, hyperemotional, undulating like a cat across the table from Mohammed, ambushing words and arguments. He manages the entire beach as he debates—giving advice to a young soccer player who approaches him, giving a contribution to a needy family, trading secrets with a party activist—a one-man band.

The two minutes passed. The conversation lasted close to four hours, and in the process it slowly became clear to both sides how much trouble they were having bridging the gap between them. It was easy for the onlooker to realize that, despite the goodwill, their first line of defense was also their last. Jojo would never give up Israel as the Jewish state; Mohammed would never retreat from his goal of full equal rights with Jojo—that is, that Israel be "a country of its citizens" and not "the country of the Jewish people."

As this became apparent, the two of them became impatient, trying to catch hold of each other, to put it into other words, words that would circumvent an abyss. They did not want the victor in this confrontation to be familiar political differences. They wanted victory to go to those nameless things whose potency and insistence could be felt when Jojo's and Mohammed's faces came close together—that same link of expression and warmth, the mirror dialogue of mimicry, and the hidden thing that synchronized the two of them, as in a ceremonial warriors' dance. It was easy to imagine them changing roles and arguing, in an opposite state of affairs—each one making the other's points with the same fervor.

Mohammed: "The truth, Jojo: you too have suffered discrimination during your life in Israel, right?"

"Suffered?" Jojo guffaws. "I *grew up* on discrimination. I grew up on inequality. I grew up with the word 'Moroccan.' I grew up with everything you've felt. Compared with the Ashkenazim, I was discriminated against here, too."

"So you are the first one who should understand the violent response of the Palestinians in the territories, and the desire of the Arabs in Israel for equality."

"No, no," Jojo rebuffed him. "Me, my whole outlook now is against violence. Ask why. Because all violence brings counter-violence. Mohammed tells me, 'You're strong in your country and weak in the Middle East.' But the Arabs are strong in the Middle East and weak in the world. The world, pal, is built like a ladder. For every strong man there's someone stronger than him, and what we're talking about is not how to be strong but how to reach an understanding. So that I can turn my back to you and sleep peacefully, and you the same. Look, Mohammed, for instance, wanted to be a lawyer. The country didn't try to trip him up, he went and learned law . . ."

"It certainly did try to trip me up!" Mohammed shot him down. "I'll give you a simple example. When I was studying they put me, in my second year, before exams, on house arrest, to keep me from passing the exams. I stayed at home for an entire year just for having quote unquote 'dared to protest' the injustices we spoke of before."

"But you studied and finished and became a lawyer, right? They didn't even give me the option you had! That is, between Jojo and Mohammed, Jojo was the one more discriminated against!"

"Look, Jojo. The Sephardim were discriminated against and are still discriminated against. When I was in school, it hurt me to see that less than 1 percent of the students in the university were Arabs, and the same for the Sephardim!"

"Not only in the university! Also in the officer corps, and in the government!"

"It's very interesting how and why they block cooperation between the Sephardim and the Arabs here, even though, from a theoretical point of view, logic says that both of us, the underdogs, should work together. Let me remind you that here in your Ashdod the government—indirectly but deliberately—uses the Sephardim against us, and when there's an Arab attack against Israelis, it's you who go out to beat up the poor Arab laborers! You, the Sephardim! In my opinion, the response of the Sephardim, so hostile to the Arabs, derives first from them not having been given an education. They were not given a chance to study. They're a simple, unsophisticated public, and when the newspaper headlines and the radio stir them up—and that's directed very well from above—that public gets hot and blows up. Second—discrimination. You and I, Jojo, both our groups get screwed here in this country, because of the historical reality that the early waves of immigration were Ashkenazim, and after a period of hardship here, they became the ones who eat the cream. Then you became disadvantaged, and it's well known that the disadvantaged—it's very simple—wants to compensate himself by discriminating against others."

"I don't agree!" Jojo jumped up from his seat. "Take the most extreme anti-Arab movements we have, Kahane and the Moledet Party who want to transfer all the Arabs out of Israel, in all their hierarchies you'll hardly find a single Sephardi! The entire leadership is Ashkenazim! Americans! So tell me, how can that be? Where's your theory? Listen to me, Mohammed, don't go looking for university explanations. When it's a matter of life or death, there aren't any Ashkenazim and there aren't any Sephardim. Everyone comes together. Just as an Arab from Sudan hates me when I send my army into Lebanon, we're all against you when you butcher one of us. And precisely because you and I have the same mentality, you should understand that, and I'll explain to you: Our behavior, Mohammed, will be different from Grossman's in many ways, different from the Ashkenazi's. If he has a guest who comes in and talks to his wife, it won't bother him at all. If a guest comes and talks with my wife, he'll never enter my house again! That means with us, with you and with me, my wife, and to put it more generally, my honor, is a higher priority than my work, before everything. With the Ashkenazi, no. First his work, first advancement. With us, a guest comes to my house, even if two hours beforehand he ran over my son, the minute he comes to my house, first I welcome him in. I'll get him afterward—but that's separate. Our commitment is to honor. Our mentality all plays accompaniment to the first violin—our honor. And I, Jojo Abutbul, don't hate Arabs, but I would make a law that every Arab who throws a stone in the intifadah should be shot. Because for me the act of throwing a stone is not just throwing a stone. I'm not afraid of a stone!" Jojo shouts, the veins in his neck bulging. "But with me, in Morocco, who do you throw stones at? At a dog! At a snake! It insults me! I'm not his dog, not his snake! And don't forget, Mohammed, that same stone you throw at us today, we grow up with it, we remember it!"

Kiwan's face went sour. "First of all, the Israeli public— and you, I'm very sorry to say, are a part of it—doesn't understand what the intifadah is. You don't understand the pathetic state of the people there, how bitterness built up to the point that—how did that writer of yours, S. Yizhar, put it— 'a nation rose up.' People had no way to remain silent any longer, so they used the stone. Not, God forbid, to insult you!

They are certainly not treating you like a dog, God forbid. An Arab will also throw a stone at another Arab. It's simply the only tool he has to make the world hear him! And besides, Jojo, you have to understand something important. When you're there, you're not a private citizen. You are an instrument in the hands of the Israeli regime . . ."

"I'm no instrument! What do you mean instrument? I'm part of this country, and because of that I'm also part of the government!"

"You're an instrument in the hands of the Israeli occupation regime! I'd expect of you, my dear friend [Jojo nods with a smile, waiting in ambush for his prey], that you, as part of the progressive Israeli public [Jojo the whole time is going, "Yes, yes . . ."], you should be saying that you refuse to serve in the territories!"

Jojo pounces. "Aha! In other words, I should rebel against the law! Against the law that I previously agreed to accept as a citizen here! And that's probably exactly what you'll do to me tomorrow if you and I have that country of equality, and you suddenly don't agree with me about the law, you'll say, Wait a minute! I'm resigning from the army until you, Jojo, agree with me!"

Mohammed: "There are laws, and there are laws!"

"No, pal!" Jojo bangs on the wooden table; the coffee cups and soft-drink bottles shake. "When I was in Morocco with you, you were my boss. Did I come crying to you and throw stones at you? There were things I didn't like there! I walked down the street and they threw stones at me, too, and they said dirty Jew and I got slapped in the face! Did I dare rebel then or say that there are laws and there are laws? I had two options then, to leave Morocco and come here or to accept what there was there, the good and the bad! You, if you don't want to live with me, as you wish, I made you a Palestinian state over there, there you have your own laws, fine with me. I'll go there with a visa, like a tourist!"

The conversation was interrupted for a moment. One of the workers from the restaurant came up to Jojo to ask him something. He was limping a bit. Jojo introduced him to us as Uzi. "Actually," Jojo explained, "his name is Awad. I changed it to Uzi. Easier for him, easier for me." A deep, heavy glance curdled for a long moment between Mohammed Kiwan and Uzi. "He doesn't feel comfortable either when I call him Awad in front of people. Look at him, Mohammed. He lives in Gaza, and because he had good relations with Jews, your friends there put two bullets through his legs." Jojo sent the man off and resumed his flood of words. "We said I'd visit you there with a visa. If you want, let me come in. If you don't want, throw me back. But here, in Israel, you and I will live in equality. According to the laws we make together. We are not allowed to decide to take the law into our own hands. If you or I start deciding which laws to obey, it will start today with the law about military service in the territories, tomorrow it will be the income tax law, and the day after it will be the law about how many wives I can have. You have to understand what the real meaning of democracy is. It's in your interest to understand, because you want democracy in the country you'll have someday. Democracy is that if I don't agree with the law I don't have a choice! And I want to hear from you now an answer to one question about all this—you, as a citizen here in the State of Israel: Will the Palestinian state, when it is established, satisfy you for good?"

Mohammed: "I accept that, with two of my reservations. That I have my basic rights, and then there's the last little problem that remains, my national identity."

Jojo leaned over at him suspiciously. "What's that? What did you say?"

Mohammed studied his fingers. "Give me recognition as a national minority. In other words, internal autonomy. In Israel. For the Arabs here."

"Oho!" Jojo erupts. "Hello, trouble! So now you've made me another problem—that you know in advance you're looking for as a problem, not a solution! Very nice! And here, from the start I've been telling you, Listen, let's the two of us bake two cakes. When it comes to how much flour, how many eggs we'll put in—about all that I'm willing to ask your advice. But the minute we've baked the two cakes, don't eat mine! And you, Mohammed, you should understand from your nature and I'm also appealing to your logic and your sense of justice—you can't take part of *mine* once I've given you yours! You got your country and flag and leadership, so leave me alone with my country and flag and leadership!"

He is breathing rapidly, wrathfully. Offended. An idea suddenly comes to him. "You know what? You want autonomy here? Fine! But all the Jewish settlements in your Palestinian state, give them autonomy, too! What you demand for yourself, demand for me, too! But listen, let it be, I'm telling you, let's not fool around with leftovers. I won't put my fish in your meat, and you won't put your chicken in my steak. Let's leave the fish to itself and the chicken to itself!"

Mohammed: "Even if a Palestinian state is established in the West Bank and Gaza—and of course I consider East Jerusalem to be part of it—there will still be our problem inside Israel. Am I forbidden to educate my son in accordance with my cultural heritage? Am I forbidden to foster my Palestinian nationalism? Am I forbidden to hope that the country's flag should reflect my national sensibilities also?"

Jojo shakes his head in anger and amazement. "Look what kind of person you are. You came here to tell me that you want your flag, your leadership, independence. That you don't want to live according to my law. And I'm saying, You're

1,000 percent right! So why don't you understand the same thing about me, that I want a flag that's all mine and laws that are all mine? Why do I need to try so hard to understand you, despite the fact that today I'm stronger than you and I've got power, and you, with nothing, you exist just in theory, you're already starting to tell me what to do here! So what will happen tomorrow when you're strong? Where will I be? After all, you butcher your own brothers who don't agree with you, so me you'll grind to a pulp! You scare me, Mohammed! You're scaring Jojo, the most moderate man in the country, who's willing to listen and to talk. What you're saying to me is, Listen, Jojo, now I'm getting something else ready for you! So what happens with people like me? They tell you, Hey, just a minute, if that's the way it is, motherfucker, I'll live my own life, and shit on all the rest! Let my kid burn out his brain with your kid in his own good time! But I'm saying no. I want your guts and my guts to stop fighting! I want to be able to look my kid straight in the eyes. I want my kid to live here, and if your kid wants to live here, that's just fine."

"Do you know that because of the land confiscations my child won't have anywhere to live in Um Elfahm? My house is already on the very edge, and there's nowhere to build for my son?"

Jojo stretches out his arms at him in an expansive gesture of brotherhood. "Hey, Mohammed, my son doesn't have anywhere to live near me either! Jojo would also like a house with ten rooms—but he doesn't have one! So what, the two of us will fight over ten rooms, or maybe we should both squeeze ourselves into five rooms so there will be room for both me and you? What do you say, Mohammed?" He gives him a smile of "Let's shake, let's find at least one thing in common to start with."

But for Kiwan this is not just a one-shot argument. He's fought his whole life for these ideas of his, and he's paid the price. So he gets precise: "Just as you said. We need to look for a way to live together. But if your basis for discussion is to equate the rights of the settlers who stole land from Palestinian peasants with my rights in Um Elfahm, where we've been living on the land since time immemorial, then there's no symmetry in your comparison!"

Jojo is again surging forward, and Mohammed's lips are already moving, mumbling his prepared answer, and it is already manifestly clear how each argument lights a long wick of memories with the other, running swiftly down the fuse of painful wounds. You can see how in each segment of their conversation the entire conflict is reborn, from its shell made of yesterday's newspapers back to Sarah the matriarch saying, "Cast on this bondwoman and her son: for the son of this bondwoman shall not be heir with my son, with Isaac." And in the background—the sea, which also, you may recall, was once assigned a role in the conflict. "You're still not answering me about that, Mohammed, and time is running out. Think about it now and tell me yes or no, in one sentence; it has to be only one sentence, from the guts; you've got a problem, Mohammed, maybe because you're a lawyer, you send it from the guts to the brain and then to the mouth, and the whole time I've been talking to you out of my nature. Will you, Mohammed, recognize without any challenge my right to one Jewish state? Yes or no?"

Mohammed laughs. "Look, my dear Jojo, from the cumulative experience of the Arabs in Israel . . ."

"He's being a lawyer again."

"Just a minute. Listen to me. After the Palestinian state is created, we'll still have a problem with you. Our land. Our education. Our definition as a national minority here. Our national symbols. I'm coming out of all this, and in the most democratic way possible trying to change the situation, trying to convince you—not violently—that my good is your good.

That we, the Arabs in Israel, will be a kind of, a canton, we ourselves will manage the—"

"Canton?!" Jojo burst out, from the heart. "Now you've killed me! Now you've actually created a state within a state!"

"Just a canton," Mohammed Kiwan blurted out, "a small kind of authority . . ."

"A canton is a state within a state!" Jojo Abutbul repeated. "Switzerland, for instance, is one country and it has cantons in it!"

"So you know what?" Jojo banged his fist in his hand. "I'll keep the whole West Bank and Gaza under my control, and I'll make cantons there! You decide what canton you want to live in!"

"I want to explain to you, Jojo, that autonomy, or a form of self-administration, call it whatever you want, does not diminish your future State of Israel; it can even augment it and be helpful to solve all the problems now, and not to leave any wounds under the skin, because I don't want to reach a situation where ten years from now, because of the country's discrimination against me, there will be an internal intifadah."

"So there can be an intifadah of Ethiopian Jews, too, and an intifadah of Russians, and of the oppressed Moroccans, too! So we should make a Moroccan canton? Listen, Mohammed, what you're actually saying is that a man like the Transferist is right. Gandhi says, I'll transfer out the Arabs, by consent or by force, but when I finish there will be only Jews here. That way I prevent any wounds under the skin! Then they'll be one wound, one earth-shattering scream, but that will finish it off and it will be healthier for everyone! You live with all your brothers in your Palestinian state. You won't have double identities, you won't have a problem that you need ten words to explain who you are, Arab, Israeli, Palestinian, Muslim, and I won't have any problems either with citizens that threaten me constantly with an intifadah."

Mohammed's face paled. "If you are such a racist and ig-norant man that you think, like Gandhi, that in the twentieth century it's possible to transfer nations, then please. I think it will fail."

Jojo: "I'm against it! But now you're coming and scaring me, and not leaving me a choice!"

"People aren't sheep to be taken to slaughter!" Mohammed shouted. "They'll oppose the transfer! There will be more bloodshed here!"

"Then 200,000 were killed and the problem was solved!" Jojo came back with a shout. "Then 400,000 were killed! But with that we've solved it for good!"

"But you already know from historical experience that that won't solve the problem! There will be a new problem!"

They pound the table furiously, shouting without listening. Two families of Russian immigrants, who might very well have arrived only a couple of days before, watch them in astonish-ment. They certainly have no conception how much this de-bate touches on them and their children. When Mohammed gets up for a moment to make a phone call, Jojo turns to me in amazement: "So there's a problem here that will never be solved! So whoever is strong will live! There's no other choice. Our leaders apparently know this problem. That's one of the things we don't know as citizens . . . So we're back at square one with them again. We're in a round room without corners. No one can sit in his own corner; wherever you sit there's no corner . . ." He whistles in amazement. "So it really has to be clear in the peace agreement that we solve this problem finally, and this is the last opportunity. If the PLO is Mo-hammed's sole representative, the PLO will have to commit itself to not having any more claims on the Galilee. We'll be sorry if that's not in the peace agreement." He rose, then sat down. "And even though I've been arguing until today that peace is the thing Israel needs most urgently, now I'll oppose it! With that kind of peace I'd rather not have it! Because then I didn't heal a wound, I only covered it up, and underneath, the wound will continue to become infected. Then my situation will be that much worse, because I've already handed over my best cards, Nablus and Hebron . . . very interesting . . . and he's honest, Mohammed, he's speaking sincerely. Someone will have to give way here, no arguing that . . . I'm starting to understand what's happening here . . . I've discovered a point of view that I, as an Israeli, never knew about."

Mohammed returns, sitting down heavily opposite him. Jojo turns to him with a now quiet, slightly wounded voice. "I always thought that you and I were equal. You and I—part of the map. Sure there are problems, sure there isn't complete equality, but we try to attain it. You are an Israeli Arab, I don't interfere with your feelings or with your religion, and I'll try to help you as much as I can, so that your son will go to a good school, so that he has a future here like my son. I was ready to put my shoulders level with yours. *But* to reach a state where one day you'll want to set up a state within a state? I don't care what you call it—canton, self-administration, the Autonomous Region of the Galilee. I, Jojo Abutbul, would be making myself a misery that I never thought of! So Jojo Abutbul is sitting and thinking that if that's the case, maybe Gandhi and Sharon really know what I didn't know and what you knew."

Mohammed's face isn't what it was before, either. With a weariness much greater than that caused by the conversation itself he says, "Linking my ideas and Gandhi's is very strange. Because if I wanted to be like Gandhi in my opinions and demands, I would have to say, Transfer the entire Jewish state of Israel! Abutbul will go to Morocco, the one from Russia will return to Russia, the one from Romania will return to Romania. But what I'm trying to explain to my friend Jojo, unfortunately not with any great success—"

"No, no, you really succeeded! God help me if I understood right what I understood!"

They sat and talked for a few more minutes, repeating their indictments and marveling at one another, trying to find a crack in the round, cornerless wall. Afterward Mohammed told of the classroom where his son studies, "in a four-meter-by-four-meter storage room, and in the winter, for there to be enough light, the teacher has to leave the door open."

"The country should be ashamed of itself," Jojo said. "It hurts me, it wounds my pride in my country, I won't accept it."

Mohammed continued to recount the daily hardships and harassments he endured as an Arab, problems deriving from the law and an abuse whose source was deeper. He told of a Jewish boy who had come up to him on the Netanya beach when he was there with his two small children and demanded that he, Mohammed, leave "because you're polluting our beach." Jojo listened. Before they parted, in an effort to smooth over—in retrospect—the sting left by the conversation, a clumsy effort but still heartwarming in its magnanimity, Jojo tried to put the best possible face on Kiwan's demand for autonomy. "If we want Mohammed and his people to be loyal Israeli citizens," he said, "first we have to be loyal to them. That means we can't take what little remains to them: their honor, their pride, the little that a man needs in order to live. We won't think only of what we want from them, we'll also think of what they want from us. They're part of us. And if there's a Palestinian state next to the Jewish state, and Mohammed has the right to choose where to live and he decides to live here anyway, that will be to our benefit, it will bring us honor that he feels good and equal here. And when a man like Mohammed comes and says that he wants that, autonomy, his canton, he, in my opinion, doesn't really mean it. He wants security. He wants a way to defend himself. That's what he means when he asks for a canton. He actually wants a lot less than that—equality."

Mohammed Kiwan accepted the hand proffered him. It seemed to me that Jojo's moving gesture was more important to him—at that moment—than standing his ideological ground. Maybe Jojo really had understood Mohammed's intent. I don't know. "Maybe, as Jojo said with great justice," Kiwan responded, "it may well be that the ideas I raised with regard to the canton were raised as a kind of shield, as the result of the cumulative and very bitter experience of the way the government here has behaved to the Arab population. But for me the most important part of this meeting was that I met Jojo the man. I felt in a very human way Jojo's willingness to understand me, to identify with my suffering, and I leave here exhilarated, not because of what we said, but because of the sublime values of man and humanity. I always believed that every human being is, when it comes down to it, human. The stigmas, the labels Jew, Arab—this conversation proved that they are as important as an onionskin. And just for that I'm happy I came."

The two of them stood, exhausted from the conversation, and then, in an impulse of the moment, embraced.

CHAPTER 9

"Sure I want to be part of the country," says Rima Othman, twenty-three, from Beit Safafa, a village nestled between Jerusalem's old and new southern neighborhoods. "And I want to feel a little as if I belong here, but they don't give me a chance. Even if there's no law that's overtly discriminatory, they always push you away here. Close the door in your face. Ask me why I so much want to get through that door they keep closing on me. The truth is that I don't want to go all the way in. I don't want to cast off all my culture and society, I don't want to assimilate. But I want to get ahead like you. I'm not saying really compete . . ."

"Why not?"

"Okay, why not. The truth is that competition makes for quality. And I think that Israeli society brings us quality and progress. If I weren't an Israeli Arab woman, if I were a Jewish woman, I'm sure I wouldn't be studying speech disorders. I'd be a secretary. But our society imposes on us a responsibility to advance, to improve ourselves. Because we need doctors, lawyers, social workers. We have to move forward.

"As a Jewish woman I'd study. What would I study?" Her eyes float through space as she smiles to herself. "Maybe I'd study business, have a briefcase, meetings, telephones, long-winded talk. But I'd be learning something useful. The truth is that I wanted to do a master's in speech disorders between different nations, but that seems too abstract to me. And we don't have the luxury of occupying ourselves for no purpose with useless things. Not only that—curing international speech disorders is too discouraging. I've stopped believing in it."

She pauses for a moment. Begins to say something. Laughs at herself. "Because I still believe. Or hope. I fool myself. You see, I'm always changing my mind . . . unstable . . . you know, in that I envy the Arabs in the occupied territories, everything's much clearer to them. They know that they are there, and know whom they are fighting against and whom they should hate. They don't have to go to a clinic and be treated by a Jewish doctor, who's nice to you and helps you, and yet maybe he's a Kahane supporter. But if I lived in Ramallah, would it bother me to hate Jews in general? What contact would I have with Jews? Only through repression. Sometimes I get upset about something and say, I hate Jews. Two minutes later I think, But I can't hate. Noa, my friend, is Jewish. And my friend Miriam is Jewish, and religious. When I studied at Tel Aviv University I was the only Arab among forty Jewish women, and it was important for them to make me feel that I was accepted. They were all so nice to me, I'd be hurt if they told me that they hate Arabs.

"The same is true in the opposite direction. Jews who don't know Arabs—it's easier for them to hate us. They know the Arab laborer, the terrorist, the Arab with a *kaffiyeh* and a knife. That's why I, when I was an Arab woman in Tel Aviv, maybe

I went out of the way to be very nice to the women in my class, to show them that I'm an Arab and you can get along with me, and if you can do it with me, there are many more like me."

She is a tall young woman, well dressed and made up. Her hair is chestnut and falls to her shoulders. She is soon to marry a man from Teibe. For the time being she lives with her parents on the edge of Beit Safafa, almost on the tracks, in a neighborhood where the walls tremble when the train, the village's timekeeper, passes by. A woman I once met told me that "Jerusalem is every place from which you hear the train whistle." Beit Safafa, by that criterion, is in the center of town.

Like Barta'a, Beit Safafa was also cut in two by the Rhodes armistice agreements. By night smugglers spirited tomatoes and potatoes across the border from Israel to Jordan, and spices and pine nuts and almonds in the opposite direction. Rima's parents were married a month before the war that united the village, and they conducted the wedding procession right along the border, so her father's sister could participate in the celebration. The village school has "Jordanian" and "Israeli" classes in adjacent rooms. When she was seventeen Rima passed the Israeli high-school graduation exam, while friends of hers took the test devised by the Jordanian Ministry of Education. She studied Bible, Hebrew literature, and Jewish history. They studied Arabic, Koran, and Arab history.

"In our civics lessons I saw that there is no such thing as a pure democracy. I saw how much you could play with the law. Still, there's nothing like democracy! During the Gulf War I was on a trip to London. In Hyde Park I argued with Kuwaitis and Egyptians—even Israel is better than you are, I told them. There was a Jordanian there who got me so mad! He told me that he blamed the Arab leadership for the Arab nation's problems. I shouted at him, And I accuse the people of acquiescing in such leaders. Because if we, the Arabs, were a courageous people we would get rid of all our leaders! You should have thrown King Hussein out a long time ago! And I told him how in the intifadah there had been a lot of excesses by the Israeli Army, and they caught the soldiers who did the excesses and put them on trial, and they wrote about it in the newspaper. In what Arab country could that happen? Suddenly I felt I was defending Israel. How did that happen to me? But I was just making a comparison.

"For us, the Arabs, it was hard to get used to democracy. We don't have any talent for it. I'll give my children a democratic education, but in school they won't see it. You need a special character for democracy, and we've become accustomed to there always being someone over us telling us what to do. We've gotten used to dictatorship. Everything with us is hierarchy and family authority. I, for instance, work with both Jews and Arabs. In staff meetings, if there's a Jewish chairman, everyone is bold, even the Arabs; everyone expresses opinions, criticizes. But if by chance there's an Arab chairman, the Arabs will submit to everything he says. So I think that if there's a Palestinian state, it will be a dictatorship at the beginning. Maybe that's what has to be in order to make things work there. Oh, we've got a lot more to do. Many long years will pass before we become real people.

"That's the way we are. From history. We never went with our feelings and with what we believe and want. Ever since the Turks, the British, the Jordanians, our nation has had no say in its own affairs. They always told us what to say. We are not a brave nation. We are afraid of every ruler, of every strong man. Take a small experience I had. We were sitting in a restaurant in the Galilee, in Turan. A young Israeli man sat next to us with a bunch of tourists; he was talking politics with them. Loudly, you know, so everyone would hear. There was an Arab waiter there, a boy in eleventh or twelfth grade. He spilled a glass of water on the table. It could happen any-

where. The Israeli yelled at him at the top of his lungs, Bring
me the manager! And when the boy went to call him, the
Israeli stood up in front of all of us and shouted, He spilled
water on me and still dares look me in the eye! How dare he
look me in the eye, that Arab! That's what they really think
about us. We're not allowed to look anyone in the eye. We
grew up with that. That's with Arabs everywhere, but here in
particular. And you see how all our talk about honor and
bravery and manliness, with Arabs—all those exist only with
regard to equals. Not when it comes to anyone bigger or
stronger than you.

"I really feel the lack of that courage. I also work in the
Augusta Victoria Hospital in East Jerusalem and there I see
how they talk with superiors, how the face goes red and the
heart pounds. When I worked at Tel Hashomer Hospital in
Tel Aviv, I had to speak with my advisor every morning, and
for three years I didn't dare ask a question. All the education
in democracy and boldness I received was still not enough for
me to have courage in Israeli society.

"I just hope," she says, "I just hope that we'll know how to
use what we've learned from you. But the problem is that we
don't actually do anything. I'm envious of anyone who lives
at one with himself, like you, an Israeli Jew . . . Sometimes
I imagine myself living as a girl from Tel Aviv, going to shows,
going out, Yehuda Poliker concerts; I like him."

"Have you been to one of his concerts?"

"I really wanted to, but I didn't go."

"Why not?"

The look she gave me . . . half the articles I read on the
identity dilemma of the Arabs in Israel try to explain that look.

"If I were to go I'd spend the whole time thinking, What
am I doing here? I'm an Arab. I'd feel that I was playing
someone else's part. I'd get upset and argue with myself. But
I like him! But maybe they'll notice I'm an Arab? So when

I'm alone I put on one of his cassettes . . ." I ask, and she hums the song "Less, But It Hurts," and giggles awkwardly. "That's our quandary, our split personality. When Israel went on daylight time, I worked until eleven in Jerusalem at the hospital for deaf and mute children, and then I'd go to the Augusta Victoria, where they work according to Jordanian time, and set my clock back. Because if anyone in the bus asks you what time it is and you give them the Israeli time, they make a big ruckus about it."

That's so different from my experience, I thought, when four years ago I went to the West Bank to talk with Palestinians. There, it was hard to find a young woman of Rima's age who wasn't tied—even bound—by a rope of passion to a single, unambiguous stake. The "pathos" Azmi Bishara talks of was in the air.

Is it really absent, as Bishara claims (with such pathos)? Can one reach any unambiguous conclusion about the current state of the Arabs in Israel? Almost every person I meet illuminates the tangle in a different light; instead of fervor and slogans there are doubts, internal contradictions, and, especially, man's empty-handedness in the face of complex circumstances. "It would be such fun if I were a Jewish woman in this country." Rima blushed, putting a fluttering hand on her mouth, shocked at what had come out of it—yet she added, "It could be really fun to live here. I told my boyfriend, There's no more ideal place on earth when it comes to quality of life, work, entertainment, view, relations between people, independence . . . if we were only Jews here."

To my credit I remained silent.

"And my boyfriend said, This isn't our country. That was when I said that our way of enjoying ourselves is different from theirs, from yours. For us, going out means going to a restaurant, shopping, but enjoying yourself can also be a nature hike in the Negev, in the Galilee. He said to me, 'Rima, if this were our country, everything would be different.' Because, for instance, there are a lot of places I've never been, canyons I'd like to see with my own eyes, not on the map. Only once in my life was I in the Negev. Or, for instance, overseas I've been in a lot of museums, and here in Israel I've only been one time, in fourth grade! I see, for example, a new immigrant from Russia, and I know that I belong here more than she does, when it comes to language, the land, heritage, in any real way, but they don't give me the feeling of belonging. There's not the peace and the security that it's mine.

"So you understand what that means, day by day? Look how I'm talking. How I jump from one thought to another. No stability of thought, of nerves. Always confused. No serenity inside. And that you'll see especially among us—we have no self-confidence. We're too unsure of ourselves. Afraid of every sip we take from the cup. I remember when I was little there was a terrorist attack in Jerusalem and we were going home on the bus. My mother told me, 'Shhh! Don't talk in Arabic!' Something like that always stays with you. When I have my own children, I already know I'll be afraid to go into town with them, to a movie, say. I'm not the type to silence my kids so they won't talk in Arabic, and I already know that a time will come when I'll do that.

"Or at Tel Aviv University, when I studied there and they assigned us dorm rooms. They didn't know I was an Arab, maybe I don't look like one, and one of the girls came up to me and said, 'Gee, your roommate's here, and she's an Arab!' On the other hand, when at work, in East Jerusalem, someone discovers that I studied at the university with Jews, he understands: 'Ah! You're from '48! And I get treated differently from then on, the face changes. I try to convince them that I'm like them—"

"Whom do you try to convince?"

"The . . . I try to convince the Arabs that with us we've

also hardly been having weddings since the intifadah, and my
uncle was arrested for a year, and I catch myself: Hey, you're
really trying to persuade them, to prove something to them.
And they don't want to hear . . .

"Or, during the war, when I went to Augusta Victoria in
Arab Jerusalem. I had a gas mask and they didn't—in the West
Bank they didn't get gas masks. Wow, what will I do with the
mask there? I was always hiding it, packing and wrapping it
up in something. Luckily there was no alert when I was there.
Every time there was an attack on Tel Aviv I'd think, Who
were the people who got hit this time? I hope no one was
killed, maybe a friend of mine. Should I call? What could I
say to her? But I didn't call, don't ask me why, maybe I was
nervous, maybe because it was a very sensitive period and every
word I said could be misinterpreted, even though during that
period I felt very much a part of Israeli society, my room was
the sealed room, and we listened to the civil alert broadcasts
along with everyone. Joy never entered my head. No one in
Beit Safafa danced on the rooftops, but still I thought that
maybe it would make the Jews wake up and think what it's
like when they blow up a house in the West Bank because a
boy who lives there threw a stone. That's the dilemma and
that's the hard part—you live in this country, and someone
attacks you, and you think that maybe someone will come to
the rescue, but maybe not, maybe not.

"My children, when I have them"—she sighs—"will not
speak in generalizations, that's certain." Her lips purse. "And
I can't take anything all the way. What little I've seen of Israel
I can't love all the way. Today, when I leave Jerusalem, for
instance, and see the mountains, I think, Oh, how much
you've been through, mountains. And I think, If the sea could
talk, if the mountains could speak. Who dwelt on you? Who
built on you? Who lived here? Who will live here? Are you
mine? Whose? And all the questions start up again."

CHAPTER 10

During one of the lessons in the twelfth-grade class in the village high school, in the center of Israel, I asked the students what they knew about the Holocaust. At first they could not figure out what I was talking about. Maybe they didn't know the word. I translated it into Arabic. Most of their expressions were still blank. One girl said hesitantly, "What the Nazis did to the Jews?" When I confirmed this, everyone remembered. They had spent four hours studying World War II, and they knew. "That they put them in the ovens? I heard that he killed six million Jews." She smiled. "That's what *they* say."

A boy named Munzir, who sat in the first row, said, "I saw a television documentary on that. In my opinion, what they say about the Nazis isn't right. They killed maybe only a million."

"What makes you think that?"

"Because human beings can't kill so many people. He wasn't as cruel as you say."

"Do you see anything good in what Hitler did?" I asked.

"First of all, he brought the whole German people together under him, and wanted to unite all the nations of the world. But the Jews were a problem for him, because they'd gotten control of all the money in Germany. Hitler wanted the Germans to be in control, and the Jews interfered with that. So he killed them. But certainly not more than a million."

Most of the students in the classroom nodded their heads in agreement. I thought, Arabs have so often accused us Jews of guilt in the deaths of the six victims of the Land Day massacre in Sakhnin in 1976. They saw the murdered men as symbols, as a myth, and made demands in their name.

I asked, "And do you think it is justified to exterminate a minority that interferes with a majority?"

"Well, not eliminate it. But deport it, yes." Munzir chuckled. "All they did was a population transfer." But here another boy, Amir, spoke up: "Population transfer isn't legitimate! What Munzir is doing is to justify the Israeli regime that wants to do that to us. After all, we interfere with Israeli rule here!"

I asked if they feel that the Jews in Israel treat them the way the Germans treated the Jews. The young people had no doubts. Cries of agreement came from all directions. When I noted that Israel is not trying to physically destroy the Palestinian people, neither from racial nor from other motives, a boy named Naim threw this out at me: "It's exactly the same thing there and here! Israel wants to get rid of the Arabs, wants to exterminate us!"

"Exterminate you?"

He thought for a minute. "Okay, maybe not physically, but spiritually! It wants to eliminate our history and literature. They forbid us to study our national poets. In a moral sense, they are destroying us!" As he spoke he grew feverish. "They want us to assimilate, to become Israelis, to detach ourselves from the other Arab nations, to forget what it is to be Palestinian. Isn't that destruction to you?"

"Of course, they don't know anything about the Holocaust," said Mohammed Handuklo, a history teacher at the Jat school. "What do they know? That the Nazis were against the Jews and wanted to evict them from Europe, and they know some of the solutions that Hitler, let's say, made use of. I'll tell you straight out, we don't give that any special attention. We study it the way we study, say, the Vienna Congress. We talk about it for as long as the curriculum says we should, give assignments; the students debate a little about whether he was right or not, if he should have done it or not. Various opinions are expressed, and that's it."

"How many hours, on the average, does the Arab student spend studying the Holocaust during his time at school?"

"There's no average." He laughed. "Exactly one lesson. I teach one lesson about it."

In other words, fifty minutes.

I asked Dr. Ali Hidar, the director of Arab education in the Ministry of Education, why so little attention is given to the Holocaust in the Arab curriculum.

"I can understand it if they don't go into the Holocaust in depth," he said. "Because it's a sensitive matter."

"Very sensitive," I agreed.

"In everything that relates to the extermination of the Jews," he went on, "the Arab teacher is afraid that they'll say that he—you know—that is, who knows, maybe some of the students will suspect him of, you know, being glad of what happened . . ."

"But the teacher can present the Holocaust objectively, according to the facts, and that way he can teach what happened there."

"No, no . . ." Hidar mumbled.

"He can find universal lessons in the Holocaust; he can also tell them that the Arabs were the next ones in line for extermination, according to Hitler's book."

"Yes, that's the way I explained it when I was a supervisor and I was once invited to a school where they had painted swastikas on the road. I explained it all to them—until they cried. But I have the background. I've visited the Ghetto Fighters Museum, and I know. But another teacher, whatever his position is, there are those, his enemies, who will claim that he taught the Holocaust and favored the extermination. With us, in the Arab sector, there's no small problem of informants."

Does the situation seem immutable? I asked. He said that he, together with Lapid, an organization that seeks to educate the public in the lessons of the Nazi extermination program, had recently begun to formulate a lesson plan for Arab teachers, to help them give their students the facts about the Holocaust. "It all depends on the teacher." He sighed. "But not every teacher is able to cope with it. It's a big problem."

"Why should we learn about it?" a girl from the Jat twelfth-grade class shouted at me. "They're always teaching us about how the Jews suffered!"

I prefer to answer her by quoting an Egyptian, Tahsin Bashir, formerly President Mubarak's personal ambassador. "The Arabs have no consciousness of the Holocaust," he told me. "At most we see it as the way you justify what you are doing to the Arabs, and for that reason we have little patience for it. Before we made peace I always argued that we lacked a serious book about Judaism in Arabic, a scientific and well-documented book. Not propaganda. We also lack any acquaintance with Israeli literature, especially that part of it that deals with the Holocaust. There is not, for example, an Arabic translation of Anne Frank's diary [actually, there is, translated by Mohammed Abassi]. How can we understand you? The Holocaust is, after all, one of the main keys to the Jewish soul.

As long as the Arabs do not hold that key, we will not be able to gain entry."

"Last year I took an organized tour of Eastern Europe," Dr. Nazir Yunes of Kafr Ara told me. "The group included the children of Holocaust survivors, people whose families had been murdered there, people who themselves had been there, and partisan fighters. Obviously, the tour was centered around the extermination camps. I heard their stories, and they'd talk on the bus rides. They made everything I'd read in books very concrete. I went with some of them to look for their old houses. I took a cab with one member of the group and we went to his hometown, in Czechoslovakia. He remembered every street and every house. We reached his house, and his nurse was there, old and blind. In the extermination camps we visited I stood in front of the gas chambers. We lit candles, and all of a sudden everything you knew about the suffering and the history of the Jews runs through your head, and you tremble, almost enough, I'd say, to make you cry. At the gas chambers I asked a friend of mine, an Arab who was there with me, 'What does it mean to you that entire villages, whole towns were erased there in a single day?' And he answered me, 'What do you want, look what they're doing to us now.'

"Now, I'm not willing to make that comparison," Yunes said, "but the link between the two things certainly exists. The principal impetus that led to the establishment of Israel was Jewish experience in the Exile and in the Holocaust. That traumatic experience affects all of life here. When you see those things you understand it in such a concrete way, and you realize how much the element of fear in Jewish society was deepened by the Holocaust. Fear of the foreigner. Fear of everything."

When Nazir Yunes was fourteen, his father sent him to

study at the agricultural boarding school at Pardes Hannah, together with Jewish children. "Father knew that we had to have strong ties with the Jews. To learn about them and learn to live with them. If we don't know each other we won't be able to live together." Nazir entered the school not knowing Hebrew, and found himself studying about the early Zionists and the 'redemption of the land,' and singing 'Hatikva' devotedly. When his father found numerous mistakes in the Arabic of his letters home, he said, 'I've lost my son.' Today Yunes, forty-four years old, is a surgeon in the general and plastic surgery department of the Hillel Yafeh Hospital in Hadera. He speaks with a perfect Hebrew accent, reads for the most part in Hebrew, dreams in both languages, and counts in Hebrew.

"If I remember that 26,000 out of the 36,000 dunams of my village's land were confiscated; if I remember that until the end of 1966 I needed a special permit to go from my village to the neighboring one, because of the military government; if my village received electricity twenty years after the Jewish settlement next door received it; if the road to Ara was paved only three years ago; if the 'nationality' and 'religion' entries on my identity card raise eyebrows in every office; if I see Arik Sharon's maps in the newspaper showing how he wants to surround me with thirty to forty thousand Jews, to cut me off like a dangerous criminal; if every day more voices are calling for my, an Israeli Arab's, eviction from the country—if I put all those together, I should hate you. But I just can't hate you." He nods his heavy, prematurely gray head. "I grew up within your culture. I was educated in a certain way. I can no longer hate you."

He is a brave man. In 1991 with Palestinian-Israeli leaders declaring that the PLO, not Israel, represents them in the peace talks, Yunes rose at a stormy political rally in Um Elfahm and said, "The PLO does not represent us. The people that should be representing me in the negotiations with Israel over my fate as a Palestinian are we ourselves, the Palestinians in Israel." This opinion is certainly that of many Israeli Palestinians, but Yunes was among the first to express it openly. In doing so he revealed the divisions among the Palestinians in Israel as to their role in the future peace treaties. Why am I relating this? Because it is all woven up with the central point, the special Israeli identity that might someday be created here.

"My children have a hard time understanding me," he continued. "It's strange for them to see me and my wife crying out of emotion and compassion when there's a film on television about Jewish suffering during the Holocaust. What do they know about the Holocaust? My daughter, thirteen years old, never heard of the Holocaust. They also don't understand how I can have a party at home and have twenty Jewish guests, colleagues from work, when the same night the Jewish army has been conducting searches and abusing people in the Nablus refugee camp, where their aunt lives. It all gets mixed up with them.

"Or one day I took the kids to the swimming pool at Gan Shomron, the Jewish settlement next to us, and bought them tickets, and the woman selling the tickets suddenly heard the children speaking Arabic and said, Just a minute. Wait outside. I have to find something out. Then she comes back and says, I'm sorry, this is a private pool.

"I took my children to one side," Yunes related. "They were already in their bathing suits. I explained to them that the woman said that it's a private pool and that we need special permission to enter. My two older children said, No, it's because we're Arabs.

"I took the woman to one side, and I told her that what really irked me was that I didn't know how to explain it to my kids on the way home. You tell me what to say to them.

"So she said, I don't know. It's not my orders.

"I kept insisting: The children want to know why you aren't letting us in. And I hope that because of this refusal my children and your children will not meet on two sides of a rifle fifteen years from now.

"She burst out crying. Afterward it turned out that she is a Holocaust survivor, and maybe she saw herself in a situation that seemed like somewhere else. I don't know. We went home. They called later from the pool and apologized, and invited us to come again, for free, but we didn't go. That is, I go there regularly. I'm the doctor at Gan Shomron. I care for them. Give their women their periodic breast examinations and stand in for the regular doctor when he's not around."

CHAPTER 11

The idea of Palestinian autonomy within the Israeli state has
churned beneath the country's surface, invisible but present,
threatening and suspicious, like a false bottom hiding no one
knows what, and it echoes in all discourse between the two
peoples. The things that Mohammed Kiwan hinted at during
his conversation with Jojo Abutbul on the Ashdod beach gave
me no rest. I searched for someone who could clear up the
haziness and put it in perspective. So I met with Dr. Sa'id
Zeidani, a native of the village of Tamra, in the Galilee.

"The Israelis always ask the wrong question, one I reject,"
Dr. Zeidani said. "They ask me, 'If a Palestinian state comes
into being alongside Israel, will you remain in Israel or will
you move to the Palestinian state?' I think that we need to ask
a different question: 'If a Palestinian state is established, how
will you, as an Arab in Israel, see your relationship to it?' This
allows a discussion of a much more complex and richer relationship. Of all kinds of mechanisms and arrangements for

ties between the Arabs in Israel and those in the Palestinian state. I don't know if I myself will move there, but I very much want there to be such a country, one that I'll be part of, or at least that I'll be on intimate terms with, even if I live within Israel's boundaries."

I asked, "What exactly is that 'intimate relationship'?"

"For instance, if I live in the Galilee and a Palestinian state is established, it should mean something to me, and not just abstractly. It should solve my problems. It should represent the Palestinian experience I am a partner in."

"How could you be a partner in it if you live in Israel?"

"That's a difficult problem. There have to be, for instance, open borders between Israel and the Palestinian state. There has to be a certain link, maybe administrative, between the Arabs in Israel and Palestine. There can't be a situation in which the Palestinian state comes into being after decades of struggle and we here remain indifferent to it, and it to us. This intimate relationship can be like that of the Jews in the Diaspora, in America, to Israel."

"There's an ocean separating the Jews in America from the Jews in Israel."

"That's right. And here we are talking about territorial continuity between Israel and the Palestinian state. So that we can have even stronger cultural, family, and commercial ties, ties of all types. Maybe a political link between us and them, maybe an administrative one."

"What you're actually speaking of is complete autonomy for the Arabs in Israel."

"The word 'autonomy' only partially describes that relation."

"So please describe it in more detail. When you say 'political links,' do you see representatives of the Palestinians in Israel sitting in the parliament of the Palestinian state?"

"If we vote for the Knesset in Israel, then of course we will not vote for the Palestinian parliament. But if the Israeli Arabs are part of the Palestinian state, then they can send representatives to the Palestinian parliament."

"Do you believe that there can really be a situation in which the Palestinians living in Israel are an integral part of the Palestinian state?"

"What do you mean 'believe'? Not in the short run, but in the long run. Still, maybe that will remain a dream."

"Your dreams also interest me, and I'll tell you why. Today [August 1, 1991], when I was driving to meet you, the American Secretary of State James Baker's motorcade passed me. He came to hear from Prime Minister Shamir whether Israel is willing to participate in the peace talks. So if there actually is a serious intention of solving the major problems of the Middle East, without leaving any smoldering embers, it's best for us to know clearly what the aspirations of the parties are."

"Look, if we're talking about real peace, about a historic compromise, about nations that truly want to live together, about equality and well-being for all, then it is possible to think of all sorts of political arrangements that the Arabs in Israel will participate in. What I had in mind when I spoke of autonomy is that instead of dividing this territory into two states, Israel and Palestine, maybe there could be one state divided into cantons. Like Switzerland. And one of the cantons would be that of the Arabs in Israel. Jerusalem might be a separate canton. That could solve ethnic problems within Israel, as well as the Palestinian national problem within Israel. That's all."

"Could you describe life in such an autonomous entity in Israel?"

"That's not simple. How can a national minority achieve equality in a society that has a Jewish majority, a country that is defined as a Jewish state, in the absence of a general Israeli nationality? How is that possible? There is discrimination at all levels and in all areas of life. The Arabs here are half-citizens, and the state, for them, is half democratic. They are in the middle—between citizenship and subjection. The doors are only half open to them in all areas of life, and there are areas in which the gaps are getting larger. And all this is after decades of struggle for some kind of integration of the Arabs into Israel. That struggle has not succeeded. So I ask you, What is the message? How should the Arabs in Israel organize themselves as a national minority in order to realize their different ethnic national identity and realize their equal civil rights? The idea of autonomy is intended to provide an answer for both those questions."

He is forty years old, and studied philosophy and English as an undergraduate at Haifa University. He received his Ph.D. from the University of Wisconsin at Madison. His major fields of interest are aesthetics and ethics. Today he is a member of the Philosophy Department at Bir Zeit University. Zeidani, like other Arab intellectuals born in Israel, has moved to the territories—he lives in the East Jerusalem neighborhood of Beit Hanina with his wife and two daughters. "It is not an ideological decision that I should be—you know—participating in the struggle and educating my daughters from within the intifadah. To say it is ideological is good for making speeches. What was important to me and my wife was to live in a Palestinian community, a normal community for us, one that does not discriminate against us. In which I have respectable work. I simply can no longer stand a situation of discrimination. When a policeman says that you've made a mistake on the road, be careful and don't do it again, okay and thank you, and I go, and then he calls me back and asks to see my identity card, and you know from that moment on you're done for. So you look at that policeman, and show him how much contempt you have for him. But inside it's not just contempt. It's so painful it kills you."

"Explain to me how he knows that you're Arab." I stray for a moment (or perhaps not) from the main subject of our discussion. "You yourself told me before that you 'don't look Arab.' Your Hebrew is perfect and you speak without an accent."

"Maybe it's something in my eyes. Maybe in my insecurity . . . I guess the uneasiness is evident. Maybe the way I walk, maybe the suspicion I feel envelops me. Maybe"—he laughs—"maybe it's really an aesthetic problem."

I asked whether his presence in the territories during the intifadah had led him to formulate his idea of autonomy.

"Only in the tactical sense. I mean, they say there should be autonomy in the territories, and I say that this is the wrong place to have autonomy. Autonomy is what you do with a national minority within a country, not in an occupied territory. But that's not the thing. What we see is that the model of integration, involvement, of coexistence that most Arab political groups have championed has failed. I argue that even were there not a state of war, it would not be possible to overcome your attitude toward us and the discrimination. So we need to look for another model. That could be the model of separation. That is, we will separate from the Jewish state and be part of Palestine, for instance. Or we'll want self-determination. An independent country."

"What they call the 'Galilean state'?"

"I think that a 'Galilean state' is not realistic. So I propose an intermediate model—that we be part of the state, but that there be both separation and integration. Look at the experiences of other countries, Switzerland, Canada, Belgium, and Eastern European countries, and you see that all along the way the integration model did not work. In Belgium they're now talking of a federative structure; in Switzerland there's division into cantons according to ethnic affiliation—Italians,

French, Germans—and it works. In Canada it's working, but it's harder."

These ideas of his have already aroused anger at him, largely from the Arab establishment in Israel. In several private conversations I heard, however—mostly off the record—favorable comments about autonomy, which they see as the only realistic solution. Sa'id Zeidani himself voices his views in a quiet and serene voice. He is a slender man of intellectual appearance, his face delicate and expressive. With each statement he dives inside himself and disappears for a moment before surfacing with the word he wants. As he speaks, quiet but firm, discerning and somewhat distant, he seems at moments detached, strange to that clay of emotions and anxieties, the mortar from which the politics of the region are kneaded. Yet at the same time I felt that his philosophical attitude, hanging in the timelessness in which anything is possible, was what really threatened me.

"I told the Arab leadership here, You are chasing after an illusion. There will be no integration here. There will be no real cooperation with the Jews. So we need to change direction. To search for another framework. And when I speak of significant and full autonomy, I am also speaking, of course, of the territorial aspect."

"But it's not realistic—Israel has no region that is only Arab."

"The border does not have to be a straight line."

I recalled the summer evening when I drove from Nazareth to Mghar by an entirely "Arab" route—through the villages of Rayna, Kafr Kana, Turan, and Ilabun—brown stony hills, shepherds with herds of black, scrawny goats, brown hens pecking along the roadside, a veiled woman picking figs, pages from Arabic newspapers impaled on thorn bushes. Later I went through the streets of Sakhnin—in the courtyards of small neighborhoods women and girls stood sifting rice, or kneeling and slicing watermelons. A green, pencil-thin minaret suddenly shot up through the long twilight, as did the jubilant voice of a boy singing a prayer duet with the *muezzin*. I drove slowly, immersed in the odd sensation of being able to watch without being seen. Present and absent. A pair of neighbors in undershirts played backgammon, and a boy served them coffee. A group of youths strutted down the street, hair greased back, eyeing a gaggle of girls out of the corners of their eyes. It reminded me of how I had encountered an identical scene in the Lebanese village of Mimas during the war in 1982. It had been this same languid summer evening hour; the boys and girls met on the village's single main road, looking, giggling, and taking measure of each other at a distance, bold and demure. The war would end sometime, after all, things would change, and you have to live those moments now, for there will be no more like them. For a moment it was possible to imagine that Sakhnin was located in the Shouf Mountains of southern Lebanon, or in Jordan, or near Nablus—the neon signs were in Arabic, the music coming from the cars was Arabic, and the atmosphere had the self-assured tranquillity of the masters of their own homes. The way people walked, their body language, was different, freer and more relaxed than what they showed when they were in Israel's "Jewish" regions. More than once this summer I noticed what happened to people when, after sitting with them in their homes, we went outside. Even one's natural environment can be foreign. Their faces immediately took on a foreign expression in order to pass our scrutiny. They unwittingly adjust themselves to our surveillance and become attenuated or, paradoxically, more blatant. But that evening in Sakhnin they were among their own. The Jews were not present, and one could even argue that the "situation" was no situation. I also had a sudden sense of relief (when I write this now, in Jerusalem, I begin to doubt myself—did I really? No fear or threat from that freedom "they allow themselves there"? No. On the contrary). An unexpected, refreshing sense of relief; after all, a burden gets taken off my shoulders that way.

"Just a minute!" The internal security officer sets off his siren within me. "Where did you get those pretty words? Don't you know that three weeks before your enchanted evening in Sakhnin we uncovered in that very village a cell that planned to blow up the Rafael military industries building, a real gang of terrorists?" You know what, I answer him, maybe not even a single group like that would have risen there had we been smarter and bolder. If the people of Sakhnin felt relaxed and free in Tel Aviv as well. Have you ever tried that line of thought?

The idea of autonomy for the Arabs of Israel celebrated its sixtieth birthday not long ago. In 1931 it was proposed by a Zionist leader: "We conceive of the regime in Jewish Israel in the following way: the majority of the population will be Jewish, but the equal rights of the Arab citizens will not only be ensured—they will be realized. Both languages and all three religions will have equal privileges, and each nation will receive the right of cultural self-determination." The speaker is Ze'ev (Vladimir) Jabotinsky, the Revisionist Zionist leader whose ideological heirs in Israel today are Yitzhak Shamir and the Likud Party, and the words come from his article "Round Table with the Arabs," included in a book with the ironic title of *On the Road to Statehood*.

Jabotinsky went into even greater detail in "The Revisionist Manifesto": "Absolute equality of rights for the two races, the two languages, and for all religions will prevail in the future Hebrew state. National self-government for each of the races in the land—in matters of community, education, culture, and political representation—must be implemented to the fullest measure" (from *On the Road to Statehood*).

On January 26, 1990, Sa'id Zeidani published his plan in the newspaper *El-Arabi*:

1. I conceive of an autonomous regime for the Arabs of the Triangle and the Galilee, including an independent elected administration that has the widest possible authority.
   a. The establishment of one or more Arabic universities in Israel.
   b. Making Arabic the official language in the zones belonging to the autonomous regime.
   c. Decision-making authority regarding construction, development, health, and environment.
   d. Decision-making authority on the issue of non-military national service.
   e. The establishment of a local police system, responsible for internal security in the given area.
   f. Decision-making authority in questions of education, and the establishment of the goals and contents of the educational system.
2. The autonomous areas will have federal links with the State of Israel. Their administrations will have a free hand in creating and strengthening ties with the rest of the Palestinian people and the Arab nation, both before and after the establishment of a Palestinian state alongside Israel.
3. The autonomous authority will not infringe on full and equal citizenship.

"Territorial autonomy," I asked Dr. Zeidani, "is generally a stage preceding total separation from the mother state. Who can ensure that after the Palestinians in Israel have autonomy they will not want to adhere to the Palestinian state?"

"Such a risk exists, of course," he responded sedately, "but, on the other hand, Israel has done everything to ensure that such a possibility will not come up for discussion. With regard to its population-dispersion policy. The Jewish border settlements, the kibbutzim, the locations of absorption centers . . . Adherence to the Palestinian state is not realistic."

"Who will control the external security of the autonomous region?"

"Israel. But in all other matters—I'm the boss. The judicial system will also be separate. With regard to elections to the Knesset, the existing state of affairs can continue. Or the canton could send ten or twenty Knesset members, in proportion to its population."

"In Switzerland, for example," I noted, "the citizens of the various cantons send their sons to the country's army."

"Autonomy is a solution to the army problem as well. So far, the Arabs in Israel have not been required and have not asked to serve in the army. But in territorial autonomy, which has its own police force and its own national guard, it is possible to speak of national service. They can compel, or ask, every boy of a certain age to serve a year or two or three in public service of the autonomous region. In other words, Israel will not require national service for its own ends. Instead, the boys will serve their own society. They could work in public institutions, serve in the national guard, in the hospitals, in the police force."

"Describe your ambitions in the field of education."

"That's what we want autonomy for, isn't it?"

"Why, if that's the case, don't you limit yourself to a demand for cultural autonomy?"

"What's cultural autonomy? Where in the world has that worked? I want an Arab university where I'm the boss, but as part of my control of my entire society. A Jewish man will not be the boss where I live. Today, say I'm interested in nuclear physics. Can I study that in Israel? And if, hypothetically, they were to allow me to study that, what work could I get afterward?

In construction? You can't separate the functioning of the educational system from what you do after you graduate. You can't detach education from the economic life of the entire population. I want, after all, to direct my own education so that it will answer the needs of my society, as I see them, and not as the Ministry of Education in Jerusalem determines for me. What are our graduates when they finish their studies? Teachers teachers teachers. They aren't taken in accordance with their abilities. Not into the universities, or the Israeli civil service, or the foreign service. They aren't given places on committees; they are not directors, or deputy directors, or senior officials, or ministers. We have no place here. I want a society I have a place in. In which there's something I can relate to and where I'm my own boss. I'll decide who my supervisor is, and according to what abilities, and there won't be anyone who will put a ceiling on my ambitions."

Were I to speak with such a man in another country, I thought to myself, with a Basque in Spain, for instance, how easy and simple it would be to feel sympathy for him. Here is a man who dares to express radical opinions, to confront a hostile regime and, more important, his own society. People like him are models of courage, self-respect, and utter intellectual honesty. And when I recalled some of the interviews I had conducted these past months—the evasiveness, the pandering, the off-the-record courage—I could not but feel a certain relief in the presence of Zeidani's openness and his egregious stand before me, before us.

"You certainly know," I told him, "that your idea of autonomy puts you straight into the Israeli nightmare, one that wakes up the dreamer to tell him, 'It is no dream.' "

"Listen. Israeli nightmares don't interest me, if they're at my expense."

"So why should your ambitions interest me, if they are at my expense?"

"I want you to feel that you have a problem with me. And that problem will explode at some point in the future. I won't go on being your obedient subject. There is a new generation of Arabs in Israel. A new potential. Ambitions open to the world. I won't let the country treat me the way it treated my father. That has to be clear. I'm a proud, modern, educated man with a sense of pride. I, to speak in Darwinian terms, am already a different species than my father was. I want to be an equal citizen, without waiting for a hundred years! I want my daughter to be an equal citizen just like your son. And if you don't want me to be your equal, go to hell."

"And if circumstances don't change to your liking?"

"Then I'll try to make your life miserable," he said simply. "If you have thousands of Arabs with Ph.D.s who can't find work, it will blow up on you. If you have tens of thousands who have no place to work in this country, and if you have more than 50 percent of the Arabs under the poverty line, even though we're barely 18 percent of the population, you can certainly expect an explosion. Listen, I'm not describing anything apocalyptic here—there are lots of problems we've waited decades to solve, and we don't see that in the foreseeable future, with the current form of struggle, we'll have a solution. So do you want me to live in a state of inferiority for the rest of my life? And the future I make for my children will be that way, too? I don't want that. I think every political theory justifies the use of different means—civil resistance, even violence—in order to achieve one's goal."

". . . so even if there are a few Jews here and there in the Galilee, there can still be Arab autonomy there! Absolutely! And the extent of the Arabs' allegiance to the state will, if you ask me, depend precisely on the distance of the Syrian tanks from the border! You saw in January 1991, in the first moment of the Gulf War, how all the truth came out. If we succeed in Judaizing the region, we will have put off the danger a little. It all depends on us."

Professor Arnon Sofer, a Haifa University geographer. For the last twenty-five years he has been sounding the alarm against the trends he sees in Jewish-Arab relations in both Israel and the territories.

"First, the facts. Human beings behave in an interesting way. Over the years the birth rate has been declining steadily, while the death rate has not changed much. There is the primitive stage—many are born, many die. Then there's the 'Ashkenazi' phase—you have fewer children because your wife wants to fulfill herself, wants a Subaru, and you put off another child until next year.

"The Israeli Arabs have sustained for almost fifty years the phase in which there is no decline in the birth rate, but a unique historical event has happened to them. We have brought their death rate down drastically over the space of four years. It happened when the people of Sakhnin stopped giving birth at home and started giving birth with us, at the Rothschild Hospital in Haifa.

"So we find a situation in which their birth rate is as if they were the most primitive people in the world but their death rate has dropped below even the Jewish death rate. Is it because they're cleaner than you are? No! It's because they are a population made up entirely of children. Here I want to touch on the worst situation, about which the public is generally mistaken. Approximately 50 percent of the Israeli Arabs are young children! Nearly 12 percent are high-school students. In other words, 62 percent of them are under the age of twenty! There are almost no old people! Because those are fellows from the Ottoman period, when the life span was short. There are very few old people in Arab society, and the great majority are young people and small children."

I remembered that pleasant afternoon with Tagrid and Abed Yunes in Arara. The two children in diapers, and the couple's argument over how many children they should have . . .

"True, true," he confirmed patiently, "there is a decline in the birth rate. We see it in the tables. In recent years, however, there has been a small rise, which is also a cause for concern, and I think it is intentional. Women have come to the hospitals—in Afula, for example—and asked to have their IUDs removed, saying that it is their contribution to the intifadah. Yes, yes—Israeli-Arab women. A pediatrician reported it to me. But that's not the decisive thing. What will be decisive will be the demographic process that I call 'momentum.' Even if Israeli Arabs today decide not to have more than two children per couple, there will still be twenty years during which the business will keep on going just as it does today, and it will explode. You don't believe me? Take their one-year-olds. What will happen with them twenty years from now? Even if we suppose that they have only two children, think of what massive numbers of young couples there will be. The coefficient will remain *horrible*.

"And there are those who don't limit themselves!" he shouts, as if outraged by some disgraceful breach of faith. "Sometimes you go to a village—and I have to tell you, these are my real friends—Feisal Zuabi in Miser, thirty children, all of them accountants, teachers. There's a village here, Hajajra, and there's a man there: when I was a student he had eighteen children, and when he was killed in an accident in 1978 he already had forty-eight children. Today he has 671 descendants in the village! Unbelievable! To put it concisely, religious Muslims continue to have children as if nothing had happened. The Druze continue. The Bedouin, too. So even twenty years from now you'll have no consolation, so don't look for it.

"Now, the main thing. In the year 2000—without counting immigration—the Jewish population will be 4.2 million and the Israeli Arabs will number 1.2 million; there will be about 1.5 million Arabs in Judea and Samaria and close to a million in Gaza. In other words, in Greater Israel, if we continue to control the territories, there will be 4.2 million Jews and 3.7 million Arabs. That's already a binational state, clear and simple.

"Even if we add a million Jewish immigrants, and add them in as if there is no emigration, and as if the big wave of immigration does not increase emigration, and assuming that the Arabs continue to act just as they do now—compute the figures and you'll be surprised. The Jews will rise from 54 percent to 57 percent of the population, and the Arabs will drop from 43 percent to 40 percent. That's the whole difference. The binational state remains."

He is about sixty years old. Tall, gangly, with glasses. He is open, patronizing. He piles the table before us with documents, studies, tables, data, with an aura of energetic, military, almost Hardy Boys–type enthusiasm. It is apparent that he sees himself as the last soldier on a mountain ridge, defending the lost cause of an inattentive and indifferent convoy. I, in contrast, in the face of the flood of numbers and maps and photographs that he stacks up around me, photographs he takes to keep track of illegal construction in the villages—I get more and more depressed.

"What's wrong with there being an Arab majority in the Galilee?" young Mohammed Daroushe of Iksal asked me bitterly. "The Galilee has been Arab for two thousand years! So why have they made such a ruckus about an Arab who bought a dunam in Kfar Tabor [a Jewish town in the lower Galilee]? He's not an Israeli citizen? He didn't pay for the land?"

"What effect will an Arab majority in the Galilee have? Oho . . ." Arnon Sofer sighed deeply. "The effect will be over a very wide spectrum of phenomena. First, the sense of being a minority, or the other side's sense of being a majority. When I go on a bus alone, I hide myself in a corner and read a book quietly. When two of us travel, we talk. And when we're seven school friends, we shout.

"Because when you are part of a group, you behave differently. In the large Arab concentrations in the Galilee 90 percent voted for non-Zionist parties [in 1988]. Ninety percent! That's not the case in small Arab settlements distant from the Arab center. You also behave differently on the road. You observe Israeli law less. There are areas in which you feel— from the driving, cleanliness, illegal construction—that the State of Israel ends there!

"Then there's the language. You won't speak Hebrew there anymore. You'll speak only Arabic. And you'll put on your *kaffiyeh*. There's already the beginning of national consciousness. If a Jewish person goes there, the Arab's territorial imperative stirs. A foreign body has entered the territory! And you ever so slowly gather strength. Then Jewish people have trouble getting there. When you, the Jewish idealist, settle in the Galilee, and everything is taken by masses of Arabs—from land, to shopping centers, to employment—because they're the cheapest labor force—and you have that great magnet, Tel Aviv, acting on you, then you'll get out of there pretty fast. You know, in the sixties the Galilee absorbed about 150,000 Jews. Guess how many were left ten years later. Guess. Thirteen thousand.

"In the meantime, all the essential components for the actualization of autonomy have been created. They have territory. In that territory there is a group that constitutes the majority. There you already have the two major factors in irredentism and autonomy.

"Technically, I can trace the borders of that autonomous entity. There is already a physical Arab continuity, including land ownership, that turns the entire area into a kind of territory. Take Arabeh, Sakhnin, Dir Hannah, Nazareth, B'aineh, Rumana. That's a continuity. And remember that the most difficult areas in Yugoslavia today, between the Serbs and the Croats, are areas of mixed population. That's where the battles began and got serious. That's where the destruction is.

"That's exactly what's simmering under our noses. And it was spontaneous. No one planned in advance the establishment of the Arab Committee for the Preservation of Land, or the Arab Mayors Committee. But how was I brought up as a Zionist Arnon Sofer? I remember how we cried at the song 'On the Negev Plains,' and the eleventh of Adar, the day

Trumpeldor fell, it was terrible, it hurt as if it had happened just yesterday! We beat the Greeks and got back at Pharaoh and screwed Ahasuerus. That's how that little Zionist, Arnon Sofer, was brought up—as a great national patriot.

"Now look." He bends his fingers one by one. "Land Day and Brotherhood Day and Home Day and Olive Day and Water Day and Equality Day. They stand at attention, they write songs, and our friend Toufiq Ziad, the mayor of Nazareth, writes: 'Here in the enchanted Galilee we have a homeland!' At their summer camps they celebrate that and draw pictures of it and cry for it, and when you go through Arabeh, you see stores painted with PLO colors, because *they're building a national consciousness!*

"I sit with my good friend Majed Elhaj, who may be the next leader of the Israeli Arabs, and he tells me, 'I won't live with you in peace if you don't change the flag. I want a Muslim color on the flag! And until you change that national anthem that does not speak of me or to me, I'll fight for a binational state!' "

"No no no . . ." Majed Elhaj protests angrily when I quote that to him. "If I were really demanding everything Arnon Sofer says, it would mean that I'm demanding fully equal rights. I'm not demanding that! Under current circumstances, there can't be equal rights. The Arabs in Israel are struggling for equal *opportunities*, not equal rights! It's important to distinguish between the two. When Jews and Arabs speak of 'full equality,' they actually mean two different things. The Jew means changing the Jewish character of the country, and he fears that. The Arab means equal opportunity as regards budgets, services, and so on. There can be full equality only at a later stage, only if—in a peace process—the country begins to think again about its orientation, and to define for itself what it wants, whether to continue Zionist nationalism forever or whether there's a new situation that allows a new social contract, in which all groups in Israeli society, including the Arabs, are partners as legitimate elements in Israeli society. Then, under such circumstances, it will be possible to speak of full equality of rights and responsibilities in all senses. Today there can't be anything like that. Not yet."

"Oh, don't be so naïve," Arnon Sofer prodded me. "That's their goal. They'll fight for it. Their goal is not equal rights. Here they're already talking about a deep national problem! Their battle won't end if Majed receives four tons of gefilte fish for Friday night! They've already built the institutional infrastructure for autonomy. But let's examine what will happen from here on out. A Palestinian state will be established —something, by the way, that I favor—and the Israeli Arabs will tell us, Hey, guys, no more excuses! Now give us full equality. Now give us work in factories and industry and in military camps! But we won't give them that. For objective Jewish reasons, we'll always think of Arnon Sofer's son before Majed's children. And of your children's education, and the new immigrant who will come to you, and not of him.

"Then the million and a half that will be in the large concentrations around Um Elfahm and the central Galilee will begin to say, as in Kosovo, that they want to be annexed to their country, to the Palestinian state. Irredentism. I ask my good friend Majed about that and he has no answer. Why should you be different from any other group in the world? Why should you be any different from the national groups in Nagorno-Karabakh and Armenia? Why should you be different, especially when you have a historical account to settle with me, and especially when we will never agree to non-Jewish rule here?"

"I am very concerned," Majed Elhaj responded in his home in Shfaram, "that all this talk of irredentism, and about the ambitions of the Arabs for autonomy within Israel, will turn into a self-fulfilling prophecy. That's because it will grant policymakers the legitimacy they need to persist with their current Arab policy, even to make it worse. It confirms their assumption that nothing has changed with the Arabs, that nothing will help, and that the Arabs' ambitions will remain, when it comes down to it, antithetical to Israel. My friend Arnon Sofer forgets, for some reason, that there are many minorities in the world and that not all of them demand their own country."

Arnon Sofer: "All I am saying is that if the Palestinian state comes into being, and they really do deserve it, let's redraw the maps of the old State of Israel. Because I say, Damn it, Jews, you don't want to live in Um Elfahm, you don't want to live in Wadi Ara? Then give them up! Let's, for instance, give them that whole area, here, the southern Triangle, with its tens of thousands of Arabs, in exchange, for instance, for the security guarantees that were included in the Allon Plan. For all the army outposts along the Jordan River!"

I read what I have just typed with eyes that have recently become somewhat bifocal. This way of seeing with a Jewish-Arab double focus helps me a lot. Without it, how could I know how to find my way when, over the thousands of kilometers I've burned these past months, I saw almost no important road sign written in Arabic as well, even though Arabic is an official language in Israel? At the grocery store, how would I be able to tell the difference between spaghetti and macaroni, between yogurt and sour cream, if I didn't know how to read Hebrew? How would I know that I should keep my children away from poisonous cleaning fluids and pesticides? Could I tell the difference between aspirin and antibiotics if I couldn't read Hebrew and English? How could I understand that a sign says FALLING ROCKS, while another says CAUTION—HIGH TENSION WIRES? (At least I'd be spared the bumper stickers on the pickup trucks that read JEWISH LABOR!

and the placards pasted up by Meir Kahane's disciples that proclaim "We propose five years' imprisonment . . . for every non-Jew who has sexual relations with a Jewish woman.")

I also read Arnon Sofer's words with my bifocal eyes. To do this I enlist the gaze of Riad Kabha of Barta'a, for instance, who works at Givat Haviva for Jewish-Arab coexistence and integration; and the eyes of Amal Yunes of Kafr Ara, who said, "I feel that I belong here, this is my place. I so much want to be a part of it, to be 'someone' in this society"; and Lutfi Mashour's wink: "I don't want autonomy here! That's all I need, autonomy: to live in a ghetto. Maybe we really deserve a ghetto, but I want to be equal. To belong!" Of course, not all the Arabs in Israel want to be part of Israeli existence. And those who do did not arrive at that desire out of overwhelming love of Israel but rather out of acquiescence and prudence, through an arduous process of formulating a new identity. Their struggle is for the achievement of civil equality. When I read the new partition plan proposed by Arnon Sofer, my Arab eyes go dark—my homeland unremittingly measures me through the lens of a *numerus clausus*, counting my babies and my dead. Switching me by decree from fate to fate, and in any settlement that is reached, no one will ask my opinion.

(Maybe on this matter it is worth asking the Jews who have come from Russia what they felt when they heard the sighs of relief of so many Russians when their homeland's door slammed behind their backs.)

"Their allegiance to the state is exactly commensurate with the distance of the Syrian tank from the border," Professor Sofer says, and for a moment I accept his words at face value, because the assertion fits in well with my fears. Then I examine his statement in the light, and I am already unsure. No, I don't think Israeli Palestinians will fight shoulder to shoulder with the Israel Defense Forces against the Syrians, but neither am I convinced that many of them will be prepared to act to exchange Israeli rule for a Syrian, Iraqi, or even PLO regime. I have no doubt that today many of them have a good sense of what Israel still has to offer them. For them, Israel's destruction will mean the end of a dream that has not yet been fulfilled but which is worth fighting for.

Arnon Sofer: "So you'll say, Very nice. You've solved the problem of the Triangle. But what about the Galilee? And I say, If—*if* there's a role for population transfer to play in this country, it's not with the inhabitants of the West Bank and Gaza Strip. It's with the lower Galilee. If! Now you'll probably ask, How is it that liberal, progressive Arnon Sofer can say a thing like that? Well, first of all, the Labor Party has done it twice already. The classic case is the Golan Heights. There we feverishly deported 70,000 Syrians in the space of two days. Now when you, sir, travel through the Golan, everything is nice, and you're a good Zionist and you can explain to your children how nice it is here. Or in the lower city of Haifa. Or in Jaffa, from which you transferred 60,000 Jaffans! Don't try to escape that! So you know what? Ten hard minutes, and maybe it's the right solution?"

"Ten hard minutes," I reminded him of what we both knew, "and afterward forty even harder years."

"Don't worry. I won't do it. You see? Here my entire model collapses, because I'm not able to take it through to the logical conclusion. I won't deport my good Arab friends. Do you think I can tell people I've known for years, with whom I work, to leave their homes? I recently told one of those friends, If something should happen, call me immediately and I'll be right over!

"So, in theory, transfer might be the right solution. With the Bedouin in the Negev, too, since they are an absolute majority in their territory. In theory. In practice, that's a different story. Because I am not morally able to carry it out. Even if my life was in danger. I can't. Even if it costs me my life. [He shouts.] What will I do? I've got a big moral problem. I don't have an answer. We're in a horrible, terrible, vicious circle. I take figures like these home each night and I can't sleep. I have no answers. All the tricks we can do can put it off only for a week or a year. The Arabs don't want us, and that's horrible!

"So what can we do? Not much, but something. First of all, get out of the territories. That's the only logical response to the demographic problem. Get out of the territories and you've created an overwhelming Jewish majority in the State of Israel. A fifth of the country's population will be Arab, and that's not a binational state. That's a normal ratio of majority to minority, like in most countries. Even if the minute after our retreat there's a bloodbath in the territories, get out!

"Then, divide and govern. Yes, that blunt, cheap trick. Cultivate the Bedouin. Cultivate the Druze. The Christians. And give. Give to whoever is good to us. If he feels good, he won't want to rebel against us."

"One of the things that really drive me crazy," says Lutfi Mashour, an Israeli Palestinian Christian Arab and a newspaper editor, "is how smart Jews make the same mistakes that others have made. The Jews will fall the same way the English fell, with the 'divide and rule' method. You, too, are always redividing the Arabs into Christians, Muslims, Bedouin, and you explain to us that we, the Christians, we're really part of the West, who got here only by chance, and that we're not Arabs at all. You said that the Druze aren't Arabs, and now you've started saying that the Bedouin aren't Arabs! And we call the Bedouin Al-Arab—they're the original Arabs, not us! Then you made a new division, and said that the Christians themselves are divided into Maronites, who are, as you know, fervent, strictly kosher Zionists; and the Catholics, who are, you know, still on probation, and the Protestants, whom you once thought of as the best Zionists, but today they're the top

PLO supporters. So you play nicely with your toys and don't understand anything."

"And what are you?" I asked Mashour.

"Me?" Mashour, an intricate, quick-thinking, and ironic man, chuckled. "When I am cursed as a Catholic, I'm Catholic. When they discriminate against me as a Muslim, I immediately become a Muslim. Ask—what about Jewish? Well, in the original sense, as I understand Judaism, I'm more Jewish. More than the Jews here, because what remains in your Israel of Jewish values?"

". . . and reinforce the Shin Bet," Arnon Sofer keeps hammering away, "and the police and border guard! A Shin Bet and police state, yes! Without any window dressing. There's no choice. We really are doomed to make a Sparta here. A country with a military landscape!

"And bang in wedges! Put new settlements between them wherever you can. Push them in here and here and here. I can be proud of that, because I am one of those responsible for the idea of Gush Segev [a cluster of small settlements in the western Galilee]. We shoved wedges in here and here and here, so that as much as possible they don't have territorial continuity.

"But in any case, all that is only a delaying action." He slowly gathered up the papers, documents, maps. "It only postpones it for a few years. If you see the future with open eyes—the demographic balance, the youth leaving the country, the deterioration of society, the defense effort that is pushing us into economic catastrophe, and the disappearing democratic forces. . . . We don't live on a desert island, and one day, when we're weak, we'll take the blow. The State of Israel, I very much fear, will be destroyed."

"So why do you stay here?" I asked.

"A wonderful question. Why do I stay here? Because I was born here. Because my parents were Zionists. Because I've buried so many here. I've buried two hundred people here—friends, relatives, students. My brother fell in the War of Independence. And mostly—I don't want to live in the Diaspora. I can't. I told my children, That's the way things are. This is my prediction. You are free to decide. I'll stay here to hold the fort."

Arnon Sofer has been saying these things for more than two decades. The Israeli left accuses him of racism, and the right accuses him of defeatism. The Arabs in Israel are angry that he suspects them of an aspiration for autonomy, an aspiration most of them forcefully deny.

To myself—through the hail of data, factors, and numbers that he pounded me with in forceful amicability, I considered to what extent the demographic question had, in recent years, become one of the central points of debate in our faded political discourse. Each side brings its own data, and even data that everyone accepts get interpreted by each side in accordance with its needs. All kinds of predictions about what year will bring equal numbers get launched—2015, 2030, 2045 (these relate to equality in all the land between the Jordan River and the Mediterranean, including the occupied territories). Many treat the numbers and percentages submissively and simplistically, as if at the very moment the demographic tie score is reached—and only at that moment—some magic, total process will begin. As if an especially determined or frightened minority, or one suffering from megalomania, cannot with its military power and advantage long rule over a majority larger than itself. As if we are not now deep in the tie score's magnetic field, turning us for all practical purposes into a binational state in which there are inhabitants of three different ranks—Jews, Arab citizens, and the Arabs in the territories. As if the only important thing is how many Jews versus how many Arabs, and not what kind of life we make for ourselves here.

Sa'id Zeidani is the only one, so far, who has raised the

idea of autonomy for Israeli Palestinians in such an open and explicit way. The idea won attention in 1989, after Arafat's Algiers declaration of a Palestinian state. The Palestinians in Israel realized that day that Arafat's "state" did not include them, and this meant that their interests were not even on the Palestinian agenda. "We, whatever happens, stay on the shelf," a Palestinian-Israeli intellectual told me. This realization, along with the sense of discrimination in Israel, with the fear of a wave of Russian immigration, and perhaps—and this is only conjecture—smarting from the PLO's failure to make any mention of the Arabs in Israel in its declarations, apparently induced Zeidani to publish his plan at the end of 1989. One may also suppose that now, with the collapse of the Soviet Union and the blow to the Israeli Communist Party—which for years led the struggle for equal rights for Arabs—some of its supporters will turn to more extreme and separatist modes of thought.

The most forceful opposition to Dr. Zeidani's plan came, as I've noted, from the leadership of the Arabs in Israel. The arguments brought against it dealt with its geographical impracticability, with the implausibility that the Jewish majority would agree to it, and with the belief that demanding autonomy would lead the country to treat its Arab citizens more harshly.

"One of the central arguments always used by the extreme right is that the Arabs don't show their cards. Now they are suddenly being given a present by Arab groups—not in foreign currency, but in gold—autonomy!" fumed Salim Jubran, editor of the Communist Party newspaper *Al-Ittihad*, in an interview with a local Haifa newspaper. Knesset member Nawaf Masalha (Labor) said, "The demand for autonomy will pull out from under us the moral correctness and legitimacy of our demands for Palestinian independence in the territories, first and foremost with regard to the Israeli left, which is our partner in this struggle. Whoever demands autonomy sabotages relations between Jews and Arabs in Israel."

"Of course they attacked me," Zeidani says dispassionately, as if he were not the target of the attacks. "I'm saying very harsh things, after all. But perhaps if for forty years you give the entire public a political education in a certain direction, you can expect that such ideas will not break through the ideological and pragmatic barriers. Their realization demands something hard and serious, and the political leadership is trying to escape into something easier. But I would like to hear," he queried, "what your opinion is, as an Israeli."

I responded that I respected his courage. That while he spoke I thought of how unfortunate it was that Israel had not been wise enough to create, for a man like him, channels through which he could express and realize himself as a real Israeli. But I agree, I told him, with only some of the opinions you've expressed. The word "autonomy" is not so frightening to me —I would like the Palestinian citizens of Israel to win maximum freedom as a national minority, to be able to manage their independent educational system, to establish an Arab university, to run their own religious institutions, instead of a Jewish official appointing the *kadis* (judges) and *imams* (preachers). I would like their young people to perform national service within and for their communities, and I would like the Israeli government to recognize, finally, their representative bodies, such as the Supreme Oversight Committee. Yet all this must be done, in my opinion, in the framework of the State of Israel, as the country of the Jewish nation, existing alongside the country of the Palestinian nation. I know that you don't agree with me, and that in your opinion there is no chance for such integration, but in my opinion, even after forty-three years, we have still not sincerely tried, with full commitment, to create integration in the State of Israel. We have still not clarified for ourselves, Arabs and Jews, the meaning and requirements of terms like "equality," "coexistence," and "citizenship." The process that took place between us up until now was, largely, one of mutual evasion and abstention. I've spoken a great deal; now I'd like to ask, in conclusion, whether you intend to take any practical measures to carry out your ideas?

"I am not a politician," he said, "and I have no ambitions in that direction. I would like to contribute to self-understanding. It is a process, and there are already far-reaching changes in the existing leadership. The ideas have made their mark. The Progressive Movement speaks of 'self-management'; the Islamic Movement is working for autonomy in education; Knesset member Daroushe has established a party made up solely of Arabs, there is a Supreme Oversight Committee of the Arab public, there is a Sons of the Village movement. All these are the germs. It's true that today autonomy is a theoretical idea. But I'm telling you that ten years from now there will be a whole range of problems that will have no solution except in that direction. Problems of employment. Economic and social problems.

"So I think that I'm presenting you with a great challenge. I am presenting a great challenge to Jewish democracy, and Jewish values, and your entire tradition. I am presenting you here with a moral demand in the name of the categorical law that is above and beyond questions of nation or religion. It is a matter of humanity!" For the first time since the beginning of our conversation Zeidani raised his voice, and his face paled a bit. "You, by discriminating against me, are saying that I am a man of less worth than you are. That I am less than a man. If you say that—and that's what the attitude of the Israeli majority implies, it follows logically—then the practical conclusion, in an Aristotelian sense, is to slap you in the face."

Early morning in Faradis, on the old Hadera-Haifa road.

The coffeehouse sits right on the street. When I come and sit there, the conversation of the men dies out. They examine me carefully. Then they disappear. Around the square the stores open with a yawn. The large village awakens slowly. It lives with the road, just as another village might live with a river —small children sit on its edge and gaze longingly at the other side; boys careen with their bicycles between the waves of traffic and navigate them boldly; a shepherd crosses with three goats and two cabbages . . .

Afterward an old woman fords the roaring flow, erect, balancing a tall bucket on her head. A wonder of concentration and direction. Her hands lie at the sides of her body, holding her dress around her thighs, and the bucket does not move. She looks right, looks left, strides swiftly, and the bucket does not move. Hundreds of generations of the oppression of women have, one might say, molded her and her burden together. I drink a first cup of coffee, the sweetest of all, and eavesdrop on the

*conversation of the men behind me. There were once two sages,
Rabbi Haya the Great and Rabbi Shimon Ben Halafta, who
"forgot words of the Targum"—the Aramaic translation of the
Bible—and "went to the Arab market to learn from them."
There they eavesdropped on the people until they recalled the
meanings of the forgotten words. In Faradis, even an Israeli
who knows no Arabic would be able to puzzle out the conversation: "Al me—ruh from department to department, jib me
a red form . . ." "Wahada mush a primitive zalameh, you
know, a zalameh in modern dress." "Ana ahadit from him
twenty cartons of tomatoes, daf'at him a down payment . . ."
"And they fi idhum an arrest warrant, wa-ana shaef, mafish
a judge's signature!" "An-nas amalu in two days, all the concrete and all the electricity . . ." And this is how they talk
among themselves.*

*I listened. I made a mental note of the Hebrew words—
VAT, income tax, down payment, bank guarantee, social se-
curity, license, fines—an instrumental Hebrew screwed onto
Arabic like a metal joint or, more often, like a clamp.*

*I thought of the rich, sensitive Hebrew I hear from people
when they speak to me. The words of Zuhir Yehia of Kafr Kara
came to mind: "Our soul is not here. Maybe our soul has gone
dormant here with you. Our soul is there, with the Palestinians
in the territories. All our soul is there, and our body is here. I
try—in order to preserve the body—to kill the soul. Or to push
it aside. I don't know when it will awaken. I don't want to
endanger the body. Maybe one day it will awaken."*

When? I asked.

*"Listen, today I'm more accepting of the fact that Kafr Kara
will not be in the Palestinian state. But even if I'm not there,
it's okay. It will make it much easier for me if there is a country
like that. My soul will reawaken if there is a Palestinian state."*

"And in the meantime?"

"According to legend, on a scale the soul weighs heavier than

the body. But with us the body is heavier. There is a soul, but in the meantime it is waiting. It's as if you are in love with someone—maybe this is not a modern example, but it could happen with us—and suddenly the family decides that you have to marry someone else. Even if it's brutal, you accept it and say, It tastes all right. You can't go on saying that it doesn't taste good."

A few weeks later I read an article by Emmanuel Kopelevitch, formerly the Director of Arab Education, about how spoken Arabic in Israel has borrowed Hebrew words. According to Kopelevitch, there are some three thousand different Hebrew words in regular use in Arabic. Sometimes those using these words are not even aware that they are borrowed from Hebrew.

The article contains a list of "the sixty-two most common Hebrew words in the Arabic of the State of Israel." Here are some of them: health fund, cab, traffic light, computer, appliance, permit, mail, cold cuts, vacation, VAT, station, report, form, office, membership card, director, theory (the written part of the driver's license examination), pay slip, driving test.

The list goes on. It includes the names of tools, automobile accessories, kinds of foods. Taxes. Forms. Appliances. Objects. Legal processes. Punishments. Various government functions. These are the impressions left on the language by this long association—which is still only a material one. A physical one.

I was the only Jew in the little coffeehouse. I was a minority. Each of us is a minority in at least one context in his life, and we all know how it feels to be the exception in a given situation, so there is no need to waste words on it. But there was one moment when the buzz of conversation around me suddenly swelled, and someone by chance bumped into my chair, and a passing motorcyclist revved up his bike too close to me, and there was the sound of choked laughter behind me. None of these, apparently, was directed at me, but something welled within me, and in my distress I bent down to my briefcase to take out my notebook (maybe I just wanted to hold on to a pen so as to draw security from it), and suddenly I understood how I would look—sitting in an Arab coffeehouse, my eyes behind dark sunglasses, recording the background conversations. I knew that if I were to take out my pen I would frighten them. They would be scared, there would be a silence, a few hearts would stop for a moment, and people would hastily reconstruct what they had said, to check if they had said something that might be misinterpreted. For a long moment I had the malicious itch to pay them back for the previous annoyances. The temptation was very strong, and from within that temptation I also realized with certainty how many times each of those sitting around me had been the victim of such simple, cheap, opportunistic malice, when within one of "us"—as within me at that moment—the domination gland secretes a single drop into the bloodstream.

CHAPTER 13

"On October 31, 1948, when I was twenty years old, the Israeli Army came to my village, Ikrit. We received the soldiers as guests. With food, drink, and song."

"Song? What were you so happy about?"

"We were glad that none of our people had been hurt in the fighting. That the war had not touched the village. Up until then we had had very good relations with the surrounding kibbutzim. We weren't for Qawukji [the commander of an Arab guerrilla force during the War of Independence] and we weren't for the Israelis. We were a Christian village, we knew that neither side cared much about us, and we wanted to live. During the week after the Israeli soldiers came, we continued to feed them. Our mothers and wives would draw water from the spring, two kilometers from the village, and bring it to the soldiers to drink. When the soldiers wanted to go to the spring themselves, we showed them the best way, so they wouldn't tread on the mines that Qawukji's army had laid. And in fact none of the soldiers was hurt."

I met with Aouni Sbeit in his home in Rama, a Galilee village of Muslims, Druze, and Maronite Christians. Aouni is sixty-three today, father of eight and grandfather of nineteen. He is a popular folk poet, making a living from composing lyrics for weddings and celebrations, an affable, paunchy, warmhearted man, wearing a white *kaffiyeh* on his head, against the heat. He leans on a cane, a tractor having run over his foot; Sbeit is now receiving physical therapy. Perhaps he is too tired to go to Ikrit?

"Too tired? For Ikrit?" He laughed, showing a full complement of white teeth.

The car has trouble following the deceptive twists in the road. Low-lying Levantine oaks and carob trees line both sides. Red peppers dry on the roofs of small villages. Aouni Sbeit (who speaks only Arabic) cannot wait for us to reach Ikrit; along the way he begins telling his story, knowing every date and name involved in his tragedy by heart.

"Then, on the fifth of November 1948, the army commander, whose name was Ya'akov Kara, came and said that he had received orders. No one knew who had given them. We did not see the paper. Orders. The children and women and old people are to be evacuated from the village, because the army wants to fight Qawukji's army, which is still in the area, and doesn't want civilians to be hurt.

"Officer Ya'akov Kara gave his military word of honor, which is always the truth, and promised that we would leave the village for fifteen days only, and afterward each one of us would return to his home. Each family was allowed to leave one person to guard their house. The priest was also allowed to stay, to guard the church.

"The army itself evacuated us in its vehicles to Rama. Did you hear that? We didn't flee. *The army evacuated us*, and we had an agreement with the army that after they finished off Qawukji they would bring us back.

"Fifteen days later we went to the authorities and they said fifteen more days. We returned to Rama and waited. Fifteen days later we again went to the authorities, and they said come back in fifteen more days. On and on. We spent six months in Rama. All the people of Ikrit. They gave us the keys to the houses of people from Rama who had fled."

"You mean that you lived in the houses of people who had also left their homes?"

"Precisely. That hurts a man at his most sensitive spot. Because what can justify my leaving my house and going to live in someone else's house? We didn't know the people of Rama at all. Then it wasn't like today, where there's a car and you drive over. Nor did we know where they had disappeared to. They showed us houses and said go on in. We went in. We saw that the houses were already empty. Thieves had entered and taken everything."

The people of Ikrit were lucky. They had roofs over their heads. The residents of Biram, another Maronite Christian village on the Lebanese border, were also asked by the army to leave their village for a few days, "until hostile forces are cleaned out of the area," the army explained to them, and they obeyed. They also knew the soldiers who evacuated them. In the weeks preceding the request to leave, the soldiers had lived with the villagers. Every house in the village assigned them a room. They slept and ate together, and the children of Biram, who have grown old in the meantime, still remember those meals, with the rifles leaning against the wall. Before the evacuation, the villagers cleaned their houses and put them in order. Then, one after another, they handed the keys over to the officers.

They left on foot in a long convoy to go to their ancient olive groves, on the mountains overlooking the village. There they lived for two weeks. It was November and there were heavy rains. The families slept on the ground. The lucky, or perhaps the strong, found caves to live in. During the day everyone would gather under the olive trees, gazing down in concern and incomprehension at their village, which military trucks kept entering and leaving. Two weeks later their patience came to an end. A delegation of elders set out for the village to ask the army to return them to their homes, as they had been promised. When they entered the village all seemed to go black—the doors on their homes had been broken. The houses were empty. Shattered furniture lay abandoned in the street. The soldiers they met ejected them, aiming their rifles. "This land is ours now," they said.

"The betrayal cut us like a knife," wrote Elias Shakur, a former resident of Biram, in his book *Blood Brothers*. Shakur was then a young boy. "Father and mother seemed as baffled as children because of that merciless betrayal. I think it was beyond their comprehension."

We pass by Alkush, a *moshav*—a Jewish farming settlement—built on the site of the former Arab village of Dir Elkasi. Then we pass another *moshav*. Even Menahem, the former Kalat Elraheb ("the monk's fortress"). Aouni Sbeit points all around. "Everything you see around us was ours. All this was Ikrit's land." They had had 16,000 dunams, most of it rocky. In the distance we could already see the Ikrit church, a white dome jutting up from the top of a hill.

"We saw that they weren't going to bring us back," he continued, "and we decided to turn to the law for help. We went to a lawyer in Nazareth and brought him the deeds. In May 1951 he petitioned the High Court of Justice, and the court began to hear the case in July.

"In July we traveled to Jerusalem. We were perhaps two hundred people from Ikrit. The case was between us and the government, over the question of whether we resided permanently in Ikrit. The court ruled that Ikrit had to be returned to us immediately."

The High Court of Justice, Israel's supreme judicial body, did not accept the state's arguments and ruled in favor of the petitioners. "We believe that the respondents [i.e., the state] can no longer deny that the petitioners are permanent residents," the court ruled, although it postponed execution of its verdict to a later date. It seemed that a barrier had been lifted and that the villagers would return to their village very soon.

"We danced with joy the entire day. In Jerusalem and in the buses home. We returned to Rama. We began to pack our things. The court said that we were residents of Ikrit! The army came and distributed keys and locks with which to lock the houses we had lived in in Rama, and we made preparations to leave for Ikrit. There were only two cars in Rama, but we were willing to walk. Then a sergeant suddenly appeared and notified us that a letter had arrived from the army to the *mukhtar* of Ikrit, and in the letter the army notified the *mukhtar* that Ikrit was now a military zone and no entry was allowed until further notice."

The army's maneuver will never be studied in military textbooks. It went like this: In court the army had argued that the villagers were not permanent residents of Ikrit because they had not been in their village when the area was declared a security zone. The High Court of Justice ruled that it was illegal to prevent their return, because the residents of the village had been asked by the army to leave, and for this reason could not have been in their village when it was declared a military zone. The army had lost the battle but was not going to lose the war. Immediately after the court announced its decision, the army got smart and sent the evacuees, who were then in Rama, "exit orders" (expulsion orders in all but name) from Ikrit. In other words, the army addressed the evacuees as if they were still living in Ikrit, as if nothing had happened, and notified them that it had now been decided—for the first time, as it were—to expel them from Ikrit. To the villagers' surprise, it turned out that not even the court could do anything to block this military ploy—formally, it was a legal and totally legitimate finger on the scales of justice.

"We didn't know what to do. If the Supreme Court made a decision and the army violated it, the story must be over for us. But we still didn't give up. Not for a minute. Just as the Jewish people suffered and were persecuted for 2,000 years, and always hoped, until they returned, so we hope also. We still do."

We pass the rusty sign announcing that this is a military zone. We turn onto a dirt road. The Lebanese border is close by. In Israel's early days this border was an excuse for evicting no small number of Arab villagers from the area—defense officials feared that the people would try to aid the enemy across the border. They feared that the people of Ikrit and Biram would forge ties with their Christian brothers in Lebanon. Today a Christian militia supplied by the Israeli Army defends the north of Israel from the other side of the border.

Aouni's son, Halil, jumps from the car and opens a barbed-wire fence for us—a barrier meant to prevent the flight of Yehuda Dari's cows, which graze there. "The last thing we need is for a cow to escape," Aouni Sbeit mumbles.

In September 1951 the village of Ikrit was suddenly destroyed by the security forces. All the houses were blown up and the site was plowed. The church, which the destroyers did not mean to blow up, was hit also. The date for leveling the village was carefully chosen—December 25. "What a Christmas present for the village!" Aouni Sbeit sighed. "While we held in our hands a court decision saying that we have a right to return as soon as it is no longer part of a military zone. Why? Because. They wanted us to give up. To hurt us when it hurt most."

The fate of the people of Biram was no better. They were living in abandoned houses in Jish (called Gush Halav in Hebrew). In September 1953, five years after they had been duped into leaving, the Biramers stood on a hill above their village. Now they call it "the hill of tears" and "the Biram Wailing Wall." Down below, not far from them, the village of their birth was abuzz with unusual activity. Military vehicles and bulldozers surrounded it, and a company of soldiers walked through the village laying out wires.

The refugees heard a loud explosion and saw their houses fly up in the air. The whole action took only five minutes—brief and efficient. For five minutes the village, with its people looking down from above, quaked and was destroyed. Then the bulldozers began leveling the ruins.

Now the whole area is silent. The air is clear. Tangled thorns sway in the breeze. A small hill, a ruin, with little vegetation, rises up over the plain. Here and there broken stones are scattered about. Above, a single structure—the restored church. We climb up a difficult, rocky path, but here Aouni Sbeit has almost no need of his cane. He skips between the stones and shrubs, using his stick to point out a rusty olive press, a small pool for collecting the olive oil that runs off the press. We step over a path of cut stones, hidden among the thorns and the caper bushes. Aouni's legs lead him without needing directions—Here was the road that descended from the village. I would go down from here. Here is the well. And from within the deep well grows a magnificent chinaberry tree.

I ask him how he felt when he came here for the first time and saw the ruins.

He turned to me, smiling benevolently at my foolishness. "Let's trade places. I'm David and you're Aouni Sbeit. Now write what you felt." He adds, "Man is not stone, hawajeh."

He calls me hawajeh, "sir." You can tell the members of his generation, the generation of defeat, by that hawajeh. Even after forty-odd years they seem not to have recovered from that huge upheaval that undid their lives and turned them from masters of their homes into barely tolerated guests. ". . . the event that emptied our heads and erased memories from our memory and blurred the contours of our world," as Emile Habibi wrote in his novel *Ahtia*. "Beyond their comprehension," as Shakur said, was this cruel awakening into a morning that was not theirs, the morning of a nation that was at the pinnacle of its new ascent, which had given birth to itself out of cataclysm and had vigorously suckled all the future that was then to be had in the region. They slowly awaken to find themselves bound in the strong cords of ingenious laws, unintelligible to them, and arguments that could not be challenged—historical justice, ancestral right, security needs —yes, who could possibly doubt the right of adversity we had then, but "then" (have I said this already?) is over.

"Returning the villages would weaken faith in Zionism, and create doubts about the justice of its claims," Prime Minister Golda Meir said in 1972. She thus placed above the justice of our claims a huge billboard that said: CAUTION: WE ARE RIGHT! Lutfi Mashour sighed, "That's what I always say: Our problem is, we're dealing with Jews."

"What do you mean?"

"That's our problem. If we had been conquered by someone else . . . but you were always better bastards than we were, stronger than us, more legalistic than us, more paranoid than us. Take, for example, the Turks. They conquered us and went to hell. They had no culture. What was their culture? Large pots! That's all they left us here . . . They didn't have the brains and the character that you have. With you it is very difficult," he said, and then grew serious. "You are a very strong nation. *Too* strong a nation."

"Here there were figs, and here olives, and here grapes." Sbeit's cane waves in the air, drawing orchards and vineyards. "And here was my house."

Now it is only a mound of wreckage next to the church. Aouni Sbeit's father had been the village *mukhtar*, and his house had been the only one with poured concrete. "Father himself chose every stone in the house. When the house was destroyed, people came and stole the stones. Not one remains." With his cane he straightens a trailing raspberry bush, pacing absentmindedly between the large pieces of dung shat by Dari's cows in his living room. It shocks him anew each time he sees it.

"If they allow you to return, would you come back here?" I asked Halil, Aouni's son, who now lives in Haifa. He shakes his head definitively: No. He has already become accustomed to city life. He's used to living away from his family. He will not return. But his father differs. "If they let me return, I am ready to sleep even on this," he said, striking a thorn bush with his cane. "Look what a crime they have committed against us. We are refugees in our own homeland. And how often we have asked to return. And how much they promised us. Who didn't promise us? Ben-Gurion and Chaim Weizmann and Begin and Golda Meir and Ezer Weizman and Moshe Arens. I said to Shimon Peres, 'Mr. Minister, let's put the Israeli Declaration of Independence between us and go over it section by section, and let it judge between us.' Yigal Allon once asked me if the children of Ikrit who were born in Rama still think about Ikrit. I laughed. I, to this day, live in a rented house in Rama. I did not build a house. Because I believe that my sons will be able to return. If you gather together all the children in Rama and ask them where they're from, the smallest of our children will tell you that they're from Ikrit. I'll take you to a pregnant woman, put your ear to her belly and you'll hear: 'I'm from Ikrit.' "

Afterward, in his home in Rama, Sbeit shows me a picture that an anonymous Jewish photographer took fifty years ago, "one who used to wander around the Galilee looking for pretty things to photograph." Aouni's wife also came to look, and her eyes immediately filled with tears. "Look what we had and where we are now, refugees . . ." She waved her hand at the bare floor of their rented house, the peeling walls, and fled. The photograph in my hand showed a village blooming with flowers and green with trees: Ikrit when it lived.

Halil: "For Father, Ikrit is memories. It's his childhood. For me, Ikrit was the escape from the Rama that didn't want us. Didn't absorb us. To this day we're considered refugees there. We're considered homeless. The people of Rama did not intermarry with us, will not give their daughters to a refugee. To this day—forty-three years later!—they make us feel like strangers. They curse us. Humiliate us. Rama is a very closed society. I have no chance of getting involved in the municipal government. If I tried to get involved, they'd tell me I don't belong."

Do the people of Rama act that way because the people of Ikrit moved into their houses when they were exiled? Is it because the people from Ikrit are Christian, while the rest of Rama is Muslim and Druze? Is it because the people of Rama wish—in accordance with instructions they received from somewhere, or of their own volition—to keep the Ikrit refugee problem alive? Halil listens to the questions and nods, but makes no response.

"Will you, despite all that, be a candidate for the Rama village council?"

He smiles. "That's the other side of the matter. The people of Ikrit won't support one of their own."

"?"

"Because they refuse to participate in the elections in any way. It is liable to be interpreted as an acknowledgment that they already belong to Rama and not to Ikrit."

Today the people of Ikrit are spread all over the country. Yet they hold their religious and family celebrations here, and the whole community gathers. The same holds true for the people of Biram. I heard of a man from Biram, Joseph Elias, who for nineteen years has worked a small piece of land at the edge of the ruined village. He goes there three times a week to water his vegetables. Sometimes, on Saturdays, there is a long line of cars along the road to the two villages. On weekdays you are also likely to find an Ikrit family having a picnic. "They come to take a little of the air here, to renew their strength." The younger Sbeit laughs.

"You should know," Aouni explains for the third or fourth time, "that the problem of Ikrit and Biram is different from the problems of other villages and refugees. We did not flee and were not expelled. The army came, was our guest, ate of our bread, drank of our water, and promised to let us return." His son shakes his head as one who knows that these are but dreams, words worth less than the air that carries them. "They don't want to return us," Halil bursts out in the end, "because that will reveal the truth about what happened in '48. You are afraid to admit that the Palestinian refugees did not flee. They were plundered. If you return us, it will shatter the myth on which you've educated each generation of your youth."

"The government," I answer, my lips unmoving, "is afraid to return the people of these two villages to their homes, lest it become a precedent."

"What do I care about your government's fears?" Halil fumes. "It's my right to demand justice for myself! Why do I have to deal with the whole refugee problem? That's a problem you made, not me!"

We descend through the thorn bushes to the cemetery. The mountains around us are covered with green, the Galilee is drunk with spring, and only Ikrit's hill is nearly bald. As if nature had decided to leave a patch of starkness here. Neither is the hand of man to be seen—the place has been declared a military area, so no one, Jew or Arab, may cultivate the fields, and they have wasted, as if the place is still staring around groggily, still in shock.

In the cemetery Aouni Sbeit shows me the graves of his father and mother. Since 1972 the Ikrit dead have been allowed to be buried in their village, and each family has established a plot of its own. All descendants of the villagers—even if they themselves were not born in Ikrit—are put to rest here. The first to be buried on Ikrit's land after the eviction was Aouni's grandfather. When he died, in 1953, his family brought his body and buried it here, in accordance with his will.

"When we left, the army came and asked us what he was doing here. We told them. They said, Now go back and take him out and take him back to Rama. We dug him up and took him back on our shoulders. What were they afraid of," Sbeit asks, "that he might rise from his grave and sow the land?"

"Evil are those who make history," said Hegel, but there, on the deserted hill of Ikrit, one could only consider how history makes people evil. I will not list all the promises made to the people of Ikrit and Biram. Promises by Labor governments and Likud governments. All were broken. Menachem Begin wrote to them to say he supported their return, but that it would be delayed because of the security situation. Most of the villages' land was long ago parceled out among the surrounding Jewish settlements, and parts have been declared nature preserves. A minuscule number of the deportees have accepted the government's offer of compensation. All of them rejected a proposal to establish new villages for them, because their original lands were not included in the designated area.

In June 1986 cabinet minister Moshe Arens declared his intention of returning the people to their villages soon. The villagers were carried away by a wave of joy and hope. They called Moshe Arens "our new Moses," and hoped that he would lead them back to their land after forty years of exile. Yet this promise also came to naught—Prime Minister Yitzhak

Shamir shot it down in a way that was described in the Likud as "a slap in the face for Arens."

Until 1948, my grandfather and grandmother, my mother's parents, lived in the Sheikh Jarrah neighborhood of east Jerusalem. It was then a mixed Jewish and Arab neighborhood. When the War of Independence began to intensify, my grandfather, Shalom Vermus, began each night to transfer his religious books and the lighter furnishings to the home of friends in the western part of the city. Afterward the war began to rage around them, and my grandfather and grandmother, with my young mother and her brother, became refugees in their own land. One evening, at the beginning of October 1991, I returned to that neighborhood to meet the Minister of Defense, Moshe Arens, in his office. "There is no justification for preventing the people of Ikrit and Biram from returning to their land. Today there are no security considerations to prevent it. Those who oppose it fear that it will be a precedent that will open a Pandora's box. I don't see a precedent here. Ikrit and Biram are special cases."

I asked him why the Israeli government should not now, with the beginning of the dialogue between the countries of the Middle East, or during the process, make a symbolic gesture and call on the evacuees to return. If it is a precedent, I said, it would be a precedent of goodwill, of generosity, and of self-assurance.

"If it depended on me, I would do it," Arens said simply. "I think that we need to do it, and I also agree with the idea that now is an especially good time for it. But there is no point in my making such a proposal now, when it is clear to me in advance that it will fail."

Today, in the estimation of people who know the subject well, the Israeli government could solve the problem with relative ease, to the satisfaction of all sides. They surmise that a majority of the villagers will now agree to accept the compensation the government offers, and that about a hundred families from each village will resettle on land assigned to them. Most of the evacuees realize that their former land will not be returned to them. An old injustice should not be corrected by creating a new one.

"And write that since 1948 there has been no one from Ikrit who has done anything against the country," Aouni Sbeit intones, suddenly exhausted as we leave the site. "All we did was in accordance with the law. And what did we get? Even a prisoner is better off than we are. A prisoner who is sentenced to ten years knows when it will be over. We don't know when our imprisonment will end."

We drove away. Halil got down to open and close the barbed-wire fence, so that Dari's cows would not escape, so there wouldn't be a scandal. Aouni, a warm man, all heart, embraced me and said, as if trying to comfort me, "We will return. There is no escaping it. We will return and build houses and plant orchards and vineyards, and compensate ourselves for what we missed all these years. And then you'll come to visit me."

I'm sure they will return. It is malicious to keep them from doing so. I know well how this sounds to sober individuals, to the experts, to the systems analysts, to politicians covered with the moss of experience, and to all those analytic brains that anticipated none of the important developments in our region and in the world. In their internal dictionary, the dictionary of life-survival, all the words of suspicion and entrapment and subterfuge are in bold type. They will say that the smallest of concessions will crack the entire line of defense. That Israel's credibility as a country that sticks to its principles will be harmed if we make even one small retreat. That it is better, even, to stand by one's errors and injustices, just as long as one does not create untimely doubts as to the justice of our case. Especially, they will say I am naïve.

That may well be, but perhaps the criminal naïveté is that of those who still believe that Israel can completely and permanently ignore the reasonable demands of its Arab citizens. Just as it can, they believe, create a "new order" in the region when it wants to, just as it can always win every war, and will certainly win American support for all it does.

How long will we prevent the Ikrit and Biram evacuees from going home? For how long will we brandish the justice of our 1948? At some point another, new process must begin. And we must fight for it with the only permissible naïveté in the Middle East, scarred naïveté, like that which may be heard in a poem by Yehuda Amichai, who also fought in that war:

> In the place where we are right
> Flowers will never bloom
> In the spring.
> The place where we are right
> Is trodden and hard
> Like a courtyard.
> But like a mole, like a plow,
> Doubts and loves make
> The world crumble.
> And a whisper will be heard
> Where once there was a house
> That was destroyed.

CHAPTER 14

Friday, five in the evening and the village of Bara hums like a beehive—tonight they are paving sidewalks here, putting up fences, repairing roads. Two hundred fifty men run through the village streets with work tools in hand, breaking stubborn boulders, heaving picks, lugging bricks, no time to stand for even a second.

A pile of stones brought from the village of Jama'in in the West Bank lies in the middle of the road. One of the foremen, a sweating, large-boned young man, consults with the members of his work detail as to where to move the heap and how to parcel it out to the other details. A tractor honks at the crew's back, passing by: it's almost dark. When the driver sees the village's mayor, Kamel Rian, he asks him at a roar to send two trucks with soil so that the new roadway can be lengthened. Best to finish it all tonight, it's a good night to work.

Rian listens, cocking his head while half closing an eye, rubbing his beard. It'll be fine. The truck drivers are praying now. Right after their prayers they'll be with you. Take fifteen

minutes. Come on, he calls to me, we'll go see how the tar
is doing.

He is thirty-three years old. Born in the village, a graduate
of the teachers college in Netanya. Three years after com-
pleting his studies he became religious. "I began to read religious books. I became close to Usrat Eljihad, "the Family
of the Holy War," the forerunner of the Islamic Movement
in Israel. Ever since then the Shin Bet has been following me.
Even if I landed a job, they would fire me a week later. What
could I do? I had an uncle, a partner in a stone quarry. I went
to work for him, and there I found what I was looking for."

Well built, bearded, with glasses. Good-natured. It's hard
to believe how he has transformed the village in the eight years
he has been mayor.

"After you set off explosions in the mountains, you have to
transfer the blocks of stone from the mountain to the work
site, where you smash them. I worked at crushing the stone,
at the hard stage of processing the stone. For two years I
smashed boulders, ground them into gravel.

"I enjoyed the physical labor, and I liked being independent.
I was completely free there. My own boss. During breaks I'd
find myself a corner, sit down, and read religious books, commentaries on the Koran. Culturally, it was the richest period
of my life. The Koran, after all, is not just a religious book.
It is also the essence of literary power. There I was my own
king. Then I also started being the *imam* at our mosque, and
I'd give the sermons on Fridays. Then I was *really* religious,"
he says, a bit apologetically.

"And today, less so?" I asked him, trying to talk over the
clamor of the trucks.

"Let's just say that I don't have the time to exercise all the
laws and precepts." He mixes and mingles, in a single sentence, slang, military expressions, and biblical Hebrew. "I miss
the days in the quarry. There I was calm. I put my trust in

Allah. I did things in perfect faith. Today I'm in politics. Do everything relatively. Make compromises, put things off . . .

"But a group from the village decided that I should run for mayor. I didn't want to. I had no chance. The incumbent mayor had had the job for twenty years. His father had been *mukhtar* for twenty years. He had Turkish roots! And he was also head of the largest clan in the village—they're 70 percent here—and I'm from a small family. How could I run against him?

"But look, 70 percent of the village voted for me, and in '83 I entered city hall, and for six months the security services slandered me in all kinds of ways, saying that I was a Khomeini supporter on the outskirts of Petah Tikva, and they quoted an article they claimed I'd written, that I was waiting for Khomeini to destroy Israel and that I was already inviting the PLO to come.

"In every government office I entered I'd see a photocopy of that article with its lies. Doors were closed to me wherever I went. They didn't give money. They tried slowly, slowly to strangle the village because of me. We didn't have money to pay for electricity; they cut our water off, too. The village didn't have a single meter of pavement then. There was no sewage. No underground water network. You didn't see a single flower. There was no place for sports, no place for culture. There was no medical clinic. Whoever needed a shot had to run to Petah Tikva! Our city hall was one room and one employee. Try working with that.

"I was young, a boy! From where do I know how to run a municipality? When in my life had I ever chaired a meeting? All that and the pressure from the Shin Bet outside. I went and studied in a program in local government at Bar Ilan University. I worked by day and studied by night. The people here helped. They suffered from the water being cut off, from the pressure, but they knew it was directed against me. The entire village would go seven to ten days without any water. We would bring water from Kibbutz Hahorshim, they helped us. The whole time I wanted to resign. My conscience wouldn't let me leave the village without water. If the village hadn't supported me, I would have resigned.

"But they supported me, and I kept going. I was twenty-five years old. Hot! I saw that I wouldn't get anything out of the national government, so I began enlisting the Islamic Movement. Here, in Bara, we held the first *muaskarat*, the first Islamic work camp; today, praise God, you find them all over the country."

I drove to Bara on a Friday, during the Jewish holiday of Sukkoth. I had heard enthusiastic stories about the Islamic Movement's work camps, and I wanted to see one with my own eyes. Along the way I started to have doubts. I'd already interviewed several of the movement's members and leaders. More than once I had come up against that invisible boundary no stranger can cross. He can only sense that beyond the faces smiling so cordially, behind the answers, which are always well-meaning, there is something else, something enigmatic, irrational—inaccessible to him.

The narrow road leading to Bara runs from Ben Shemen to Rosh Ha'ayin, northeast of Tel Aviv, along the marches of a marginal, forsaken land, a land of limestone and chalk, roads full of potholes, past abandoned quarries where huge cutting and crushing machines rust. The settlements scattered there, Hagor, Beit Nehemia, Givat Koah, are preparing for the Sabbath—children becoming formal in holiday clothes, a woman putting a cake out on the windowsill to cool. What are you looking for at this hour in Bara? What does the Islamic Movement's Sabbath cheer have to do with you?

I picture the members of the movement I have already met. They are young and dynamic. They are feeling a growing sense of power. They are aware of the apprehension they arouse in secular Arab circles, and they are no less attentive to the tremors of anxiety and distrust the Jewish public feels about them. They chart their course with great discretion and awareness. "We have the ability, and the opportunity, to search and scrutinize the Islamic constitution to find the conditions and the means appropriate to our circumstances within Jewish Israel," explained Ibrahim Sarsur, mayor of Kafr Kassem, one of the movement's leaders. "The Islamic Movement in Egypt and Hamas, the Islamic Movement in the territories, oppose any move toward peace, and they also draw their ideas from the Koran and the Sunna. But I can understand the Koran and the Sunna as I wish, and I can prove to you that the Koran requires me to negotiate, and to solve the problems between us and you, between us and our enemies, in peaceful ways."

" 'Our enemies'?"

I could hear his brakes screeching: "Just a minute! I'll retreat! I take it back!" He raises a finger in front of me, closing his eyes as if reciting. "Even though the Israelis are always saying 'our enemies the Arabs,' and in doing so they make no distinction between Israeli Arabs and Arabs from the territories or from Syria. But I still take it back! I'm a human being like you, and you are like me; I'm not willing to have even the spark of a thought that you are my enemy enter my head. Under no circumstances!"

His eyes stay closed tight, and it is clear how that sophisticated, pragmatic mechanism works. It was certainly this way, with eyes shut tight, assimilating new conditions, that the Islamic Movement decided to turn into a law-abiding organization, to raise itself up out of the ruins of the Family of the Holy War underground, after that movement's members and leaders were released from prison eight years ago. It is really this internal control, this self-programming, that disquiets me. The Islamic Movement smiles broadly at me, but with a twitch in its cheek, and when Ibrahim Sarsur again looks at me with his bright eyes, I know that he has already jotted down a warning to himself.

"And if Hamas believes in expelling the Jews from their homeland, from Israel, then they are also the enemies of Islam!" he added. "Anyone who wants to expel the Jews from their country is my enemy as a Muslim, an enemy of Islam, an enemy of humanity."

So says Sarsur, one of the leaders of the movement, but in *As-Sirat*, the movement's monthly magazine, printed in Israel, there was recently an article stating that "the problem of Palestine and its Muslim nation is a purely Islamic problem, which may be solved only by means of fundamental Islamic solutions." Another article declared: "Palestine is not merchandise to be sold and bought in a slave market, on the principles of profit and loss . . . Palestine is Islamic holy land . . . It is not the property of the Palestinians, or of the Arabs, but of all Muslims of all past and current generations, and no man, whoever he is, has the right to abandon or concede one inch of its land."

"Hey, you're treating those sentences as if they were straight from the Koran! Very good!" Sarsur spun threads of ridicule around me. "It's good that you take us so seriously! Here, I'll give you some *tafsir*, some commentary, of a modern type. It says there that the Palestinian problem can be solved only with fundamental Islamic solutions? I agree! We, as an Islamic movement in Israel, believe that the Jews have a right to exist in Israel, which is part of Palestine! Even Salah ad-Din Ayyoubi resolved with the Crusaders that they would remain on the coast. Can I come and tell you today that Salah ad-Din Ayyoubi, a celebrated leader, a [winking] fundamentalist—did he really give up part of Palestine to infidel Crusaders? Or was it an entirely different matter, one of shrewdness and tolerance? And the Crusaders, you know, had no right to this land, unlike the Jews, who really do have a certain connection, they have a history and a well-known right here; but the Christians, they're from Europe, they claim that Jesus' grave is here. And I thought Jesus ascended to heaven, didn't he?"

Thirty-two years old. A graduate of the English Literature and Linguistics Departments at Bar Ilan University. His face is pleasant, candid, his forehead high and glistening, his voice musical. Quick of thought, swift of speech, enjoys an argument. "If fanaticism means devotion to the principles of Islam," he says, quoting Sa'id Kutub, the ideologue of the Muslim Brotherhood in Egypt, "then the entire world should know that I am a fanatic. In order not to be a fanatic, I must really be torn. I must tear away all the roots that connect me with Islam. If you think that when you call me 'fundamentalist' you are insulting me, you are very wrong! The word in Arabic is *asuli*, 'rooted.' So I am proud to be a fundamentalist.

"But you"—he nods at me—"your Western eyes see another fundamentalist, an evil one, with a big beard, a shaved mustache, wearing a robe, with a sword in his hand and blood dripping from the point of the sword. That's how the world sees fundamentalism today. It's in the West's blood."

I asked, "And whoever says, 'You make compromises over money, compromises over property, but you don't make compromises over the soul of the nation,' and by that he means land, what is he in your eyes?"

Sarsur chuckles. "Who said that land is the soul of the nation? I'll give you an example. Mohammed was in Mecca, at the Kaaba, and he heard a Muslim praying, raising his hands to the sky: 'Allah, *bihak el-Kaaba!*' He was asking Allah's aid and invoking the name of the Kaaba, that Allah answer his petition. So the Prophet took him to one side. Listen, he said, you are calling on God and invoking the Kaaba. You should be doing it differently—you should be calling on God in your own name, your own personal name! 'Because he who raised the sky without pillars, the name of the believer is for him more sublime than the name of the Kaaba,' so it is written in the Koran. So do you want to tell me that this dirt that they call Palestine is more important than the Kaaba to a Muslim? If the Kaaba is no more important than a human being, then Palestine isn't either."

"What I just quoted you on the soul of the nation," I admitted, "was said yesterday on television by a Jewish settler from Hebron."

"You played a trick like that on me?" He laughed long but silently. "Oh, a Jewish settler said that? With fundamentalists like that we'll really find ourselves at war, God willing."

I said, "Your slogan 'Islam is the solution' is too cryptic for my tastes."

He said, "What's cryptic? What's unclear? It's very simple and straightforward: Islam is the solution!"

"Still," I insisted, "I was once the subject of a solution, so I'm a little suspicious. A solution to what? A solution for whom?"

"David, David, don't be scared. We're not the Islamic Movement in Jordan or the territories! We live under other conditions. They have the opportunity to fight the occupation in their own way and to save themselves. We have the opportunity to find other ways and interpretations to live together with you. As a Muslim, I now accept the existence of Israel as an established fact. We have nothing to say about this given. God forbid, you should say we're against the country," he warns me with a smile, always a smile. "We're against the policy, not against the country. After all, under today's conditions it would be foolish to expect the establishment of an Islamic state inside Israel. So we act within the framework of the law."

"And what is the nature of your ties to Hamas?"

"They are there—we are here. Each one functions in his own reality. Listen, there is not a single regime in the Arab world today that will allow its country's Islamic Movement to progress and develop. We're fought against everywhere in the Arab world. They know that if we gain control it will be the end of their regime. Our luck is that in Israel the regime is different from those in the Arab world. Despite it being a Likud government, there's democracy, and if you don't undermine Israel's security, if you are aware of the limitations imposed by law, you have a chance to act. We had a certain experience with that in the eighties when Sheikh Abdallah Nimr Darwish and other leaders and members were accused of various things, of supporting the Fatah, and were imprisoned. Since that experience everything with us has changed completely, and there has been a 180-degree turn."

"You mean," I asked, "according to what you said, that Israel is actually the only country in the Middle East that allows its Islamic Movement to act freely?"

"Of course! I admit it."

"And what about the commandment to fight a *jihad* [holy war] obligatory on you as a Muslim?"

"Good thing you asked. What is a *jihad*? There are many forms of *jihad*. Seven or eight gradations, maybe even twelve. The military *jihad* is only one of them, and it's the last one. If I improve my life in the village, and hold a work camp— that's a *jihad*. If I add rooms to a school—that's a *jihad*, too. If I sit with you and persuade you that it's worthwhile for us to live in peace—isn't that a *jihad*? Now, the most important thing: if I have the possibility of liberating the part that was occupied in '67 peacefully, then I'd be guilty, a criminal, if I caused the blood of a Muslim to be spilled in a war, when I can obtain the same thing with a *jihad* of peace. That's what Sadat did, after all, when he liberated all of the Sinai peninsula, without spilling the blood of one Muslim!"

"And what about the territory that the Muslims lost to Israel in 1948? Here you make a tactical concession in your faith?"

"We don't deal in tactics. In 1948 there was a war, and there was a decision of the United Nations about dividing Palestine into two countries. As a Muslim today, I accept the existence of Israel as an established fact. We have nothing to say about this given. The occupation of 1967 is an occupation, according to all the countries in the world and according to the U.N. But if Israel does not offer its hand in peace and does not withdraw from the occupied territories, and does not return the land to its owners," he declaims in his pleasant tenor singsong, giving *everything* he says the same strange amicability, "only then must the Palestinians and Muslims all over the world fight Israel in accordance with the precept of the *jihad* and expel it from their land."

"Does that include you, within Israel?"

"No. We are not part of the Islamic nation which is required to fight against Israel. We live as a minority that cannot fight, and according to the principles of Islam, we are not required to fight Israel. Islam says: When you are a minority, you are not even *allowed* to behave in a way that will undermine the security of the ruling nation—on condition, on *condition*, that it allows you to live as a Muslim. If the Knesset comes and decides that I am not permitted to pray, if it decides to damage the mosques, in such a case Islam compels me inexorably to fight and to maintain our rights. So long as that does not happen, we do not fight."

I examine him carefully. There were no surprises. He does not deny his ambitions. He is pragmatic and sober. Islam does in fact concern itself first and foremost with the well-being and security of its adherents. After the death of the Prophet Mohammed, the community of believers was torn apart by a great and traumatic civil war, the *Fitna*. Ever since, Sunni religious sages have advocated refraining from rebellion against the ruler of a Muslim country, and all the more so when the Muslims are a defenseless minority. Ibrahim Sarsur is without a doubt giving me the interim truth. But in his fluent Hebrew discourse I hear also the echo of far mosques, and the roar of the aroused crowds in the streets of the Sudan and Iran and Algeria, the sound of the bullets that Muslim fanatics fired at President Sadat. And it was not long after this conversation, in the winter of 1992, that three Israeli Arabs, members of the Islamic Movement, butchered three Israeli soldiers with knives and a pickax—the most serious act of terror yet perpetrated by Arab citizens of Israel. I listened attentively as Sarsur testified: "I am worth nothing without the Islamic Movement. I am zero without it. Whatever it tells me to do, I will do."

The sun is already setting in Bara. The village roads are boiling. Steam rises from the sidewalks as they are leveled by steamrollers. I compress a lump of warm, sticky tar in my hand. Wherever I look I see people working, eyes sparkling, bodies heaving. Boys run between the workers carrying trays of cold drinks and coffee. The neighbors beside whose houses the sidewalk is being laid invite the laborers in to get their wind back. In the afternoon all the workers eat at the home of one of the neighbors. Two sheep were slaughtered. Two hundred people squeeze into the yard. It is a privilege for a Muslim to slaughter a sheep when a son is born to him. But this privilege, the *akika*, may be "saved" for another opportunity. "What's better, to give the meat to satiated, celebrating people or to people who are working hard?" asks Kamel Rian. "So we 'save' the privilege, sometimes for half a year, until the Islamic work camp." Two other villagers have asked to host the work details for meals tomorrow. The day after, there is a problem—too many villagers are fighting to host the meals. Most of them do not even belong to the Islamic Movement. "It looks like

we'll have to extend the camp for a few more days." He roars
with laughter.

I'd bring activists from poor neighborhoods, people from
urban renewal programs, mayors, here to learn from this young
man. How, without any experience and, especially, without
support from the national government, did he turn this backward village into a place it is a pleasure to live in? I'd bring
the Arab mayors whose towns contain neighborhoods of luxurious houses lying along miserable dirt roads, stained with
sewage, where no one lifts a finger to help himself. Rian, one
of the people, sharp, tolerant, omnipresent, picking up every
piece of trash from the ground, hugging the whole village to
his barrel chest. I rush after him to one of the distant fields
outside the village. Bulldozers are working there, their head-
lights lit, conquering another detour. The trucks dump earth.
"This is soil I kept from the roads we built during the last work
camp. Instead of throwing it away I saved it, and now I can
use it for this new pavement."

The two bulldozer operators descend toward us in the light
of their vehicles. Sweaty, grimy, glowing. Nidal Sutani from
Tira, and Ali Abu Sheikha from Ara. They have come for a
week. Staying with friends in the village. "I can sleep wherever
I want. Wherever I want, they'll let me eat," Ali says. He is
working here as a volunteer. He is sacrificing a week's profits
from work on his Volvo BM tractor and a week's salary from
another job. He even pays for the bulldozer's fuel. "I've already
learned that if I do a good deed here, I earn more afterward
outside." His friend adds, "In these camps I've learned what
the power of religion is, what the power of work is when you
do it for yourself and help yourself. Look at how the people
here are giving with all their hearts. I got up this morning
when it was still dark, at 4:30, I prayed, and ever since I've
been working, and we'll keep working until we collapse."

Over the last seven years the movement has succeeded in

"conquering"—a characteristic term—seven local authorities, a most respectable achievement. It is also well represented in the councils of two cities and twelve villages. It is steadily gaining power in the Histadrut labor federation; it has founded an Islamic soccer league (with prayers at the beginning and end of each match); it has founded dozens of nursery schools, youth clubs, and clinics. Um Elfahm, inspired by the Islamic Movement, is about to establish fourteen separate classes for boys and girls in its high school, and Teibe is establishing a religious college. As the feeling of discrimination and frustration grows among the Arabs in Israel, an ever greater number, it seems, seek the solution to their troubles in religion and in the Islamic Movement. As faith wanes in the power of the Arab leadership in Israel to achieve real progress, the movement is reinforced by new recruits. Perhaps, instead of listing all its achievements, I should have noted one detail—during the last decade more than one hundred mosques have been built in Arab settlements in Israel.

Sheikh Abdallah Nimr Darwish, founder of the movement and among its most prominent leaders, sighs when I ask him how the great power he wields affects him. "In politics, when a man my age takes up a position of power, that's a big thing for him. I'm looking to resign now. Enough already! Enough!"

"Are you tired? You haven't accomplished enough?"

"No, no. Everything I've planned I've achieved, thank God. I even achieved what I didn't plan. I didn't think that in the 1990s a man from the Islamic Movement would be the mayor of a city like Um Elfahm. If we've already achieved Um Elfahm, I don't think it's at all impossible for us to win *the* city. The big one, Nazareth."

"And after that?" I asked.

The sheikh flashes me a smile, direct to the dungeons of my fear. "Afterward the government, no? Relax. All of you, relax. Nazareth is something very important for us. We don't think beyond that. If we do, we need to build an Arab society in Israel that will fight on two principles: to achieve all our legitimate rights and not to break the law. If we achieve that, that's the society I'm seeking."

"If that's the case, why so far have you refrained from entering national politics to achieve your rights?"

"I don't reject that. But we haven't yet decided to do it. I hope that within two or three months the Arab leadership in this country will sit down and decide to present a united Arab slate of candidates for the Knesset. As long as there is no such slate, I have no interest in national politics."

"Will Jews be accepted into such a party?"

The sheikh, emphatically: "Arabs. *Arabs*. That's enough. Enough already."

"That's racism."

He shakes his head angrily. "Whoever wants to talk about racism should take a look at most of the Zionist parties! You'll find racism there. All those parties, except for Mapam, the United Workers Party, put Jews in the Knesset with Arab votes! Show me one Zionist party that gave an Arab a chance to fill any important position! One government minister! One deputy minister in a serious job! We're 18 percent of the population! I'm not a racist. I'm a believing man who knows that racism is Satan's creed. Satan said explicitly, 'I am unwilling to accept man, because you created him from sand, and I am made from fire.' That's racism." He leans forward, his eyebrows slightly arched, forced upward. "And if in the end there's an Arab minister in the cabinet, you know what they'll make him? Minister without portfolio! Do you know what humiliation we feel when they appoint us a Minister for Arab Affairs? Hey, do you have a Minister for Jewish Affairs? And why do the police need an Officer for Minority Affairs? Isn't just a regular officer enough? Let him investigate the minorities and the majority. Why, everywhere I go, do you make me feel—

Stop! You enter afterward! No. No. This time I want to enter first. To be the first to enter the hall in which they are deciding about me. Deciding my fate."

Why has the Islamic Movement refrained from putting its own slate up for elections to the Knesset? One possibility is that today it enjoys ever-growing esteem—some estimate its electoral power as the equivalent of six of the parliament's 120 seats—but that it is cautious about getting a precise measure of that support. Another possibility is that participation in Knesset elections would imply *de facto* recognition of Israeli sovereignty. Its Knesset members would have to swear loyalty to the Jewish state and to the laws of the Knesset, which are, according to Sheikh Raad Salah, "opposed to what God commanded and bestowed upon us." Participation in Knesset elections would force the movement to publish an official platform in which it would have to take clear positions on many issues; apparently it wishes to refrain from this. One may assume that they prefer to leave many fundamental matters touching on the life of the zealous Muslim in a Jewish state to speculation, confidences, and silent prayer.

Participation in local elections however, is permissible, even desirable, in the view of the Islamic Movement. In town councils they can determine the character of Arab rule over Arabs, and it is a step of sorts in the direction of the independent, autonomous rule that Islamic Movement activists "ever aspire to, but do not actively pursue," as Sheikh Kamel Rian diplomatically puts it.

Sheikh Darwish receives guests in his home in Kafr Kassem in a gray robe and black plastic slippers. The house is simply furnished. A few armchairs, a single couch, a wood table, and a bookcase with volumes of religious books. A large urn filled with cold water sits on the windowsill. There is one spot of color in the room—a poster the sheikh received in Mecca when he performed the *haj*, or pilgrimage required of all Muslims. It shows a Chinese child gazing longingly at the Kaaba and at the Dome of the Rock. There are 31 million Muslims in China.

"So ask—how many Palestinians are there in the world? Five and a half million. Arabs? One hundred sixty million. Muslims? One thousand two hundred million! What, you're not afraid that a day will come when all the Arabs will be sick of you? Not only the Arabs in Israel, but those everywhere! What behavior!"

It is generally hard to catch him angry. Even when there is an outburst, it seems to have been premeditated. He is generally calm and possesses a kind of serenity that radiates power and security, a leopard-like serenity, I thought, and then recalled that his name Nimr means leopard. He is very conscious of himself, frequently speaking of himself in the third person: "Sheikh Abdallah always says that . . ." A relatively young man, forty-three, with close to twenty years of public activity behind him. His beard is cropped close to his cheeks, and his face is a fascinating one. Sometimes, in the course of a single phrase, an entire range of ages fans across it, from childhood to old age. At one moment it is saturated with craftiness and evil, and experiences that are greater than his years; at another it is simple and innocent. He is certainly not naïve. More than anything else, one sees in him the desire of a very strong man to dispel apprehension about him by means of a demonstrative effort to appear more disarming. When you meet him, it becomes clear how much the entire movement has internalized its leader's mode of behavior.

His six-year-old daughter, Bara'a, enters the room. A full-bodied, lively girl with black hair. She cuddles him, pulls his beard, assaults him, and he accepts his suffering with love. I ask him if he remembers himself at that age.

"I was an unquiet boy. I wasn't easy. I made problems for my mother. I was ill from the age of eight months. Polio. To this day my left side is paralyzed. I was with my father and mother all the time, and I felt—and they made me feel—so spoiled, special. I remember very well [he pulls his head into his neck, going red with laughter], I don't know whether to tell you . . . Father and Mother were young, about thirty, and I slept between them . . . day and night [he was laughing heartily, his face glowing]. Maybe the way I felt they behaved with me is the way I behave with Bara'a today."

I asked whether his illness, which struck him in infancy, had influenced his life.

"How should I know? I only know that always, ever since I can remember, I behaved differently from everyone else. I, for instance, even before I was a believer, never drank. Never! Because I'd see drunks and the way they acted, and I didn't want to be like them. I'd say, In any case I have to do all sorts of things to look more or less like everyone else, so how would it look if I were drunk?"

He halted for a moment. Sank into himself. "Look," he said in the end, "I was just thinking that maybe I've made a mistake. In all I've said and written my entire life, I've never mentioned the handicapped. I think that has been an error. Maybe I should do it every week! Understand that I did not myself suffer. I did not feel alone as a child, I did not feel inferior. Maybe because my family was an important one so people didn't dare. That's our mentality, but now, after having spoken about it, maybe I'll start talking about it outside, writing about it."

I reflected on how such an unequivocal political and social consciousness had developed in him at such a young age. It spurred him to fight against restriction and arbitrariness. Out loud, I said that sometimes a disadvantage of that kind can give a person a certain sense of election, of having been set apart.

"Maybe it is a key," the sheikh said, "that enables you,

unconsciously, to open yourself. More and more I think of
how I, at age twenty, studied under a certain teacher, a wise
man who taught me Arabic literature, and of the texts we
learned that year, especially the poets—one blind, one deaf.
Disabled. That lit a candle with me—hey, what's going on
here. Why them? I read their poems eagerly. All of Arab
literature from the early days of Islam, and from the Middle
Ages, was founded on those writers. So I, at the age of twenty,
began to think, Maybe that blind man, because he doesn't
see, has the opportunity to think more? To understand more?
To feel more?

"So, at that young age, I decided to shut myself up in a
room, not to see people, to be alone. To read. I read, in one
year and three months, all the important books of Islamic
philosophy. I wouldn't leave the house except to pray in the
mosque. Without people. Without arguments. It was easy and
good for me that way. I had the chance to understand the
spirit and depth of Islamic thinking.

"To this day I maintain that—what can I say, it is impossible
to be modest about it—I can say that in the commentaries on
the Koran, Sheikh Abdallah is among the best, *the best*,
maybe, in the entire region! Because to interpret the verses of
the Koran you have to have mastered the Arabic language,
Arabic grammar, Arabic literature. And the wisdom of the
Islamic judges, their way of thinking. Because what is the real
teaching of Islam? The teaching of Islam is peace for all human
beings. Period."

In 1980 the Shin Bet uncovered the Family of the Holy
War underground. Its members had a vision of an entirely
Islamic Palestine, with whatever Jews remaining in it playing
the role of an obedient minority. The Family of the Holy War
set fire to fields and forests in the Negev and the Galilee,
uprooted orchards, and stole weapons from Israeli army bases.
The members of the group, which advocated a violent holy

war, or *jihad*, against Israel, considered Sheikh Abdallah Nimr, Darwish their spiritual leader. Sixty men, Sheikh Darwish among them, were convicted in a military court in Lod. The details of that trial are still classified. According to a leader of the underground, Farid Abu Muh, the prosecution was unable to prove that Darwish was indeed the ideological leader of the group. He was sentenced to prison and released after serving about three years.

After his release, he and his fellows founded the Islamic Movement, which committed itself to obeying the law. Its declared goals were much more moderate than those of the Family of the Holy War. The sheikh wisely found a special path his disciples could walk securely in Israel. They could declare their loyalty to Israel without infringing on their national identity. They found their national identity at a deeper level than Palestinian nationalism does—in the essence of the entire Arab nation, in Islam. It was possible to hear those gears whirring when the sheikh referred to the enthusiasm of the young Muslims of the work camps. "While all of them work under the green flag of the Islamic Movement, many of the young people don't belong to us at all. Because even those young people of whom it is sometimes said that they are materialistic and not active, they, too, are searching for the opportunity to give of themselves. To contribute. And what other opportunity does the democratic and glorious State of Israel give to contribute voluntarily? To identify with an idea?"

By the light of projector lamps volunteers in Bara are preparing the foundation for a sidewalk in the southern neighborhood. They pour in the foundation and the gravel. They consult on how most efficiently to coordinate the work of the steamrollers that have been brought from other villages. The plan is to pave 3,500 square meters of sidewalk in four days. Since morning, up until this hour of the evening, they have paved 1,200. In the schoolyard a teacher and his pupils complete the planting of a small grove of trees. They survey their handiwork in the dusk: "We didn't want to plant cypresses, because cypresses look like missiles on launch pads." They planted eucalyptus instead, the tree used by Israeli pioneers to drain swamps. At that same moment a long file of children passes, half running, carrying pots with saplings in them. A special work detail is already preparing, on the sidewalks, the squares of edging stones to form boxes for the young trees. Bara is a green village. "Arab villages generally don't pay much attention to green things; they plant today and it withers tomorrow. But I wanted it to look nice here," Kamel Rian says. "And it turns out that if the people themselves plant the trees and the grass, they continue to take care of the tree near their house and the nearby lawn. If someone in the village dares pluck a leaf from a tree, everyone gangs up on him. Why? Because they themselves planted it." As we speak we reach a pretty building, large and proud, lit in green light. Bara's cultural center.

"Now tell me, have you ever seen such a building? Guess how much time it took us to build it."

I answered that nothing he said would surprise me.

"Listen to the story. We were busy planning a volunteer operation in the village, and one of the planners died of a heart attack. He was young. I left him at one in the morning, and at three they called and said he was dead.

"I, at the height of the first three days of mourning, called my friends together here and said, Let's change the plan. Let's build a community center named after him. We checked and saw that the cost of putting up such a community center was more than $200,000. We didn't have it. Where could we get it? The town council's development budget, you know, was $4,800, for 1,400 residents. And I had to use that money to make a reception for the Minister of the Interior, who came here with fifty people, and they demanded that I bring a kosher cook from Petah Tikva, and there went the $4,800! That's why I never invite any of those thieves.

"So what did we do? We set up a national team. We brought five engineers, from Kafr Kana, Um Elfahm, Kafr Kassem, and one of our own. That was the steering committee. We created five committees, one responsible for materials, one for labor, one for equipment, and so on. On the fourth day of the mourning period we'd already begun to work. We collected $35,000 from the people in the village: people withdrew savings. Women took rings from their fingers, gold earrings, we filled up a bag with gold and jewelry."

"Just voluntarily? There are rumors that you force people to contribute."

"Everything was voluntary. We are forbidden, religiously, to force a man to pay. Besides, what power do we have to take by force? I've got only peer pressure behind me. Everyone around you gives, you give, too. There are political parties that oppose us, but when we lay a sidewalk next to the house of an opponent, do you think he doesn't come out to help? Of course he does!

"To make a long story short, eighteen days later we'd poured the last concrete for the community center. We worked day and night. Twelve-hour shifts—you finish, go to sleep, get up and work. It's more than 700 square meters. A public library that will hold, God willing, 20,000 volumes. A huge conference hall. A stage for the Islamic Women's Theater that we have in the village. And on the bottom floor, two private day-care classes that cost $13 a month per child."

I saw the nursery school. Happy rooms, full of color and stimuli and places to play and equipment. "Sure. Because the budget doesn't come from the Ministry of Education. It comes from us. From a charitable society we established. What do you think, that we can't have a separate educational system, like your religious people?"

He ticks off on his fingers: Today the village has a senior citizens' center, there is a regulation basketball court and two public playgrounds with the best equipment. We finally put the cemetery in order. We constructed a sewage system. Roads. Streetlights. The Ministry of Education hasn't built a single room in the school since I've been in the village, he notes, with no tone of reproach in his voice. The whole school had two bathrooms. The teachers go together with the students— what kind of thing is that? We built twenty bathrooms. We added classrooms. In my village the Islamic Movement did what the Ministry of the Interior won't do for the next fifty years. Even if it doubles our development budget for fifty years, it won't attain what we've already done in the village. Today's project will cost me $22,000. If I had it done by outside contractors, it would have cost me $130,000.

Of course we want autonomy, said the men—each in his own way—with whom I ate a sumptuous supper during one of the breaks from work. "We talk about it a lot," said Sheikh Kamel. "Everything's moving in the direction that in the end will bring us autonomy here. The establishment is pushing us by force to want it." His fellows, in chorus: Take the matter of the appointment of the religious judges. How can a bureaucrat in Petah Tikva who doesn't know Arabic appoint a kadi for a village, especially when everyone knows he's a drunk and was appointed only because he's a Shin Bet informer? How can you appoint an illiterate imam? Why do I have to wait ten years before I can build a nursery school out of the municipal budget? You've seen what we can do ourselves. Why don't they let us set a traditional Islamic curriculum for ourselves? Why don't they accept our soccer team into the league? The Islamic League was established for lack of any alternative!

"Little by little," Kamel Rian sums up the furious shouts, "our private projects add up and give us a sense of independence. The Islamic Movement today already has its tools and its institutions and its representatives. These things push us in the direction of independence."

We continue to run. The time is short and the work great, and you are the master, and that, apparently, is the secret. The air shivers with emotion. Now I understood why I had to come and how pale words are when compared to deeds. I recalled the *ziker* ceremony of the Darwish sect I once attended in the Old City of Jerusalem—for several hours the men of the *zawia* fired themselves into an ecstasy. A hint of the same internal fire and addiction is here tonight. Everywhere you look hammers clang and picks strike. The odor of asphalt sticks to the skin. Piles of gravel and sand disappear in the whirlwind of a few minutes. An old Zionist pioneer song ran through my head: "We will dress you in concrete and cement." Facing us, in the dark, is Petah Tikva, rejoicing in the Sabbath, gathering around the bowls of soup, and here where we are, that is, where they are, a truck unloads another heap of stones, and the "stone detail" charges to distribute the stones to the "fence detail," and in different parts of the village six bull-dozers, twelve trucks, three cement mixers, and steam shovels are all working, and amid all this commotion a three-year-old boy named Wasim deals a blow to the asphalt in front of his house with a yellow plastic hoe. That child's tool reminded me of another boy of his age who aimed a yellow plastic rod at me at the Deheishe refugee camp and shot me because I was Jewish. That boy is already eight today, and if nothing has happened to him he has presumably graduated from plastic to stone. Wasim is enchanted with the asphalt. With great seriousness and dedication he smooths a little hill, sniffs it, touches it with his hand—an unforgettable sensory experience. Maybe, without his realizing it, his political and religious consciousness is being fixed within him.

Beside the small post office the village manager scrubs

splotches of cement from the new fence with a stiff brush. "The finish is important, too," Rian says, sharing his concern for detail. It makes me think of that expression "Arab work," Hebrew slang for a sloppy and badly done job. Nearby, before my very eyes, in the space of two hours, a narrow dirt path turns into a broad, comfortable, tree-lined sidewalk, and the team responsible for painting the curbstones charges at it, and after them the clean-up crew to cart off the debris, and the frames are already going up around the saplings, and the trash cans are already being put in place . . .

A different, almost forgotten spirit. A kind of momentum that a stranger finds difficult to face. "You asked if we're connected to Hamas," Kamel Rian reminds me. "What's for sure is that we have a connection with *hamasa*, with zeal."

What if they ask me to join them? What if someone hands me a hoe or a pick? How tempting it is to forget what lies beyond them and to surrender to that patriotic fire that blazes in the heart. How is it possible, in that all-encompassing storm that sweeps you off your feet, to refuse a human hand offering you a work tool? It's such a complicated question; it asks, through intermediate stages of evasive and roundabout translations, one thing: Do they and I have the same goal?

Yes, yes, they are building the country. No, because I feel that they are not building my country. Yes, because they are doing exactly what any Israeli group with initiative and vision would do. No, because that *hamasa* is part of an entire web of desires and beliefs that are not mine, and only for now is that fire being used to heat the huge tank of asphalt. A brawny man with kinky hair approaches Kamel Rian. His hair is white with dust. He is in charge of the asphalt. There's an unexpected problem—because of the quick pace of the work, the asphalt has run out. Seventy tons. Some 1,700 square meters of sidewalk have been paved in a single day. Everyone marvels. Torpor begins to seep into their movements. Kamel scratches his head as if just waking up. "Everything's gone? But it was for two days!"

"The Islamic solution is for us, for the Jews, and for all of humanity . . . There is room for only one country between the river and the sea. That country will be Muslim," I read a week previously in the Islamic Movement's newspaper, *Sawt Elhak Walhuria* (*The Voice of Justice and Freedom*), but under the existing conditions in Israeli-Arab society, passivity and abnegation, it was hard not to be impressed by the deeds and not to understand the secret of their attraction for so many. There, in Bara, across the way from the drained swamps of Malabis in which the water buffalo once waded, out of which the very earliest Zionist pioneers built the first new Jewish village in Israel, Petah Tikva, the Gate of Hope, it was possible to sense and understand this Muslim Petah Tikva, and to feel a surprising pang of remorse, a longing for ourselves as we once were.

"Come on, what are you dreaming about?" Kamel Rian had already recovered. He grabbed me by the hand and pulled me after him. "Come see something you won't believe."

But I stopped and stared ahead. At the edge of a dark empty lot I suddenly made out many, many figures, swaying silently. I saw only their backs, kneeling and rising and kneeling, their faces to Mecca.

CHAPTER 15

In January 1986, in an interview with the magazine *Politika*, Israeli writer A. B. Yehoshua said the following: "I say to Anton Shammas—if you want your full identity, if you want to live in a country that has an independent Palestinian personality, that possesses an original Palestinian culture, rise up, take your belongings, and move 100 meters to the east, to the independent Palestinian state that will lie beside Israel." Shammas is a Palestinian-Israeli poet, translator, and writer in both Arabic and Hebrew, known for trenchant and ironic newspaper articles in which he takes Israeli society to task for its occupation regime. He responded sharply, lumping Yehoshua, known for his liberal views, with "his brothers, the members of the Jewish terror organization." He also gave notice that if and when the Palestinian state is established, "I do not wish to leave my country and my kindred and my father's house for the land that he, in this case, A. B. Yehoshua, will show me." A little tempest blew up, smaller than it should have been, given the subject—the nature of Israeli identity and the Arabs' place therein. In one corner of this debate over the nature of "Israeliness" was Shammas, who aspired to create a single Israeli nationality common to all those living within the borders of the state, both Jewish and Arab; in the other corner was Yehoshua, for whom Israeli identity is the consummate expression of Jewish identity. Part of the Israeli left was shocked by the position taken by Yehoshua, who is one of the Israeli left's most prominent and bold spokesmen. There were those who saw his "rise up, take your belongings" as a call for the expulsion of the Arabs from Israel, and some annulled his membership in the left. What was interesting was that in the verbal violence that Shammas and Yehoshua kicked up around them it was possible to feel, even in their passionate public attacks on each other, an ever-present thread of mutual amity, a thread that was not broken even after the debate was over.

Six years passed. Shammas in the meantime published his Hebrew-language novel *Arabesques*. It is a sad and very beautiful work, "a novel disguised as an autobiography," which begins in Shammas's Galilean hometown, Fasuta. In recent years Shammas has lived in Ann Arbor, Michigan, teaching at the University of Michigan. He has been preparing a collection of articles on the Middle East, written in English, for publication.

Yehoshua, nicknamed "Buli," has in the interval published two novels, *Five Seasons* and *Mr. Mani*, and is now working on a new novel, a love story.

At the beginning of January 1992, Shammas came home for a short visit, and the three of us met at Yehoshua's home on Mount Carmel. Shammas entered the house and Buli rushed to meet him. They embraced, looked each other over, embraced again—maybe to ground the electric charge of the meeting. Anton, balding, of delicate manners, wore a blue sweater, round glasses, and a kind of poet's economy on his face; Buli, fifty-five years old, his mane of hair already gone silver, always tensed and stormy, warm and physical, wore a red flannel shirt with the simple, direct prosaism that is his.

You haven't been here for four years, I said to Shammas, and he said, "Only four? You could say that for forty-one years, ever since I was born, I haven't been here . . . What, have *you* two been here?" And Yehoshua: "I've always been here too much . . . I wish I hadn't been here a little . . ."

Shammas: "A line from a poem by Nizar Kabani, the Syrian poet who served his country as a diplomat in Spain, just came to me: 'In the narrow alleys of Cordoba I would extend my hand and look for the keys to our house in Damascus.' I don't feel that way anywhere. There is no real home. You ask if I was 'here.' I understand the word 'here' in its geographical-Hebrew sense. I was not here in the Arabic sense of 'here,' because they have taken the ground out from under me. When you say 'Galilee,' what is that word for me? The Galilee is yours; for me it is the *Jalil*; the change in pronunciation makes all the difference; without it my entire semantic security in my sense of homeland is unsettled."

Then he recalled an article he had written some years ago, in which he referred to the experience of being "a guest in the language": "With what might have been destructive cynicism I compared myself to the Harold Pinter type of character who appears suddenly in one's house, remains for dinner, washes the dishes, and stays the night, and the next morning he is already starting to take over. And I said, But I will try to be well-mannered. I arrive in the house of the Hebrew language under the banner of good manners."

I asked him if there had been any moment in his life in which he had felt that he had the "key" to a home. He had

sensed it, he said, when *Arabesques* appeared in Hebrew—
the writer Amnon Shamush then published a review of the
book, concluding with an allusion to Shammas's ironical "declaration of good manners": "One makes up a bed for the guest,
Anton my friend, my brother, and one hosts him in the best
tradition of good hospitality; but one never gives him the keys
to the house, or the deed to it." Shammas: "Then I understood
that *Arabesques* is my key. But who knows if they won't change
the lock."

We sat and spoke, and Yehoshua closed an old account
with Shammas: Why had he chosen to call one of the characters in *Arabesques*, an unpleasant Israeli writer, Yehoshua
Bar-On? Shammas laughed and denied any connection between A. B. Yehoshua and the character in question, except
for the name, he said; and anyway, the book had been written
before the debate. This brought us to the subject of that encounter, of who had supported Yehoshua and who had supported Shammas, and we inevitably changed tracks from
literature to politics. Here is the conversation, with necessary
condensation:

"The struggle for equality is certainly an important one,"
A. B. Yehoshua said, "and we should have begun it immediately, without waiting for the conflict with the Palestinians
in the territories to end. But my problem and debate with
Anton are not about equality but about identity! Because as a
national minority in an Israeli state—"

"What's an 'Israeli state'?" Shammas interrupted him,
"there's no such thing!"

"What do you mean there's no such thing?" Yehoshua said,
mystified. He smiled the slightest bit because here it was,
beginning again. "For me, 'Israeli' is the authentic, complete,
and consummate word for the concept 'Jewish'! Israeliness is
the total, perfect, and original Judaism, one that should provide answers in all areas of life. The term 'Jewish,' after all,

came into being a thousand years after the concept 'Israeli' existed in practice, and it was created to describe a fraction, what remained after everything the Israeli lost in the Diaspora, until he turned into a 'Jew.' That whole mess has no connection to the Palestinian or Arab issue; even if there were no Arabs here there would still be the problem between the two concepts 'Jewish' and 'Israeli.'

Anton Shammas shakes his head grimly, and from the twist of his lips it is clear that we have gone back six years. He corrects me: Not six, forty years back.

"You see Israeliness as total Jewishness," Shammas says, "and I don't see where you fit me, the Arab, into that Israeliness. Under the rug? In some corner of the kitchen? Maybe you won't even give me a key to get into the house?"

"But, Anton, think of a Pakistani coming to England today, with a British passport, and telling the British, 'Let's create the British nationality together! I want Pakistani, Muslim symbols! Why should the Archbishop of Canterbury preside over the crowning of the Queen? I want there to be Muslim representation as well! Why should we speak English? There are a lot of languages here!' Think of him coming and making demands! The English tell him, 'No, my good man! We have no objection to your speaking Urdu, and you may receive—as a minority—schools and mosques, but the country's identity is English, and you are a minority within that nation!' "

Shammas: "Buli, the minute a man like you does not understand the basic difference between the Pakistani who comes to England and the Galilean who has been in Fasuta for untold generations, then what do you want us to talk about?"

"I don't understand you," Yehoshua sighed. "If there hadn't been anti-Semitism in Europe, you wouldn't even know how to write the word 'Israel'! Let's suppose that there hadn't been a Herzl and that Jews hadn't come here. You would have had a few Jews in Safed and Hebron, and you would never have

heard the word 'Israel'! You speak of an 'Israeli nationality' as
if, I don't know [Yehoshua expands his chest], your life's wish
has arrived! This entire Israel fell out of the sky on you! Why
this longing for an Israeli identity?"

"Because you conquered me!" Shammas thunders.

"Okay, so I conquered you, and I imposed Israeli citizenship
on you—"

"So you've got the responsibility—"

Yehoshua: "My responsibility is that whoever is within the
country's borders must be a citizen, and all obligations and
rights apply to him, that's my responsibility to you."

Shammas: "And have you lived up to that responsibility?
Did anyone even intend to live up to that responsibility?"

"Look," Yehoshua says, "this new country's immediate
grant of citizenship to its Arab citizens in 1948 was an act of
courage and a certain liberality. Just think—the Arabs who
remained here had been shooting at us the day before! Yesterday they fought and wanted to kill us, and a month later
they've already received from us the right to vote for prime
minister! Put your claims in proportion! Ask me, did they
receive everything? Of course not! There was a military government, there was prejudice, but show me one other country
that would give citizenship and social benefits and social security to its sworn enemy a month after a war."

"I," Shammas responded, "always said that Zionism's most
serious mistake in 1948 was that it kept the 156,000 Arabs who
did not run away and were not expelled. If you really wanted
to establish a Jewish state, you should have kicked me out of
Fasuta, too. You didn't do it—so treat me as an equal! As an
equal in Israeliness!"

Yehoshua: "But you won't receive one single right more for
belonging to the Israeli nation. On the contrary! I'll take away
your special minority rights! I'll impose additional duties on
you! For instance, you'll have to study the Bible, just as in

France all citizens study Molière and in England Shake-speare!"

"But as a literary text!" Shammas cuts him off, "not as a Jewish text!"

"What do you mean?!" Yehoshua shouts from the depths of his armchair. "We have no Shakespeare or Molière. We have the Bible and Talmud and Jewish history, and you'll study them, and in Hebrew! Everything will be in Hebrew! You can't want, on the one hand, your own cultural preserve and on the other hand be part of the nation! What would happen if a school in some wealthy Tel Aviv suburb should say, 'I want to teach in English! Our children will spend a lot of time overseas, and it's best for them to learn everything in English!' The Ministry of Education wouldn't allow it! And if they should want to teach computers instead of Bible, the Ministry wouldn't agree! They have to study as part of the Israeli nation, which receives its sewage and health services and education from the state, and that's the way it will be with you, Anton. If you are part of the nation, you sever part of your culture!"

"If that's the case," Shammas responds, "then Judaism also has to be separated from Israeliness, and you'll oppose that by force of arms."

"But how is that possible?" A. B. Yehoshua asks almost voicelessly. "Try, for instance, separating France from Frenchness—is that possible?"

Shammas: "France and Frenchness come from the same root, but Judaism and Israeliness is a different matter! That's why I advocate the de-Judaization and de-Zionization of Israel!"

"And are you willing to de-Palestinize the country that will be created in the territories?"

"I'm all for it! I won't agree to finding solutions to the Israeli national state in the framework of Jewish religious law, just as

I will oppose finding the Palestinian constitution in Islamic religious law!"

Yehoshua: "Then you should also oppose a Palestinian Law of Return for the Palestinian state!"

"I'm in favor of a Law of Return if it's limited in time," Shammas specifies. "Only for fifteen years—give an opportunity for all the Jews and the Palestinians in the Diaspora to decide if they want to come to their country, to Israel or Palestine, and then close the gates, and the law turns into a regular immigration law except in cases where it is clear that there is immigration caused by hardship."

Yehoshua: "And what about the 350,000 Russian Jews who came this year? If there wasn't a Law of Return, and if I had to ask your permission, maybe they wouldn't have been able to come here!"

"They'd get in! They're hardship cases!"

"What hardship? You'd tell me that it's only economic hardship!"

"Listen, Buli," Shammas sympathized. "That's not the problem. The problem is that I'm asking you for a new definition of the word 'Israeli,' so that it will include me as well, a definition in territorial terms that you distort, because you're looking at it from the Jewish point of view! But the minute we determine that *the country is an entity that exists in a certain territory*, then everyone who is in that territory is an equal part of it, and then an Arab in Jaljulia is Israeli just like A. B. Yehoshua. What you're telling me is because we called this country 'Israel,' we have some debt to that name, and that's idol worship to me! Don't put me into that Jewish hairsplitting of yours. If 'Israeli' is a symbol of Jewish totality, then Jaljulia can't be a full partner, because it's not Jewish, period. It can live here, use your sewage, but on the level above sewage there's a debate, and you apparently haven't learned anything in these six years, and I guess I haven't either."

"Look what you're doing," Yehoshua explains after a short time out. "The name 'Israel' is 3,500 years old, and it fell on you suddenly in '48, and now you're saying, I want to peel off all its roots and leave only the piece with the Declaration of Independence, which we'll turn into a constitution, and from that we'll make ourselves a nation. But leave my name alone!" He suddenly boils over. "You're pushing your way into the name, too? It's as if I were to intrude into your Palestinian identity and say, I'm also Palestinian, please revamp it so that I can identify with it, too! [Yehoshua turns to me.] Look how he's not satisfied with one country and one identity—he wants to be together with me in one people and one nation! He hungers to get me into one common nation with him!"

"It's not hunger, just pure rationality!" Shammas laughs, hinting to Yehoshua that still, despite the hundreds of debates he's had on the subject, he can rise like a tidal wave, with all his might, on questions that seem to be "only" about general national identity. "You know what your problem is, Buli? You think that 'Israel' is a *hungry word . . .*"

For a moment the definition flapped in the air, like the dress of a passing woman, and three writers were entranced by it. Really, I said, maybe for us, the Jews in the country, "Israel" is a somewhat hungry word. It awakens hunger and extremism and possessiveness in us. After all, we refuse to allow the Arabs to participate not only in our internal identity but also in the external manifestations of "Israeliness." When it comes to the basis of formal citizenship, it is hard for us to be more generous to them, and this poses a delicate question to the Jewish people in Israel: Do we still not understand Israel, in our hearts and in our consciousness, as such a fragile, almost naked, almost wondrous entity, an "essence" or "spark" forged in a fate so unique that no stranger can be appended or taken in? Even just a formal association of citizenship, of equal opportunities, of equal budgets? And another thing, I added, maybe we should take a look at what went wrong with our definition of ourselves as Israelis, and to what extent this definition has been imposed, despite itself, on many others who do not think as Anton does. I related how, from the minute I was exposed to the sense of suffocation Palestinian Israelis feel within the definition of "Israeli," that family name worn around their necks as in a forced marriage. Israeliness for me also became a little cool to the touch, and was already like a garment, not skin. Who knows, I asked Yehoshua, maybe the fact that Jews in Israel are still unable to create for themselves a clear, harmonic national identity, as you would like, is partially the result of their being forced to apply this identity— even if only because of its official name—to another element, in contact with which the definition is dissonant?

"That really is a problem," Yehoshua said, "and we have to consider: do the Arabs interfere with defining our identity? It seems to me only in a certain sense, but not in the long run. That is, at first Israeliness as an identity is infringed upon, because we need to apply it to Arabs as well. So when Anton comes, or the Druze, and they say, 'we're Israeli, too,' it complicates matters, and something in that identity becomes foggy. Then it's easy to retreat immediately into Jewish identity, and that includes the willingness to live in the Diaspora. Yes . . . at first it impinges on the clarity of the identity, but if you ask me about the Israeli concept of identity as I see it, as a return from Jewish fractionality to the Jewish totality that is Israeliness, then the Arab presence is a meaningful element of it. Just as for the French, Corsicanness and Bretonness are part of the Parisian menu. Yes, the Arab presence is a facet that leads to daily moral obligations, in the attitude of a majority to the minority within it, and it is also a facet that colors the Israeli language with nuances. It is that presence that also gives us the sense of territory—I myself have absolutely no sense of territory here in Israel without the knowledge that the

Arab is part of it, and just as one of the components of my territory is the scent of citrus fruit and the special air of Jerusalem, and the goats, and the cactuses, the Arab presence also lives within it."

"Maybe we've gotten into a vicious circle here," I said. "On the one hand, the Jewish people have not been successful in fully forming Israeliness, because they have 'partners'; on the other hand, as long as they don't succeed in formulating a strong definition of Israeliness that will also relate to the Arabs here, they are doomed to remain more Jewish. Look how hard it is for us to feel like a sovereign majority here. We face the minority as if we are a minority in our land—in the struggle for survival that we still wage in our hearts against it, in the battle for all kinds of 'territories' in the country, in the difficulty in being generous and sure of ourselves."

"You're right," Buli responded. "But even if there were no Arabs in the land of Israel I would still have serious problems with this Israeliness of mine, because the major front in my struggle for my identity is not with Anton but with you, David, because of your sweeping legitimization of the concept 'Jewish,' which in my eyes is a fractional concept, and because of your desire to make that fractionality a permanent element of Israeliness. As a result, you never leave out the word 'Jewish' when you speak of Israeli."

I answered him with a line from his novel *Mr. Mani*—not the obvious one about how the Arabs are "Jews who have forgotten that they are Jewish," but the one about the "Jews who cannot forget that they are Jews." But since this was not the subject of our conversation (and it may well be that there is no way of resolving the ongoing debate on the relationship between "Jewish" and "Israeli" without first resolving the question of the relation between the Israeli Jew and the Israeli Arab, the question of "who is an Israeli"), I asked Shammas what he thought of the definition that was proposed to and rejected by the Knesset in 1985, according to which Israel is a "Jewish state and the country of all its citizens."

"If it is a Jewish state because the majority is Jewish, and it puts more emphasis on the Jewish part, I have no problem. I have no objection to the educational system reflecting the makeup of the population. These are legitimate political power struggles as part of the game of democracy. But the minute you tell me that not only is the country's ambience Jewish but also its very character as a national state; the minute the law faculty at Tel Aviv University drafts a constitution for Israel that opens with the sentence 'Israel is the eternal state of the Jewish people'; the minute the Knesset inserts a racist definition into its amendment of the Knesset Basic Law, as it did in 1985, then I've got a problem with you, because you exclude me from that definition."

"I'm not excluding you." Yehoshua leaned over him. "My Israeliness includes you and all the Israeli Arabs as partners in the fabric of life here. Partners in that you vote for the Knesset, in the creation of Israeli citizenship as a whole—"

"I don't vote for the Knesset!" Shammas raised a finger. "You want me to vote for the Knesset so that you can show off your democracy to the enlightened world. I am not willing to be a party to that. I know that all I can do here is vote for the Knesset, and nothing more. I know that my mother was never able to see me become Israel's Minister of Education."

"If your mother had voted for the Knesset instead of picking olives on election day . . ." A. B. Yehoshua sighed. "Oh, I'll never forget how we sat and did figures during the '88 elections; you could have put thirteen members in and changed the whole political map. Oh, I'll never let you forget that olive harvest . . ."

On Rosh Hashanah, the Jewish New Year, in 1991, Shammas published an article in the Jerusalem local weekly newspaper, *Kol Ha'ir*, in which he announced that he was "weary of and disgusted by" the never-ending debate over "the Israeli nationality," "an idea that (on a good day) maybe thirty righteous Jews believe in, along with even fewer (if any) righteous Arab citizens of the State of Israel." "It is the best prescription for killing time and raising the blood pressure. And since life really is short, it is better to spend it making one's garden grow." He added: "I know today that 'Israeli citizenship,' as recorded on the first page of my passport, is all that the Jewish occupation state wants to and can give me. It is even more than I want. As for Israeli nationality—I am no longer interested. From this day forth, in the interests of all relevant parties, I adopt the national definition—I am a second-class citizen, a Palestinian without the nationhood of the Jewish State of Israel." And here today, four months after he slammed his passport on us and retired like Candide to his garden, he is again making a no less determined charge on Israeli nationhood.

Shammas shrugged. "What I wrote there was, of course, a kind of tactical maneuver . . . Of course I'm not weary, it's a life-or-death case for me." I asked him why he had stayed away from Israel for so long, and what he meant to express by this absence throughout the entire intifadah, the climax of the Palestinian struggle for definition and identity. "I suppose that in my defense (I've got a list of charges against myself, as well) I would say that in Ann Arbor I am closer to the intifadah and can follow it through the media better than what the Israeli media would allow me to know from my house at 7 Menorah Street in Jerusalem. So, with the exception of going out into the field, as you did in *The Yellow Wind*—something I'd never in my life do—" "Why not, actually?" I asked, and he responded, "Look, I once tried to live there. I lived for a year in the territories, in Beit Jalla."

Yehoshua, listening in silence, went taut. "Really, Anton? I didn't know . . . What, you went to live in the territories? When was that?"

All three of us thought about that "rise up, take your belongings, and move 100 meters to the east."

Shammas: "In 1978 the rents in Jerusalem jumped, I didn't have money, so I looked for an apartment in Beit Jalla. I lived next to an olive press there. That experience was enough for me. After that year I know with absolute certainty that I will never live in the West Bank, as that man," he said, pointing at Yehoshua, "wants me to do."

Both of them laughed, and Shammas continued, "Not that I have a trace of feeling superior to the people in the territories. It's only a sense that it's not my geography there. Not my cognitive, spiritual, or mental map. I work according to other codes, my head, my imagination, my emotions." I asked him to explain what had been difficult for him there. "If we return to the house metaphor, it begins with the process of looking for an apartment, the negotiation, and signing the contract. And the interpretation that the idiosyncratic landlady gave to that contract. What bothered me more than anything else in Beit Jalla was the gradual discovery that my neighbor spoke Arabic but not the same Arabic I did. An invisible but most palpable semantic Green Line ran between us. I suppose it's as if a Hebrew Macintosh program were fed into your IBM word processor. I would guess that the neighbor had the same feeling—that here was a 1948 Arab speaking, really, a foreign language. Aside from that, the daily commute to work in the shuttle cabs running the Hebron–Nablus Gate line, and the commute back in a bus full of Jewish settlers going to Hebron, and the times that the driver refused to allow an Arab to board the bus and I didn't say anything, I just sat inside and let it build up in me, gritting my teeth—"

You didn't say anything? I asked.

"I didn't say anything. And I felt that on the most primitive level, without any fine points of ethics, I would expect the Arab to pull out a pistol and shoot the driver. I really felt that way."

And you sat and said nothing? I said in surprise. If Buli or I had been in the bus and had said nothing in the face of such abuse, you would attack us rabidly in the newspaper!

"I wasn't silent," Shammas responded, mocking himself. "I wrote an article! I wrote a piece describing a similar incident. Listen, I have no knife, and even if I had one I wouldn't use it. I have words."

That's a defense strategy, I said.

"What's the charge? That I don't feel all that much a part of it, of the intifadah. Not that I repudiate it, I'm an enthusiastic supporter; on the contrary, it should be escalated! But it's not my intifadah. It never was and it never will be. Were I a refugee in Deheishe, a writer, I don't know what I'd do . . . It's all hypothetical, I didn't grow up there, I'm not a refugee or the son of a refugee, I don't have the basic psychological makeup of refugee suffering that grows and grows and makes you explode. But if I were there? I wouldn't wish on myself to be forty-one in the Deheishe refugee camp, that's the last thing I'd wish on myself. I'd do something desperate . . . I'd steer a Tel Aviv–Jerusalem bus over a cliff."

I reminded him that in that same Rosh Hashanah article he advised an Arab from Nablus whose picture album had been confiscated by the Shin Bet and then gotten lost to set out on a spree of violent revenge. I asked what action he would advise the Palestinians in Israel to take in an ongoing situation of discrimination.

"My real ideological war will come the morning after the establishment of the Palestinian state. Only then will I have the absolute moral right to demand complete social and political equal rights from Buli, as was promised me in the Declaration of Independence. In the meantime, I wait patiently for the big conflict to end, and then my conflict will begin. Then I'll open my mouth. I'll shout for a year, two years, and if it's not solved, I'll make an intifadah."

I asked whether, among the Israeli Palestinians he was meeting as a guest passing through, he sensed the fervor and the commitment necessary for such an uprising.

"In the villages I feel the frenzy. I know that deliverance will not come from the Arabs of Haifa and Jaffa. Nor from people like me who live in Ann Arbor, or who sell candy, the corrupt bourgeoisie of Nazareth. But in the villages there are still people who lived through the Arab revolt of 1936–39, the people who live in Fasuta, and fifteen years from now, when they discover that they've been methodically screwed since 1948 and that they are going to keep on getting screwed, they will rise up and they will burn tires and they will think about bearing arms."

"Will you return from Ann Arbor to participate in it," I asked, "or will you follow it from there?"

Shammas: "I think I will return. I will return to participate, first in the ideological war, but when all other ways are exhausted, I'll join"—his transparent voice rises momentarily— "the rebels in the caves in the mountain by Fasuta! And I will write their marching song!"

Yehoshua listened to the conversation, his writer's eye wandering over Shammas's face.

Afterward, after a brief lull, we returned—like someone who keeps touching a wound—to the question of identity. Yehoshua said, "The Israeliness of the Arabs here is big and strong, but part of it has been severed. I, for instance, am linked to my sources and history, and from them I construct my identity. Let's take, for example, the question of how a prison should be built in Israel, how to treat jailed drug addicts, and so on. Now, I ask myself what the general theory of a

Jewish prison should be, what the purpose of such a prison
is." "Interesting that you chose prisons of all things," Shammas
interjected in parentheses, and Yehoshua continued, "Should
I give the prisoners vacations, what is Jewish punishment, and
for that I have to go to my sources, to the sources of Jewish
law and to the experience of the past, in order to construct a
tradition of a Jewish system of justice and punishment. And
here, if Anton were to ask, 'Where am I in all this?'—in other
words, can Anton take Muslim or Christian judicial systems
and insert them as codes within the Jewish philosophy of punishment and justice?—he can't! In other words, at this point
he is no longer a partner. That's the difference between my
identity and his. But when, in the Palestinian state, he has to
construct a judicial system for himself, they will have to give
it their own nuances there, in contrast with, for instance, Saudi
or Libyan or Egyptian justice."

Shammas asks, "So what am I here, if not a partner?"

"You are a national minority! God Almighty, is it so hard
for you to accept that? There are dozens of national minorities
all over the world!" Yehoshua flashed. "Do you know what
your problem is, Anton? That the Arabs were never a minority!
You're actually shouting your non-minorityness at us. Where
in the world were the Arabs ever a minority? Listen to me,
Anton, minorities have special rights, and they are also frustrated that they are not majorities. But the Palestinians will
have a state where they will be the majority, and there you'll
have a place where you can experience your full identity—
but here you will remain a minority!"

"In other words," I put the echo into words, "you are again
saying to Anton that if the reality you are proposing is not to
his liking, let him take his belongings and move 100 meters
to the east."

"*If!*" Yehoshua called loudly, "*if* he wants his full Palestinianness! But he doesn't want it! You heard it yourself—in Beit

Jalla he feels awful! There he had really deep Palestinianness, close to the land, to the fabric of life, right? There everyone spoke Arabic, and all the memories are there, and the united family . . . but he doesn't want that! He wants to live on Menorah Street in Jerusalem! And I say fine! I'm very happy he's here! He gives me a lot of happiness and joy by being here! But if he wants his full identity . . ."

He didn't finish the sentence—he had already said it scores of times, as Anton had, and it was all in writing and in memory. Like another debate this book presents, the one between Jojo Abutbul and Mohammed Kiwan, the two of them continue to circle within a circular wall, unable to find the proper distance from which they can relate to each other, one to the identity-in-formation of the other, bewildering each other like magnetic poles, since the creation of an identity is a process of emphasizing the unique and the distinctive, of differentiation from another identity, and here, still, everything is itself blurred and confused—Israeli identity, Jewish identity, Palestinian identity, Palestinian-Israeli identity—and each of them must crystallize out of some painful contraction of its territory in favor of another, opposing identity.

"He's a strange animal." Yehoshua chuckled, gazing at Anton fondly, with fatherly bewilderment. "He pierces like a laser beam and discovers the problematic of every system . . . that's to his credit. But most Israeli Arabs support what I say; you know, after all, that you are almost a lone voice among the Palestinians. For them, what I say is absolutely clear and natural and just. They don't want to be part of the Israeli people or nationality! Or look at the members of the Islamic Movement, with their clear and different identity; they don't want to be integrated into the Israeli nationality either! The Arabs here want to have equal rights, but they want the status of a minority! While you, Anton, you want to take my Israeliness, which is an ancient concept, and be a full partner in it! And I say no! You are a minority. So let's write down in a big book what the rights of a minority are, over and above the rights of a citizen—"

"I have no problem with that," Shammas replied. "But on condition that you declare that Israel is an enlightened apartheid state."

"Why apartheid?" Yehoshua was wounded. "You're a minority just like the Basque minority in Spain!"

"No no no!" Shammas howls. "The Basque in Spain is offered the possibility of being a Spaniard, of being part of the Spanish nationality!" The word "nationality" he said in English, and Yehoshua followed suit: "You also have Israeli nationality!"

"Good God!" Shammas lets loose. "For six years I've been trying to explain to you, Buli, that citizenship is not nationality! That's the major problem between us!" He clarified it for us slowly and painstakingly: "The minute we carry out our conversation in Hebrew, it imposes certain semantic usages on us that bind us. When I debate with you over what it is to be Israeli, both of us are victims of the fact that the Hebrew word *le'om* does not translate into the term 'nationality.' 'Nationality' has no translation in Hebrew, because the Zionist founding fathers thought of a nation-state only from the point of view of the Jewish, Hebrew nation and not in terms of the European concept of nationality at the end of the nineteenth and the beginning of the twentieth century.* The term has no trans-

---

*Even though the two disputants here are, perhaps, the two most fluent spokesmen in this debate, and even though this was not the first time they trudged through it, it was fascinating to realize that they still have not succeeded in reaching a set of common definitions and clear concepts from which the discussion could move forward. This impasse is even more interesting to me than the semantic polemic itself, and it points out an authentic and emotional problem of the overlap of concepts in the Hebrew language and Israeli existence. Concepts such as "people," "nation," "citizenship," and even "Jew" and "Israeli" still suffer from heavy psychological obscurity and subjective interpretation.

lation in Arabic, either, since Arabic was not, like other languages, exposed to the reality of the nation-state. For instance, a Corsican's passport states 'Nationality: French.' But in our passports it says 'Citizenship: Israeli'!"

Yehoshua: "But a state grants citizenship, not nationality!"

Shammas: "But Israel defines itself as a nation-state, and a nation-state has to give me nationality! That's the root of our debate! Take out your identity card and look at it for once!"

We all took out our identity cards, and Shammas took his passport out of his suitcase, and we examined them. The young faces that looked out at us asked, "You're still having that same argument?" Yehoshua was about to call the French embassy to ask what was written in French passports, but it was Sunday and the embassy was closed. The more Yehoshua refused to accept Shammas's demand for a "nationality" in its English sense, something superior to mere citizenship, at least to what Israel offers its Arab citizens, the more upset Shammas got, and it was obvious that within him, as within Yehoshua, this "external" debate, seemingly over nationality, was setting off an internal tempest that was being carefully steered, just as with Yehoshua, into a semantic, linguistic, abstract channel. I admit that I am a bit suspicious of this channel. For whatever reason it seems to me that debates over semantic precision are not always really concerned with calling something by the right, true name but are intended, rather, as a defense from it, while the most important thing remains unsaid. Perhaps

---

The force and truth of Shammas's comment about the problem raised by the lack of a Hebrew equivalent of the term "nationality" became plain to me when A. B. Yehoshua, after reading the transcript of the conversation, explained that he had used the term "Israeli nation" (*le'om Yisraeli*) only in a moment of absentmindedness, when the traditional use in Hebrew would be the "Israeli people" (*am Yisrael*) or "Jewish people" (*am Yehudi*). Yehoshua asked to insert this change retroactively, inserting "people" wherever he had said "nation." To his mind, he said, this would represent "the clear nature of the total expression of Jewish identity as I see it in the concept 'Israeli.'" I note this change with the consent of both participants.

for Anton Shammas the main thing is concealed in that "Israeli hunger" of which he accuses Yehoshua; or maybe it is hidden in the epigraph that Shammas chose for the first chapter of *Arabesques*, from G. B. Shaw: "You told me, you know, that when a child is brought to a foreign country, it picks up the language in a few weeks and forgets its own . . . Well, I am a child in your country . . ." From those three dots at the end one can divine, as with ants, one can follow the riddle of the internal confrontation with Israeliness, the apparent enemy that is also the source of abundance and stimulation. Perhaps it is actually this two-facedness that may awaken the pressing need to rub up against, to be cut to the point of pain and ecstasy on this barbed wire that divides the identity; and perhaps reality as offered in the Hebrew, foreign translation sharpens and clarifies the original for him. I am a child in your country . . .

It was finally agreed that Yehoshua would call the French and Belgian embassies the next day, and if it was true that these enlightened nations write the word "nationality" in the passports of their citizens, Yehoshua would "agree" that in Shammas's passport a similar definition should appear—"Nationality: Israeli," and peace came to the land.

"If only you had patience," Yehoshua grumbled, "If you would wait until we finished with the Palestinian problem and we established here a majority-minority covenant for fifty years, a common identity would slowly take form, and then you would see Arab cabinet ministers, and intermarriages, and we might even return to the situation of the First Temple period, when Jewish religious identity was not at all a necessary element of Israeli identity. After all, King Solomon, builder of the Temple, did evil in the sight of the Lord and married foreign women, and an Israeli king worshipped Baal—that is, he didn't act only in accordance with Jewish religious codes. He had another culture, and was even linked to a different religious system, and that worked for a thousand years, and not so badly, it would seem. In the end, if we do this, if we return to the situation in which those who reside in the country become the framework for national identity, and along with it larger frameworks come into being around us, like the European community or a regional community here, this nationalism that so bothers us today will be much more moderate and subdued. Then there will be cultural symbiosis, and a flow of identities, because the common Israeli identity will be natural and will come up from the grass roots rather than being imposed. We will arrive at it gradually, in stages, through an attitude of respect between minority and majority and not by a sudden shock. Then maybe we will reach the point where you, Anton, will feel yourself so much a majority here that you will long for the time you were a minority."

Shammas's response was: "In the long run there may be a congruence of our visions, Buli, but we have vast differences in our understanding of the present and past, and especially on the steps leading to realization of the vision. I think that when we begin something in error, we will never reach anything, and for me the root of the problem is that Israel does not define itself as the country of its citizens."

"Israel as the country of all its citizens is the definition of my Zionism!" Yehoshua decreed.

Shammas: "Do you really believe that the State of Israel ever felt the desire to be my country, too?"

Yehoshua: "Yes, I think so. Look at what it was created from and you will understand its difficulties. Look at France, whose identity was crystallized like a diamond. Today, when it has three million non-French citizens, look how it's squirming. And you take this country of Jews who came from Holocaust and war, and had to find common ground between Yemenite and German Jews, without a common language, and with the Arabs on the border and the Arabs inside. With all that, you expect some kind of omnipotence from us? Don't you have any historical perspective? You come to me with demands from within your private little hurt, and you forget—"

"Little? Why is it little? Don't you measure my pain for me!"

"It is little compared with the horrible pain, yes, compared to, first of all, the pain of those people from your own Fasuta who were uprooted from here and ended up in refugee camps! Compared with the pain of Jews who were at the ovens and came here! You stayed on your land, you weren't uprooted, they didn't force you to take up arms to fight your brothers— we defended you in that—they did not strip you of your identity, of the Koran, of the church—you're spoiled! . . . Anton is a spoiled boy, spoiled at home. His mother spoiled him too much! I say that it is our honor that such a spoiled boy has risen to flog us, and we're all amazed by him and read his *Arabesques* with such an appetite!"

Shammas: "The minute you start talking on a large scale, my pain is obviously small. My pain, and that of the Palestinian in the refugee camps, will never be heard, because it always has to pass through the filter of the Holocaust. But I am continually trying to draw you out from your pathos, from your pathos of tormented Judaism, to say to you that it makes no difference what the magnitude of my pain is. What is important is the reality we define for ourselves together, so that our grandchildren will not have to continue coping with the mess being created today. I am telling you that your dream of creating a minority that will find its ethnocultural, even linguistic place here, such a framework is unacceptable to me, because your entire view of reality is Jewish, Buli, *Jewish!* You see only yourself and forget the other components. How can you want to make me a partner in an Israeli identity, if Israel is the totality of Judaism?"

"You know what?" A. B. Yehoshua sighed. "Let us suppose that I am ready to give you this 'nationality' that you want, an Israeli nationality. From here on out you can become integrated into my identity, just as a French Jew integrates into France."

"No! No!" Shammas cried. "Because there is a French nationality but there is still no Israeli nationality!"

Yehoshua: "A French Jew has many French values, some of which are Christian and some traceable to the French Revolution, to Napoleon, and to Louis XIV. He internalizes it, and that is his Frenchness."

Shammas: "That's a false equation, because the French Jew's passport says that he's French, and only after that can he define himself as a Jew!"

"So I'll give you that!" Yehoshua erupted. "Done! You will receive 'nationality' from me! You came here at 10:30 and you're leaving at 2 p.m. with nationality! But Israeli identity you won't receive. You won't receive it from me! Why do you need my identity anyway?" He was inflamed. "You have Palestinian identity! You can't have five identities! Wait a minute—will you give up your Palestinian identity?"

Shammas: "Yes, I am prepared to give up my Palestinian identity in the sense of 'nation,' as in 'nation-state.' In other words, I am ready to give up being a national of the Palestinian state that will be established. I am prepared for my Palestinian identity to be an ethnic identity, the same as your Jewish identity."

"Oh, really, really," Yehoshua said dismissively, his hands spread over his head, pointing ten points of incredulity and contention at Shammas. "Suddenly you're bringing in ethnicity, American concepts that are valid only in a small part of the world. I don't need that folklorist ethnology. What interests me is whether your identity teaches you how to run public transportation. How, for instance, do you make a Palestinian traffic light?"

"What are you talking about, there's no such thing!"

"There is such a thing! The French have a little traffic light at eye level that you don't have to strain to see. That's why their traffic flows and doesn't get backed up like in England. That's the greatness of the French, that their identity is expressed even in a little traffic light."

Shammas: "I bet some Algerian invented it, there is no such thing as a French traffic light, Buli."

"Sure there is. A French traffic light and a French police force and a French place for a French policeman to carry his pistol, and French cooking and French foreign policy, just as there are Scandinavian ways to fight unemployment and Dutch ways of treating drug addicts. All those things, Anton, believe me, are important. They are significant. And they are constructed and cultivated from the past. They are life, and that is the meaning of life within an identity. I don't want my identity to be nothing more than my going once a week to see a Jewish show at Beit Ha'am. Identity is not a bookcase, Anton! I want to get out of the bookcase, and bring the bookcase into my life!"

Shammas: "If you want to share all those things with me, give me a feeling that Independence Day is my holiday, too. Okay, Passover and Hanukkah are religious holidays, but make some civil holidays, so that I'll want to go out on Tu Bi-Shvat and plant a tree!"

"I want that very much," Yehoshua said simply, but immediately shook himself. "But Passover is not just a religious holiday for me! It is a holiday that defines me in relation to freedom, it gives me important moral values! It's not only eating ethnic matzah! For an American Jew, Passover is an ethnic holiday, but for me, in Israel, it is a holiday that also should be establishing my relation to you. That's how my identity is constructed." "In which I have no part," Anton said. "In which you have no part," Yehoshua said.

"So we're back to square one," Anton said.

Gentlemen, I said, it is time to sum up. What has changed in these six years and three and a half hours?

A. B. Yehoshua: "Anton speaks about some great, far-off future; Anton is a kind of bird that has come here from some period fifty years hence . . . a soul born too early that passed by us on its way. It could be that what he's saying now will then be much more relevant and comprehensible to us, and I'll seem outdated, living in the past. I can only hope it will be so. But then they will say that we got through those fifty years thanks to my precise position, which also saw the evolution but didn't allow it to make the kinds of jumps that would destroy the entire country. Because if we don't formulate the concept of Israeliness most carefully, we will remain forever with two fundamental concepts, Jewish and Arab, which will ensure the permanence of the conflict. Yes, that is my summing up—Anton is the man of the future, and I protect the present for that future."

Shammas listened with a smile and said, "I would add only that Yehoshua is a nostalgic man, and I am a utopian man."

"I haven't got a trace of nostalgia," Yehoshua protested. "Check all my works—not a drop of nostalgia! But I want to tell you, Anton, that in the reality of Israel, if you've got an ally deep down—deep down!—it's me. More than David, even. Because he, with all his liberalism and *The Yellow Wind*, with all that, I'm more your ally, because my conception is Israeliness, while he still sees himself as Jewish in a partial way, tied by obsession to some Yiddish ghosts from Poland which you'll never be able to share, they'll drive you crazy . . ."

The next day A. B. Yehoshua called the French embassy and was informed that French passports indeed contain the classification "Nationality: French"; similarly, the passports issued by the Belgian government state "Nationality: Belgian."

"Anton wants 'Nationality: Israeli,' and I'll give it to him," Yehoshua said, a bit surprised at the results of his research. "But without identity! Identity, no!"

I asked, If so, what does such nationality mean to you, if it has no component of identity? A kind of advanced-level citizenship?

"Precisely," Yehoshua said. "Advanced-level nationality is precisely it. It satisfies Anton's need to receive something that is more than just the paper certification of citizenship. It seems to me that nationality is a concept that Anton has built specially for the bubble in which he, and maybe not just he, lives. A kind of framework in which he can be an Arab who lives together with Jews, an Arab who writes in Hebrew and lives in Hebrew, so he's made this definition for himself. It's hardly a coincidence that there is no equivalent word in Hebrew or in Arabic—that, apparently, is the comfortable position for him. Even so, the debate achieved something, some sort of movement. It advanced the matter of nationality, which is something I was unable to 'give' Anton up until now. It contains a certain advance toward the component of identity in the definition of the Israeli."

I then called Shammas and informed him that he'd "won" his Israeli "nationality."

"You have no idea how happy I am," he said, really sounding happy. "I've been asking Buli to do that for six years."

I noted, bringing him down, that in my opinion Yehoshua had made only a small change in his position. He was still unwilling to bring the Arabs under the wing of the concepts of "the people of Israel" and "the nation of Israel," as he, Yehoshua, understood them, nor under "nationalism" of the type that Shammas dreamed of. He was willing to grant only nationality, something Yehoshua saw as vague and somewhat hollow, a kind of honorary title.

"It's not important, it's not important!" Shammas responded elatedly (I was sorry I could not see his face at that moment). "I am a great believer in the power of words, and from my point of view the debate was very important, because it forced Yehoshua to see the problematic nature of the concepts we use in our discussion, and you'll see that that 'nationality' will be a self-fulfilling prophecy!"

CHAPTER 16

To what extent are the Arabs themselves responsible for the bad state of affairs between them and the Jewish majority? What is their part in the failure? Are they prepared to examine their own dereliction with a critical eye, or is it easier for them to blame the Jews?

"It is very natural for a minority to have grievances against the majority," said Rafat Kabha from Barta'a. "If an Israeli Arab comes and you tell him, 'Here, there's progress toward equality, there's an improvement compared with past years,' I don't think there would be one Arab in Israel who would tell you, 'Okay, you're right, I'm not discriminated against.' That will never happen. Have you ever seen a minority that didn't complain?"

The situation itself, the state of being a minority, almost inevitably creates feelings that cannot be assuaged or resolved—resentment and fear, suspicion and bitterness. There is something in the existential status of a minority that is liable to imprison it in a spiral of indignity—that is, an ever-present readiness to be hurt and insulted, followed by exploitation of the insult and wallowing in wretchedness, in a never-ending cycle.

Seniors at the high school in Jat pointedly complained about how they are not allowed to study the poetry of Mohammed Darwish, the Palestinian national poet, in school, and how this encroaches on their national heritage and Palestinian consciousness. This is a familiar and, in my opinion, legitimate complaint, but it was hard not to notice that the boys and girls were voicing their grievance in the very same words and expressions I had heard elsewhere in a similar context. To put it simply, they were repeating something they had learned by rote.

I agreed with them that they should be allowed to study Darwish's poetry, and Palestinian history and culture in general. Then I asked who among them had tried to study this subject on his or her own. No one responded. I thought that they had not understood the question, so I asked it again: Have any of you tried to find reading material about the Palestinian people? Silence. One student—out of thirty-five—said he had once leafed through the *Palestinian Encyclopedia*, which is published in Arabic in Israel. The others studied their desks. They giggled. A girl mumbled that she had once read a book called *The Palestinian Holocaust*. Another had begun reading a book called *The Tragedy of a Palestinian Girl*. Have you discussed these things that are so important to you with an adult? They exchanged glances, began to guffaw, and turned contentious. It was clear that they had never considered that they themselves could cross the line that had been drawn by the accusation they made against the Jewish establishment. Indignity had become a slogan, producing rationalization instead of rationality.

I told this to Rasem Hama'isi, an urban planner born in Kafr Kana. Today he lives in Ramallah—a dynamic, active man, gravitating toward the future. He was long since sick of such stories, his expression said.

"I've had enough of always saying that everything is because of the government. We are also guilty! We're not so quick to criticize ourselves. I'll give you an example from my life. My niece, in fifth grade, showed me her geography notebook. I took a look and saw that two answers were wrong, but the teacher had checked them and signed it, as if everything was correct. I went to the teacher and asked him, Why did you do that?

"He said, 'I don't correct. I just sign to show that I checked to see that she did her homework.'

"I said, 'That's all? Maybe she copied out lyrics to a song by Um Kulthum [a popular Arab singer].'

"He started saying, 'No . . . Look, we always do that, that's the way it is.'

"And that's a young teacher who should know better, given the system of values he believes in!

"This culture, this avoidance of responsibility, exists among us, and one of the terrible things is that we always have an alibi for it: Because we're a national minority! Or: External factors don't allow us to progress!

"So, true, sometimes that's justified, but a lot of times it's just rationalization. Once a boy came to me and I examined his notebook and saw that he had copied one exercise. He began reciting this excuse: 'I want to finish. I want a degree, they don't let us progress . . .' I told him, That's an excuse. Don't try to give me that line. You want to be a teacher, right? How can I allow you to teach my children? What will you teach them? What values?

"So if you always limit yourself and say in advance, They won't let me progress, you enter the destructive process of a people weakening itself and wearing itself out. Maybe there are some who enjoy feeling that way, wretched and insulted all the time. It gives them an excuse for all kinds of personal shortcomings. But I don't want to educate my children and my society with such concepts."

When he said that, I meditated on the extent to which offense is an emotion that—more than any other, perhaps— returns us to childhood. When we are angry, for instance, we do not revert to being children. Nor when we are bitter or sad. But when we are insulted, we are children again. Something vulnerable and helpless, burning and self-righteous rises from the depths of our memory and chokes us. So permanent indignity is liable to keep a person—or a group—in a kind of petrified childishness. It was, in fact, this very tone—childish, helpless, even spoiled—that was in the voices of the high-school students and in the voices of certain adults I met who lamented indiscriminately on the injustice Israel was doing them. It was depressing to encounter it among older people, older than I am, people with families, some of them teachers of young children. They were childish in the negative sense of the word, unable to take responsibility for their personal destiny, obediently adapting themselves to definitions dictated to them from outside, passively accepting grownup obsessions.

This is how the Palestinians in the occupied territories were for years. The sovereign states around them, the "grownups," determined their destiny for them. They were given no right of self-determination, most of them were not allowed to carry a passport, most do not even have citizenship in any country—they are refugees with no home to call their own. Everyone treated them like children or minors, and never conceived they could suddenly become belligerents who would stand their ground. For many years they internalized this attitude. The intifadah was an act of self-deliverance—of a return to their chronological age and of linking up with adulthood's sources of strength, the full integration of their national personality. Just as the Six-Day War had been a kind of collective Israeli "coming-of-age ceremony," nineteen years after the country was founded, so was the intifadah, twenty years after the occupation, the "coming-of-age" of the Palestinian people in the territories. Perhaps it is no coincidence that it was the young people, the boys and girls, who made the revolution in Palestinian consciousness. Sometimes, meeting them, one can sense the extent to which they have managed to blend the energies of adolescence with those of nationalism, and how much each has served the others.

Rasem Hama'isi is the first Palestinian in Israel to win a competition for planning a major urban center, and today he does strategic planning for cities, including Arab cities. He is short of stature and slightly balding, his eyes full of life under a jutting, convex forehead. He is sharp-tongued and expansive, and you feel right away that time flows through his veins.

"Listen, we're way behind . . . The gap between the so-phisticated tools today available to mankind and the values and knowledge our children receive is very large. This gap creates something terrible—*that you don't live the time in which you live!* What I mean is that, when it comes down to it, you live only half a life! What a waste! Today you have a telephone in your car, a fax machine at home, there's a computer that can connect you to anywhere in the world, but the big question is how do you translate that into your own thought processes. How can I translate that? Because time will not wait for me!" (Arab, Jew—when he said that, we were just two people fighting the only fit enemy, the real enemy.)

"Our internal ability to adapt to these things, to the conceptual world they create, is very limited. We still do not ask ourselves the important questions about our responsibility to society—for how many generations onward are you responsible, can you see only the end of your own nose? Are you responsible for the future of your children? Do you want to do something that will have an effect on your children's children as well?"

Rasem Hama'isi.

I asked others as well. Again and again I asked how it could be that the state's attitude of rejection could so paralyze the Arab minority. Why did the Arabs in Israel not react differently to this rejection? Other minorities in the world, in similar circumstances, react with an ambitious foray into the majority society's centers of power and influence, into its elite. They are rejected but charge again, until they impose their presence on the majority. They transform the natural bitterness that every minority feels as a result of its circumstances—the "minority toxic syndrome"—into a powerful fuel, into an enzyme that magnifies their competitiveness and drive to excel, until they force the majority to attend to them. The Jewish and Japanese minorities have done this in the United States. So has the Chinese minority in East Asia. So have the Palestinians themselves in the Arab countries. Here are some of the answers I received.

Nabih Kasem, fifty-one, teacher and writer, Rama.

"I say to my students, First of all you have to be the vanguard. Be a good student. But know your limitations. There are things that you can never be in Israel. Not a member of the cabinet or director general of a ministry or a pilot, nothing that is really important to Israeli society. This is what I say to them, This is what you should know. Dream up to this point and not beyond. If you dream too much, you'll ruin your future."

"How can you tell a sixteen-year-old, Dream up to this point? After all, that's the age of dreams."

"Listen, he has to face reality. If he goes out without facing reality, in the end he'll destroy himself. He has to know that he must achieve his rights, but he must also know that he cannot reach a key position. Why are you looking at me that way? . . . Dreams! I didn't dream too much either."

That attitude was addressed by Dr. Majed Elhaj, a sociologist at Haifa University. A young man, very eloquent, who some see as the future leader of the Arabs in Israel.

"The Arabs do not have to concede anything," he said. "They are 18 percent of the population, and the state does not exploit their potential in all fields! It's a huge loss! How can the Jews not understand what that means? More and more the country is losing a part of itself, because the Arab elite finds doors closed to it, and there is no employment, and first preference is given to immigrants and to Jews. So the gap grows, and with it alienation and bitterness."

Elhaj himself was underprivileged in childhood. His mother was widowed, and he often had to stay home from school to help her sell vegetables in the Wadi Nisnas neighborhood of Haifa. He returned to his studies only because his teachers pressured him. He received his doctorate at the Hebrew University. He did postdoctorate work at Brown University, in the United States.

"I don't think that the Arabs have to acquiesce in that. I think that there's a mutual interest in having the Arabs fight to achieve in all fields. So I'm now addressing the subject of fostering excellence among the Arabs in Israel. Without developing a superior elite among the Arab minority, it is doubtful whether the Arabs will ever be able to take a place in Israeli society. The average Arab today has no chance of being absorbed into the Jewish sector. Only an Arab who excels, who can make a really unique contribution—as has happened in the theater, as has happened in sports with Zahi Armali [a Palestinian-Israeli soccer star]—succeeds in breaking through.

"So one of the messages I take today to my society is how to develop excellence. The fact that most of the population in Israel lives under the illusion that it can ignore you shouldn't make you surrender and disappear. Because I think this tendency of the Arab minority in Israel to isolate itself, to be insular, is suicide.

"It may well be that this will not please several Arab leaders in Israel," Elhaj says, "but I feel a duty to say it objectively: We, the Arab population, have a part in this failure. We did not invest enough in the individual. In our schools education is not geared toward excellence. There is no education toward making this generation a part of our struggle to open up society. Education is geared toward achievement, not excellence. Neither excellence as individuals nor excellence as a group. We need to create an intensive educational program for this. We need to choose the gifted students in school from preschool age. To foster the young leadership.

"This is a great challenge for us. We need to overcome a great despair, especially among educated Arabs. Because even if you are the very best, there is always a boundary to your dreams. There is a ceiling you will not be able to pass. So why excel?"

Naim Araideh, a poet and literary scholar, said: "It's not really the Arabs' lack of desire to be involved. It's a great apprehension. It's fear. Because here we're talking about two entirely different cultures, and real exposure to another culture completely changes all the channels of thought and of the soul. On one hand, you do not want to assimilate. On the other hand, you want to be like them. The Jewish and Arab establishments really do not encourage such mutual involvement.

In almost every country in the world where there is a majority and minority, the minority wants to outpace the majority. Here—no. Here it's only in the technical things, the external materialistic things, that the minority wants to overtake the majority. So this one wants to build his own house, and that one wants a VCR and a car, but nothing more than that."

Araideh, forty-one, is a member of the Druze community, born in the village of Mghar. He has published books of poetry in Hebrew and in Arabic, and is writing his Ph.D. thesis on the fiery nationalist Zionist poet Uri Zvi Greenberg ("No, I can't say I haven't been upset by some of the things in his poetry. His nationalism. Yes, it upsets me, but I regard him as a genius whose poetry is great, extraordinary, a flood of genius, who is allowed to make a slip of the tongue every so often"). He once spent six months in jail in the 1970s because he knew about but did not report the Syrian spy ring led by Israeli radical Udi Adiv.

"Take Jewish society and take Arab society and compare—in your society there is a tradition of self-criticism. If you read the Bible, the first thing that stands out is that there is no idealization of reality or of characters. There are false prophets, and there are the horrible sins of King David, and Abraham lies to the King of Egypt and tells him that Sarah is only his sister. That's nice. It expresses the most human conflicts, doesn't paper over anything. And when one of your prophets feels he is burning to pronounce his prophecy, he fears no one, because he has heaven behind him, 'Because my Lord has spoken!' It's already rooted in your consciousness, it's an integral part of you.

"With us—and allow me to limit myself now to my field of study, Arab literature and poetry—the Arab poet or writer cannot criticize his society. Nor is he expected to do so, because his traditional role is to support society. If society lies, the writer is supposed to promote the lie, and then everyone forgets that they themselves created it and they begin to believe it. There are some exceptions among us, important authors unique in their generation—Mohammed Darwish, Emile Habibi—but the others? Court poets. Rhymers. Real social criticism, or a real challenge to society, will not come from them."

Here are the words of a woman of about twenty who asked to remain anonymous. She is the daughter of a Jewish mother and an Arab father, and when I commented that she could be a classic example of coexistence and that she is the person, perhaps, who can unwaveringly say, "I am Israeli," she laughed. "I'm not all that sure. I have so much pain with regard to Israel . . . everything that happens to me happens to me because of that. And I'm always feeling guilty. If something happens, they immediately accuse me—as a Jew, as a Palestinian . . . Maybe I really can say that I am Israeli, but only from the point of view of being messed up. But maybe that's what it means to be Israeli."

She, my momentary ambassador to the fault line, has black hair, very blue eyes, thick eyebrows like two soft bows over her beautiful, red-cheeked face. Her speech is muted with the bashfulness of a young girl. "Sometimes I am the only one among my Jewish and Arab friends who can see how much the preconceptions of both sides are similar, how each side uses exactly the same kinds of preconceptions and stereotypes with regard to the other, and I am always careful not to take sides. It's very difficult, especially in this situation, when everyone has to identify with a side, because otherwise you barely exist."

By profession she is a graphic artist, and she says that her graphics are Western. The same is true of the music she likes; the literature she likes is written in Hebrew and English. Arabic literature is, for her tastes, too caught up in what is happening here, the struggle, daily life; it is too polemical. She prefers to express herself in Hebrew. From within the internal contradiction of her situation she has developed her own identity, not Jewish and not Muslim. "Ever since I was little, I have always thought that I was all those things together, that they are inside me. Not that I'm part of them. Because they always tried to affiliate me with one side or another, and I didn't want to belong but to make them mine. To make them all part of me."

She has harsh and severe things to say about Arab society in Israel. "The Arabs here, in my opinion, are in a bad state," she says. "What by now can be important to them? After all, they don't have an identity of 'I myself,' they have no clear idea of who they are. What they really want. What they are allowed to aspire to. So either you compensate yourself by crystallizing a certain identity as an individual, distancing yourself from what is important to society, and thinking only of yourself, or you realize yourself materially: 'I have a house, I have a car, beautiful children, we go overseas from time to time, my cousin is a doctor, he is a lawyer'—all that materialism is just compensation for the emptiness you made."

"You're ignoring," I stopped her, surprised at how judgmental she was, "that in Arab society in Israel there is, for instance, a great appreciation of education. I've met illiterate parents, destitute, who would not think of giving up their child's education and private lessons. And every family tries to send at least one child to college."

"That's very nice," she responded, composed but resolute, "but again, that education is a college education and no more. It's not internal education. Not intellectual in the full sense of the word. There is no spiritual richness. There is no real curiosity. In the end, that also is a part of the struggle for survival. They prefer not to think a lot, only to live. Only to get through this situation in one piece. Because to contend with difficulties such as they have in the territories—I don't know any person here who would be willing to put up with those conditions. People here just want to live well. They want to survive. They want to go on living, no matter under what conditions, no matter what the cost. They'll say what they're told to say in order to continue to live here, to build their house, to send their children to college. And the result of all that is assimilation. You assimilate into another society that is not yours. You lose your identity. You're just a body, you're not a person on the inside, just a creature who lives according to what others define for you. They tell you what is good and what isn't good, what is allowed and what isn't, and, most important, what's easy. You don't fight. Don't demand. You don't say what's in your head. You don't say what you are. You no longer *know* what you are."

In conclusion, I wish to present the words of Ahmed Abu Esba of Jat, a graduate of the Kadouri agricultural school, a former teacher and former mayor, and today manager of an iron factory he built.

"We have a basic defect that makes us into people lacking initiative and self-assurance. It begins at home, where the parents' desires are imposed on the child, not allowing him to develop his own personality. That's a general Arab prob-lem—from the time they're small, we don't encourage our children to take initiative, to create by themselves. What comes out is a person who always depends on others. A parasite. A person who requests only an answer or order from his parents, or from whoever is responsible for him."

We sat and talked in a shack by his factory in Jat. Abu Esba's voice is warm, hoarse, full of power. He is fifty-six, strong and solid, sure of himself. Unlike many others, he does not stand helpless before the Israeli establishment. For example, when the mayor of Teibe is requested to prepare a comprehensive development plan for his city, he instead writes, on a single sheet of paper, a list of all his demands from the Ministry of the Interior for the next five years. Abu Esba stands out as one who has quickly adjusted to the rules of the Israeli bureaucracy. "Ariel Sharon, when he was Minister of Commerce and Industry, told us that he was different from the other ministers! With him an orderly request was sufficient, and he would immediately go out in the field and get things moving! I said, Sir! Let's see you do it. Let's try an experiment. The next day I dashed off a letter to him: 'Mr. Minister, we have an approved industrial zone, and I need infrastructure, and I request that for a brief period of four years you grant us the status of a development area, class A, in order to draw in entrepreneurs.' I prepared detailed material together with an engineering and planning consulting firm, an organized plan, with figures on road construction, electricity, sewage—everything. He immediately sent me his aide, who came, looked. I even gave him a Jat flag." He swallows a smile. "He went over all my plans and said, 'Hey, you're really ready to go!' I told him, 'My friend, I'm serious about my business. I don't like to sit around and gossip.' "

Unfortunately, the end of the story is very familiar: "That was five years ago. I haven't seen him since. And Sharon? He's building settlements in the territories now, he doesn't have time for old problems. He only has time to make new problems."

But we were talking about impotence.

"Look what's happening with us at our school," Abu Esba added. "The school is new, modern, and it has to encourage the child's initiative, his creative thought, his ability to express himself, but with us, since the teachers were educated that way, they prefer to continue with the same old methods. Instead of giving a lesson with a discussion and thought and conclusions, they give dictation: 'Listen to me and write down what I say!'

"The lesson is supposed to be what he and I work out and formulate together! But it's hard, it's a challenge to the teacher! The teacher will have to prepare himself, learn the material, think what unexpected questions the children might ask, and that threatens him. Why should he do it? Since there's no supervision, and since no one ever asks him how he's teaching, he prefers the old method. And if he fails with that, too, he makes slogans against the authorities, puts them into the children's heads, to excuse his own failure. So a kid reaches his senior year and he's afraid to give you an answer. He searches your eyes for what answer will please you.

"Another part of the problem is the woman's place in our society and her role in education. Because even though we teach the women, the girls, they finish high school, and a teachers college or B.A., but her character doesn't change. She only knows more. Then, when she becomes a teacher herself, she gives the children her character, not her knowledge.

"So I look ahead, to my grandchildren's generation, and I'm telling you that not much will change with them, either. How can it change? Who can educate them otherwise? Can a woman give her sons a character other than hers? And her daughters, what will they have to give? We're in a vicious circle.

"So if there's a change it will come very slowly. Not in a revolutionary way. And the gap between us and Jewish society will remain, will even grow. A long time. That's reality, and we have to recognize it. There are advanced societies, and there are less advanced societies. We need a general revolution, of ideas and action. And the state can't help us with that. I can't put the blame on that, not on the Jews and not on the government. What happened, for instance, in Turkey? When Kemal Atatürk wanted to change society, he took the babies, kept them away from their parents from birth, so they wouldn't receive their parents' character, and educated them the way he wanted. Redesigned them. Now, you can't do that kind of thing here. And we have to start coming to terms with what we are. That's the way we are. That's our character. We weren't educated to know how to help ourselves, and it looks as if we're unable to do it on our own."

CHAPTER 17

These are the voices. Years of cautious and deliberate existence, the living memory of the trauma of 1948, and the sight of their brothers rotting in the refugee camps have taught the Palestinians in Israel not to go to extremes—in anything—and not to take any irreversible position. Every acrobat knows the secret of walking a tightrope over an abyss; the Arabs in Israel have learned something even more difficult—to stand still on the wire. To abstain, for years, from any hasty movement. To live a provisional life that eternally suspends and dulls the will.

Thus, for many long years, has the Palestinian acrobat in Israel stood in place on a high wire—one foot in the air, never set down. He glances out of the corner of his eye to the audience below, which never stops shouting its warnings and its anger. Jewish shouts, Arab shouts—he dares not make a false move.

So he stands still on the tightrope. He has come to terms with Israel's existence but still does not feel part of it. His

identity is Palestinian, but he is too cautious to demand minimum national rights. Yes, he is a Palestinian, but he refrains
from taking part in his brothers' struggle, the struggle of those
who are one flesh with him. Officially he is Israeli, but he is
afraid to demand for himself, with full force, as is customary
in Israeli pressure politics, legitimate rights as an Israeli. Were
he to dare to demand civil rights forcefully, he would immediately be accused of nationalist extremism. If he demands
nothing and wishes for nothing, he will be accused of alienation and separatism.

So it has been for decades, for hundreds of thousands of
acrobats. Sleeping on the wire, in midstep.

In such a situation it is so easy to engage in "self-suspension," a reduction of the "surface area." It is so tempting to
shut oneself off from a complex external reality, whether
apathetic or hostile.

There is no glorious past to long for. The past is linked with
a difficult defeat, with being disconnected from the rest of the
nation, with a sense of guilt for having learned to live with
Jews. There is not too much hope when it comes to anything
touching on full self-realization in the future, as Israelis and
Palestinians. So, sprawling between their demands, suspicions,
and their contempt for and anger at all the camps that follow
their movements, many of the Palestinians in Israel stick with
the existing and the immediate.

"We have more material things than those in the territories,"
Zuhir Yehia of Kafr Kara said to me. "More money, more
property, nicer houses, savings in the bank. But material things
cannot support a consciousness. If you've got material things,
maybe you look different, prettier, better dressed, you wear
glasses; our water is sweeter, but that's not depth. The Palestinians in the territories are now more concerned with content.
We have only the body; there they have the soul."

Many of them are attached to those material things with all

their beings, out of what sometimes looks like despair, despair that has become a habit (an odd but appropriate expression here). They are inclined to opportunism, pragmatism at any price, materialism, and utilitarianism (expressed, for example, in the fact that 42 percent of them voted in the last elections for Zionist parties, including right-wing ones). They outwardly imitate Jewish manners, they foster provincialism (something that can be seen, for example, in the Arabic newspapers published in Israel, which give almost no attention to world events, or even to events in "Jewish" Israel, being almost exclusively concerned with events within the four walls of Palestinian-Israeli society). One looking in from the outside would think that many, very many, of the Palestinians in Israel create for themselves a narrow present, constricted and escapist, a kind of *sumud* (endurance) of the moment.

In one of the early chapters I told the story of the "present absentees" among the Palestinians in Israel. One may also say, without any risk of grave error, that the Jewish majority in Israel treats all its Palestinian citizens as absent presences. This is how they are conceived, and how they are depicted in the media—as a collective absence, as a group that exists but is faceless and nameless, of uniform traits, most of them negative. If in 1948 the Palestinians in Israel were "those that are not but actually are," they have over the years turned into "those who are but actually are not."

Now, in these past months, I have had a growing feeling that in some subtle and complex way this attitude has been internalized by the Palestinians in Israel themselves, and has even in some turned into a sophisticated defense mechanism against the disappointments with which the state has surrounded them. Yes, sometimes it seems to me that there are those among them who find their absent presence useful. They cloak themselves in it, to shield themselves from the face that the state presents to them—a clenched face that pursues them always, the face of a stingy and suspicious hotel proprietor.

What is so depressing, so ingrained in the relations between us, the Jews in Israel, and them? Maybe it's that the state of the Palestinians in Israel is so convenient for us Jews. It is convenient for us, pure and simple. It is easier for us to operate in such a complex situation when "our" minority is so passive. It is easy for us to postpone any real and penetrating confrontation with ourselves when there is such a partner. "What an ideal minority!" sociologist Majed Elhaj sneered bitterly. "The quietest minority in the world."

I write this again, to check. In Israel there live almost a million citizens, men, women, and children, whose suspended animation is convenient for us, the Jewish majority.

I should have imposed quotation marks on "convenient," but in the war room of our consciousness, the consciousness of the survivor, there is no room for such fine points, there is no space for a look that will see beyond the current moment. The little security officer in all of us likes the reports he receives from there.

If they are quiet—it is convenient. If they do not take part in national affairs—that is convenient. If we see to it that they have minimal rights, and they are careful not to demand additional rights that legally they should have—it is convenient for us. If they let out their frustrations by satisfying material desires, or with religion—that's their business. If they are prepared to continue to cooperate with injustice and prejudice and do not force us to change anything—it is very convenient. If they, by their own testimony, do not find among themselves the necessary strength to break out of the fossilized framework of their past, do we have an obligation to help them do that?

"There is something interesting in this story of the Arabs in Israel," said Azmi Bishara. "Our failure to struggle against discrimination and humiliation does not necessarily derive from fear. Yes, from fear also, but mostly it derives from the feeling that this is not our country. We are strangers to it. So what should we protest about? Who has any expectations of this country? Who says that it will ever grant us equality?"

If that is the situation, senior figures snort with collective vapidity, why should we awaken in them the need to shake themselves out of it, to redefine themselves, to be an equal part? We have enough problems as it is. It is very convenient.

Is this guilt, or just failure? A temptation that a nation in our circumstances found it difficult not to give in to?

It seems to me that the Israeli Jewish and Israeli Palestinian failures have met, and that this was one of the most potent and exhilarating contacts that has ever occurred between the two peoples in Israel.

Of this doubtful coupling twin guilts were born. Dr. Sa'id Zeidani, among the bravest and most open people I have met, described them: "The condition of the Arabs in Israel does not awaken one's respect. The self-castration. They don't educate the Arab in Israel to be proud of himself. There is no self-assurance, or any sense of duty or consciousness that the injustice should be opposed in a determined way. They say that power corrupts, but so does lack of power, and weakness, maybe more than power does. We are not creating human beings who take their duties seriously. Education has created people who see no social challenges for which they would be willing to fight. They leave the fight to the parties, to the political forces. I think that what Israel did, connived to do, was to rule in this way—to intentionally create an Arab society that would be quiet, that would not rise up. They did not educate it the way you educate free and thinking people."

Yes, it is a "convenient" minority that lives among us. It generally speaks to us in very cautious language. But that does not release us from the obligation to face honestly up to Sa'id

Zeidani's blunt words, to what sounds like a quiet, defeated lament rising from among many of the words in this book.

Has Israel indeed made the Palestinian minority "quiet," obedient, dormant? Has the state, through its apparatus, worked to neutralize expressions of vitality, of force, identity, and ambition? To create a deliberate dullness? It is hard to believe that this was an intentional policy. That people sat down somewhere and drafted a plan to bring it about.

Then the *Koenig Report* comes to mind. This secret document—later published—was written in 1976 by Yisrael Koenig, the chief of the Ministry of the Interior in the northern district, along with three Jewish mayors. Was it unique? The report proposed to the government a set of policies regarding the Arabs in Israel:

Central institutions should give preference to the employment of Jews instead of Arabs.

In order to take from the Communist Party the leading role in the national struggle and the representation of the Israeli Arabs, and to provide an outlet for "fence-sitters," a sister party to the Labor Party should be established that will put an emphasis on ideas of equality, humanism, culture, and language, social struggle and the pursuit of peace in the region. [Governing] institutions should organize to establish an invisible presence in and control of this party.

. . . a special task force (Shin Bet) should be appointed to investigate the personal habits of Communist leaders and other negative figures, and to bring the findings to the attention of the voting public.

Proper arrangements should be made with the directors of industries operating under the Capital Investment Act in critical areas [the country's north] so that the number of Arab employees will not rise above 20 percent.

We should reach an arrangement with the central marketing groups of various goods to neutralize and hinder Arab dealers, especially in the north, in order to prevent the dependence of the Jewish population on these dealers, especially in times of emergency.

The government must find a way to neutralize grants to large families among the Arab population, whether by linking [this benefit] to economic status or by removing these grants from the purvey of the social security agency and handing them over to the Jewish Agency or Zionist Organization, so that they will be directed at Jews only.

But why bother with Koenig's recommendations? Reality plants itself in front of our faces in a much more blunt way. Who recommended a policy that causes 55 percent of the families under the poverty line (in 1991) to be Arabs? Or one that ensures that Arab villages receive 6 percent of the development funds available to non-urban local authorities, even though they represent 30 percent of the population living in such settlements? Or that the budget per person in these local authorities is only a quarter of that in Jewish settlements? Or that fifteen of the largest Arab municipalities have not yet had their zoning plans approved by the central government, causing delays in granting business licenses, preventing investments, and forcing the inhabitants to build illegally? Furthermore, the zoning plan for Nazareth, the largest Arab settlement in the country, was last reviewed and approved in 1942. Who are the people who constructed a reality in which the water allocated for Arab agriculture is only 2.4 percent of the water available to Israeli agriculture, even though Arab farmers cultivate 17 percent of the agricultural land? The water allocation for an agricultural unit belonging to a Jew is 14,000 cubic meters of water, while a unit belonging to an Arab gets only 1,500 cubic meters. How can it be that the Ministry of Labor and Welfare has established only one institution for mentally retarded children for the entire Arab population? That in the Ministry of Justice only 3 out of 1,000 employees are Arabs? That there has never been an Arab among the

Supreme Court's twelve justices? That there is only one social worker for every 5,000 Arabs, but one for every 1,800 Jews? That in Sakhnin, a town of 18,000 residents, there is no social services office? That of all institutional places available for handicapped children in Israel, only 4 percent are set aside for Arabs—who make up 24 percent of the children in the country?

The Arab educational problems cited in the last chapter were certainly known to government officials, experts, and policymakers. True, the compulsory education law applies to Arabs just as it applies to Jews, and there is a high literacy rate among Arab high-school graduates in Israel—93 percent among men and 78 percent among women (as compared with, in Jordan, 80 percent among men and 63 percent among women, according to the *Israel Statistical Yearbook*, 1990). True, there were only 7,000 Arab children in school on the day the state was founded, while in 1991 there were more than 220,000. Then there were 170 Arab teachers, and today there are about 10,000. A large number of schools have been established in Arab communities (in 1949 there were 45 Arab elementary schools and one high school; forty years later there are 410 schools—this according to data from the Central Statistical Bureau). But this impressive growth is misleading—the need is much greater than the supply. According to the report of the Director General's Committee on Arab Education, submitted to the Ministry of Education in 1985, if the conditions in Arab schools were equalized with those prevailing in the Jewish schools, the former would need 50 percent more teachers. A field study carried out by Dr. Majed Elhaj reports that, in 1989, Arab students lacked 1,231 classrooms. An internal Ministry of Education report revealed (in May 1987) that 77 percent of the rooms rented as classrooms (which almost always fail to meet the standards set by the ministry) were being used by Arab students, because of the lack of any organized plan to erect school buildings in Arab communities.

There is no point in starting to detail the physical privation of the Arab schools. That is not the root of the Arab education problem. The question is, What could jar Arab consciousness and help those who wish to do so to extricate themselves from what impedes them? Here, at this point, precisely on the subject of education, it is necessary to examine the facts with a very sober eye, so as to discern when the country's disregard is not coincidental, when banal apathy is no more than a cover for a flexed muscle. And while a string of numbers and data is liable to numb the mind, a story hangs by them.

In the framework of a program for disadvantaged children, the Ministry of Education has added a total of 40,000 annual teaching hours since 1970 (according to Elhaj's survey, "The State of Arab Education," 1988). Not a single one of these hours was allotted to any Arab school. Yet, according to studies by senior educators such as Professor Yosef Bashi and the late Dr. Sami Mar'i, most Arab students meet the criteria for being disadvantaged, given their low socioeconomic background and the large number of students who drop out of the Arab schools. The official explanation for this discrimination was that Arab students did not need this assistance because they, unlike Oriental Jews (for whom the program was intended), "did not suffer due to the transition from one culture to another"(!).

Eighty percent of the Arab pupils in need of special educational frameworks continue to learn—mostly for lack of funds—in regular schools. This may be the reason that at the high school in Jat, for example, three hired thugs roam the schoolyard armed with thick batons. "One is a deaf-mute, one is a shepherd, and all three are illiterate," Ahmed Abu Esba, a former teacher, described them. "Is there another educational institution in Israel where order is kept by force? Sometimes, when a teacher has to confront problem students, he calls on them to beat the student in the classroom! Even in Brazzaville in the Congo there's nothing like that!"

Of the 42,000 teaching hours allocated by the educational system as part of the "long school day program," only 3,300 (8 percent) were given to Arab schools, which make up 20 percent of the educational system as a whole.

The Arabs in Israel have no real vocational program in electronics and computers. There are, however, many programs in auto mechanics for boys and sewing for girls.

Only 4 community centers have been built in Arab communities, as compared with 126 in Jewish municipalities.

According to data given me by the Ministry of Education personnel department, there is not a single Arab employee in the following departments of the ministry: the neighborhood rehabilitation department, the educational television center, the adult education department, the textbook unit, and—no less important—the road safety unit. Arabs (thirty-three of them, all told) work only in the division of Arab education and culture.

And where are the VCRs and the computers that you can find in almost every Jewish school? Where are the laboratories, the workshops, the sports facilities? Where are the counselors? Where are the psychologists (there are only twelve psychological treatment stations in the entire Arab school system; only ten positions for psychologists have been allotted to Arab education out of a total of 416 such positions in the educational system as a whole)? Where are the educational television broadcasts in Arabic, where is the advanced technological vocational education (it does not exist in Arab schools in Israel), where are the special-projects classrooms and the college preparatory programs? And what about enrichment like music, visits to museums, drama clubs, and reading rooms? Where are all the teaching aids that can stimulate thought and imagination and open new horizons?

And I've still said nothing about the subliminal messages that the Israeli educational system pours into the Arab student's consciousness. According to Dr. Majed Elhaj, formerly a pupil in the system he now studies, these are messages meant to "create a submissive Arab, ready to accept his inferiority and Jewish superiority, thereby weakening and destroying Arab-Palestinian identity." Azmi Bishara seconded: "Maybe the thing that pushed me from a young age toward social action was that, in eighth grade, in our grammar book, it said, 'Decline in singular and plural forms: Jewish teacher, Jewish teachers; Arab shepherd, Arab shepherds'; that's what I had to learn."

At what point does ongoing dereliction become active negligence? What would the fair-minded person say upon reading the following lines from the notorious *Koenig Report*: "We should encourage referring [Arab] students to technology and the exact and natural sciences, because these leave less time for occupation with nationalism, and the drop-out rate is high . . . We should facilitate trips overseas for study, and make it difficult for them to return and find work—such a policy can encourage emigration."

Something flickers behind these appearances, and invites us, the members of Israel's Jewish majority, to once again ask whether several factors have not mated here to place a cunning and dangerous trap at our feet.

We have already said that we have an "easy partner." There is an interest and a motive—even without a volatile Arab minority steeped in manifest nationalism, it would be difficult for us. Our interest and motive also have wide backing, tacit and vocal, from large parts of the Jewish public. And the State of Israel has, without a doubt, the most sophisticated and ingenious overt and covert mechanisms to ensure the "obedience" of the Palestinian minority, to keep it under control, to threaten it, and to try to bend it to our wishes, the security and educational systems in particular.

More important than all these together is that Israel today does not have the psychological force or the moral power to deal with the problem of the Palestinian minority. On the face of it, the problem seems insoluble, and a combination of circumstances has made the problem seem dormant. The slightest touch is liable to waken it. So it is best to tiptoe around it and pray that it fades, or melts away, on its own. Or something.

It is very hard to put one's finger on the right words. After all, we are not talking here about a single, dramatic event. It is an ongoing, complex, ambiguous state of affairs. Every one of us can open this locked door with a different key and see only what he or she wishes. Israel can also point to achievements in its treatment of its minority. When it comes to living conditions and certain civil rights, the position of Israeli citizens, even Arabs, is far better than those of Syrian, Iraqi, Libyan, or Jordanian citizens. The Palestinians in Israel have indeed come a long way since 1948. Many Palestinians have found places for themselves in Israeli life; there are points of contact between the two peoples and joint ventures. Still . . .

I put together all the factors I have mentioned—the motive and the partner and the justification and the tools, and the temptation to forget it all; alongside I list the factual data known to me, some of which I have presented here, a long and depressing list of minuscule budgets, sparse services, discriminatory and one-sided legislation, social and cultural alienation. Faced with all this I ask whether one can reasonably deny that the manipulative process of suspension, or "active deferral," or "pacification" has been going on for years and is going on now, performed by the Jewish majority in Israel against the country's Palestinian citizens.

After all, exploiting the weaknesses—or building up the failures—of another is "legitimate" only toward someone for whom you wish ill, whom you wish to destroy—the enemy.

"But they really are the enemy!" many Israeli Jews—maybe even the majority—will assert.

Are they the enemy?

How do we decide who is an enemy? According to his secret desires? According to the way we interpret those secrets? According to what we know of human nature? According to our anxieties? According to his deeds?

I tried to obtain from the Israeli police precise details about the involvement of the Arab citizens of Israel in terrorist activity inside the Green Line, but the police (the investigations division) refused to give me information. While they annually publish data on terrorist activity in Israel, the data is presented in a misleading way: the official statistics do not state how many of the attacks were carried out by Arab citizens of Israel and how many by Arabs from the territories. My repeated requests for more accurate information were rejected. For some reason, after my limited experience of recent months, it is hard for me to believe that this fudging of the facts is coincidental.

"During the forty years of Israel's existence only .4 percent of Israeli Arabs have been accused and convicted of hostile activity against the state. So 99.6 percent have proven their loyalty to the country," said Shmuel Toledano, formerly the prime minister's Advisor on Arab Affairs.*

*Radio interview, Voice of Israel, second channel, March 21, 1988.

"If you had a choice," Jews and Arabs were asked in June 1989, in the framework of the first study of its kind on peace proposals, "would you prefer to live your life outside the State of Israel?" Some 80 percent of the Jews and 75 percent of the Arabs responded that they would not want to live outside Israel. Of the Jewish citizens surveyed, 53 percent believed that Jewish-Arab coexistence is possible in Israel. Among the Arabs a majority of 83 percent believed this, and 96 percent of the Arabs supported, according to Dr. Elhaj, one of the researchers, a "two-state solution" (the study was carried out by the Guttmann Institute for Applied Social Research).

Every so often there are surveys that check the attitude of Arab citizens to the country. Some of the figures are disturbing (17.6 percent of the Arabs surveyed in a 1987 study by Professor Sami Smooha rejected Israel's right to exist). They show that a minority of the Arabs in Israel might be enemies, and might even participate in violent activity against the state and its Jewish inhabitants. Yet the direction of the surveys is clear, and an unscientific but open-minded look at the familiar Israeli reality confirms this. The great majority of Palestinians in Israel have decided in favor of integration into the state, in favor of a struggle for equality in the framework of Israeli law. Out of all the choices and options for action and behavior available to Israeli Arabs, most of them have chosen to accept reality.

"And I already know—even if an Arab prostrates himself twice a day on some rabbi's grave, even if he eats gefilte fish to break his Ramadan fast, he won't be equal and won't be an integral part of Israeli society. It just can't be!" sighed Majed Elhaj. "So I say to myself, Listen, I've come to terms with the existence of the state as a state. But it hasn't come to terms with my existence as a human being. True, it took the Arabs in Israel ten years before they began to accept Israel, but there are many Jews in Israel who still live in that period of anxiety and disquiet. Something ingrained in them says that an Arab cannot be an Israeli. He must be a potential enemy of Israel. An Israel hater. He won't think twice if he's given the opportunity to do harm to Israel. This is incorrect. And it is liable, paradoxically, to push the Arabs into alienation and extremism. I don't want to repeat that obnoxious sentence: 'The Arabs have again proven their loyalty to Israel.' As if they always, at every moment and in every event, have to prove that they are always loyal. 'What does it mean that we've "proven" it? We're citizens like every other citizen!' But the new generation, my children, will no longer accept it. We, perhaps, were a kind of intermediate generation, our parents always took us back, we were educated by the generation of the defeat. But our children have been educated by a generation that has political awareness and national pride, and they will not accept everything we accepted."

"The Arabs should be judged according to what they might do, and not according to what they have done," said David Ben-Gurion at the beginning of the 1950s, formulating the state's fundamental attitude to the Arab minority. Yet forty years have passed since then. For how many years will we continue to "convict" the Arabs until their "innocence" is proven? Forty years or more is certainly cruel and unusual punishment.

For the moment they are still waiting for us. Waiting with amazing patience for the country to decide once and for all what it wants from them, and what it sees in them—stowaways? a fifth column? a security burden? an unwanted pregnancy?

It is making no decision. Or, more correctly, Israel has not, since 1948, fundamentally changed its *internal* judgment of the Arab minority within it, even though today's circumstances are so different. This judgment—expressed in many ways—

prevents Palestinians in Israel who so wish from becoming allies and partners. Israel is liable in the end to doom its Arab citizens to fulfill its fears of them.

How long can a relatively large minority be assumed by the majority to be an enemy without in the end actually turning into one? How long can the state exist as a stable political framework if this is how it treats a sixth of its citizens?

Slowly and steadily, as if slumbering, Israel is missing its chance to rescue itself from a horrible mistake. It is creating for itself the enemy it will run up against after its other enemies have made their peace with it. And war (as the Serbs and Croats teach us today) means war.

THE END OF THE BEGINNING

How can it be that I knew so little of how the Palestinians in Israel aspire to autonomy? I had, after all, heard of them in the past, but still, I didn't know. I read about it—but I didn't know.

Had I put myself in their place, in their circumstances, for even an hour, I would certainly have known. Had I but imagined myself, for example, as a Jew in another land that rejected me, watching and restricting my every move, I would certainly have felt the desire to separate myself from that country.

And why was I unable to arouse within me the sense of primal family ties between the Palestinians on both sides of the Green Line? How could I not have ever exposed myself, until now, to the tangle of emotions and anguish of the Arab who wishes to be part of the Israeli reality yet finds himself endlessly rejected, suspected, detested? And why was I unable to estimate the great comfort and reward that religion gives to a people with a national handicap?

I did not, I knew not, I remembered not, and I thought not.

In all that touches on the Arab minority, the collective Jewish consciousness in Israel is like that of a city obliged to house within it a large institution for criminal rehabilitation.

On the face of it, life goes on as usual. But people learn to avoid the neighborhood where the institution is situated. Good citizens like us can live our whole lives without going near that neighborhood. In our imaginations—if we are forced to think about it—it is a violent, dirty, hostile place. Everyone there dresses the same. They have no individual names, only one collective name; they have no faces, only "characteristic features." It is important for first-class citizens like us to know that "they" are always under supervision; that they are carefully counted; that with prudence, and in ways that will not disturb our self-image as enlightened persons, their access to the rest of the city is carefully controlled.

When we good citizens meet them outside, in our territory, we treat them suspiciously, as if they were a mobile enemy enclave. We display a sense of civic concern—can they really be trusted? Will some primal instinct not suddenly overcome them? To what extent are their relatives in the criminal world (that is, the Palestinians from the territories and the Arab world) liable to influence them? Will they, when put to the test, prove their loyalty to Israel?

Yes, I know—over the last decades real friendships, relationships of deep and symmetrical fraternity, have been established between Jews and Arabs in Israel. But these are exceptional. In general, "good citizens" have but a functional, restricted contact with Arabs. "My Arab" is, generally, the mechanic, the gardener, the plumber; the metal worker or construction laborer or the tile layer, and sometimes, the student at the university. "My Arab," working where we good citizens live, is no more than an inmate of that institution permitted to work outside (for wages lower than what we would normally pay). Generally, he has only a first name, like a child. There is food for thought in the difficulty Israeli Jews have with Arab names, so common in life in the East. (It is hard here to overcome the temptation to ask whether the Israeli reader can remember even three of the names that appeared in this book? Two? One full name?) "My Arab" 's good features are, for his Jewish friend, startlingly exceptional in the society from which he comes (His Hebrew is amazing! He's so sensitive! So clean! And honest!), and his negative characteristics confirm everything the good citizen always knew.

It is not only individual names that the Arabs in Israel lack—the Hebrew language also lacks a correct general term to indicate our complex relations with the Arabs in Israel. Our problematic relations with the Palestinians in the occupied territories already have a plethora of names. Some we have counterfeited, and some have been imposed on us. We say: the problem of the territories, the question of the territories, the Palestinian problem, the intifadah, the occupation. In each of these smolders a sense of disquiet, even unrest.

When is the last time that someone in Israel explicitly referred to "the Palestinian problem within Israel"? Or "the national aspirations of the Arabs in Israel"? Or even just "the Palestinian national minority in Israel"?

They all exist.

The people themselves are alluded to in Hebrew as "Israeli Arabs," a name that is in no way innocent (even if some of the Arabs themselves use it, maybe out of linguistic absent-mindedness, just as the Palestinians in the occupied territories sometimes call themselves, when speaking Hebrew, "the Arabs of Judea and Samaria"). A more widespread term is "minorities," which is at first glance a factual label. Its greatest distinction is, however, that it is "clean"—it avoids the word "Arab," and whoever it was that coined it toward the end of

the 1940s also knew well how it sounds to the Arabs themselves—it is a standing reminder of their humiliation. (By the
way, in the country's official statistics, the term used for the
Palestinians in Israel is "non-Jews.")

The most commonly used term is "the Arab sector," another
seemingly neutral delimiter. Still, for some reason it rings in
my ears as a description of something that has a dotted line
showing where it is to be cut out.

At most, people will say "the minority problem" or "the
Israeli-Arab problem." In general, the speaker does not mean
the whole range of the relationship but rather only the narrow
security issues involved.

There are no correct names—there are only a few terms
created by the military, the bureaucracy, and the legal system,
sterile forceps with which to grasp what the hand dares not
touch.

Only four years ago, at the outbreak of the intifadah, we
discovered the price of this self-delusion. From 1967 onward
we had gradually ceased to find new words to describe our rule
over the Arabs in the occupied territories. As the situation
worsened, we stopped telling what was happening there; our
power to find new words, words charged with heat and vitality,
words that would describe the situation as it is, was sapped.
We called it all by fictitious names, using laundered words.

Since we lost our ability to use words to describe reality
there correctly, we woke up one day to a reality that was hard
to describe. Israel had become so good at fooling itself that
the army did not even have contingency plans for confronting
mass demonstrations; in the intifadah's early days its agents
rushed out to the most questionable markets to buy net throw-
ers and rubber bullets and gravel blowers and other nasty toys.

After all, any country that conquers and represses another
people ought to be prepared for large demonstrations. Israel
wasn't ready, because it did not know it was a conqueror, did

not think it was being repressive, did not believe that there was a people there. This was a lesson for us—if you do not continually ask yourself the new questions that problematic reality imposes on your cowed, lazy, noncommittal consciousness, that reality will vanish from your mind. But only from there.

Moshe Arens, the Likud Minister of Defense, said, "There is no correlation between the time the cabinet has devoted to discussing the subject of the Israeli Arabs—perhaps a thousandth of its meetings or even less—and its importance. Neither have Israeli governments had a firm general conception of a policy regarding the Israeli Arabs. This derives from a mixture of lack of understanding, lack of interest, and lack of desire."

The Nazareth poet Michel Hadad once wrote that after the 1967 war the Arabs in Israel discovered that they had been "living with a single lung." This painful image applies to Israel as well—in abdicating its Arabs it seems like a country breathing with one lung, leaving the other collapsed. Nearly a fifth of the Israeli organism is in suspended animation, "lying on the shelf." When you get close to that Arab society you discover what ought to be obvious—it is a world unto itself. There is a special pleasure in meeting people who are, largely, a collective foreign entity, a sealed package, bound undoubtedly in preconceptions, stereotypes, and suspicion, and here it is unbound before you, and there are faces, voices, body movements, weaknesses, pains. I met myself also, not always happily—the bounds of my tolerance of the stranger, the other; my own deceptions and twisted anxieties. The temptation to say "we" when you cannot bring yourself to admit that it is actually "I."

And mostly on this journey (and sometimes it really was a

journey to an unknown land) I met my country—people,
Palestinian men and women, whom I would like to see everywhere in Israel. In the cabinet. And the army. (The previous
Minister of Defense, Moshe Arens, was already initiating such
integration with the Christian Arabs, and aspired to the voluntary enlistment of Muslims as well.) In the cabinet? In the
army? You're not afraid of that? Yes, I'm afraid. Like the fear
you have before setting out on a long hike. Like before beginning the composition of a new book.

I met people with whom one can build a country. People
from whom Israel could benefit if they were to contribute their
abilities and minds and talents, as well as the special cultural
nuance they could bring to our Western, technocratic lives.
A country as meagerly endowed with natural resources as Israel
is cannot afford to give up a large part of its human ore. Why
should it keep Rima Othman, Tagrid Yunes, and Sa'id Zeidani
from the center of activity—not only within the narrow bounds
of their community, but in the entire range of activity in Israel?
Of course, the Arab population, like the Jewish, contains those
who are not "constructive citizens," and sometimes these are
even a burden. But the country carries that burden anyway.
Why should it not benefit from the good the others can—and
wish to—offer?

As I've noted, one cannot ignore the objective reasons that
have created this special situation. But for several years now
new conditions have prevailed in the country and the region
—reality invites us, Jews and Arabs, to make use of their
potential—and we are still prisoners of old conceptions. Our
strength is gone.

In many ways, overt and covert, Israel puts the minority
within it on hold and blocks its chances—and ours—for integration, for mutual resuscitation. If, for instance, out of the
5,100 full-time university faculty members in Israel only
twelve are Arabs; if out of 13,000 employees in the eight most

important government ministries only 5 percent are Arab; if among the 400 prosecutors in the Ministry of Justice there is not a single Arab; if the Department for Muslim Affairs in the Ministry of Religious Affairs is headed, still, by a Jew; if there is not a single Arab on the managing committee of the Israel Broadcasting Authority, meaning the Arabs have no influence on broadcast policy; if the director of the government's Arabic-language radio station is a Jew; if 44.9 percent of all citizens in the bottom tenth income level are Arabs; if according to the standards of the social-security system, a Jewish child in a large family is "worth" two Arab children—if all this happens here, what will happen here?

Does Israel act this way because it is sure that this is the correct way to realize its goals or simply because it does not have the strength to search for another way, and because it knows no such way? Sometimes it seems as if Israeli-Jewish DNA, after being modified by long generations of oppression and pogroms and blood libels and mass extermination, contains no gene for any other attitude toward people who might also be dangerous, even if their deeds, for almost half a century, prove the exact opposite. Professor Arnon Sofer says, "Their [the Arabs in Israel] loyalty to the country depends precisely on the distance of the Syrian tanks from the border!" I met too many Arabs during the last few months to be able to second such a sweeping statement. In any case, the distance of Syrian tanks from the border is the army's responsibility. The border is the legitimate and necessary arena of the instinct for aggression and survival. For this reason the country has an army to defend it. But as for the citizens *within* the country, citizens who have performed their duties for forty-three years—Israel cannot continue to relate to them according to the laws of the struggle for survival only. These citizens are not enemies.

Understandably Israel, cramped within such narrow borders, feels that it is all border, that it is in a state of permanent siege, that "the whole nation is an army," but we may, finally, rise up against this way of thinking. Precisely because such large parts of our lives are so close to the border in every sense of the word, because they are omnipresent, we must struggle so that in the little space free from the border we will make a real life for ourselves that contains spiritual space and expansive thinking and a place for us to discard some of our rusty armor. It must be a life in which—unlike on a border—one may stray from the main road and try others; in which it is possible to err and be of errant imagination; in which it is possible to be generous to and tolerant of the differences of the other, differences that do not have to be hostile.

I write these lines on December 1, 1991. Twenty-five years ago today, the military regime that the Arabs in Israel lived under from 1948 onward was dismantled. Under the military regime, the country had been divided into regions, and the Arabs in each region were the subjects of a military governor of almost unlimited powers. The governors could order deportations, the confiscation of property and belongings, curfews, the destruction of houses, arrests, and restrictions on movement. To go from Ramla to Tel Aviv—a fifteen-minute drive—an Arab had to obtain a special permit that was given, or not given, according to the whim of the regional governor. When it was given, payment was demanded—in the form of "goodwill" on the part of the recipient. Obtaining a driver's license, a construction license, or a teaching permit involved proving one's loyalty to the regime—that is, to the Shin Bet. It is hard today to believe that it was only in 1962 that the Druze were allowed to move freely within Israel, and that it was only in 1963 that Arabs were allowed to spend the night in areas where they had previously been allowed only during the day.

How much fear, how much suspicion and hatred were poured into those who supported the continuation of this regime, which provided complete, tyrannical control of every moment and every action and every word in the lives of the Arabs in Israel. Then the military government was abolished, and none of the dark prophecies of espionage and terrorism came true. On the contrary, the elimination of close supervision released pressures within both population groups and drained off some bad feelings. I am sure that many of us today would rather forget the position they took then in the endless debates over whether Israel could allow itself to abolish the military government.

In recent months I have incessantly heard from Israeli Jews that whining sentence: "No way." "We'll give the territories to the Palestinians, there will be a Palestinian state, and even if Israel behaves as fairly and as equally as it can to its Arabs, they'll still, after a time, want to live their life in a framework that does not restrict them because they are not Jews. Here, within Israel, a new uprising will explode, demanding autonomy. And if that is our doom, why should Israel try so hard, go to such great lengths, in order to improve the living conditions of its potential enemies?"

This question has to be taken seriously. Yes, it is natural for man and natural for a nation to aspire to the greatest possible control of their own affairs. All over the world national minorities are now demanding the right to govern themselves. Even if the Palestinians in Israel are, for various reasons, still outside that "spring of nations," the day may well come when they will ask to live as an autonomous national minority.

First, it should be noted that the voices calling for this today are few and far between. Maybe that is but an interim position, but it certainly may also be seen as an expression of the judicious acceptance by the Palestinians in Israel of the fact that their lives will be lived in the State of Israel, within which they will fight for equality.

But even if we examine the worst possibility—and no one can evade it—there will be a fundamental difference if Israel's stand against Palestinian separatism derives from a solid sense of justice. Today, with Israel ruling over 2.5 million Arabs on both sides of the Green Line, and with its leaders denying that line's existence yet discriminating against its minority in almost every sphere, what can we say to the Arabs among us who see themselves less and less as citizens and more and more as plundered of their rights? Can there be any wonder that they want to cut themselves free?

Israel's position will be decisively different if it faces an Arab minority with many rights, with varied channels of expression and self-fulfillment, integrated into all the country's elites, taking part in determining the country's character and responsible for its decisions—yet despite all this demanding to go its separate way.

You haven't convinced me, my interlocutor will say. Look at Yugoslavia. Its various communities were reasonably balanced. There were tensions, but each group had its channels of expression, there was equality for all (or inequality for all), and there was osmosis between the elites. Yet look what is happening there. And here, where we are—

I can respond to that only by making one assumption: that there will soon be a peace agreement in the Middle East, at least between Israel, the Palestinians, and Jordan. If no such agreement is reached, if the current negotiations end without granting concrete rights—in particular, the right of self-determination—to the Palestinians, who knows what will happen.

But let's assume that an accord is reached, and that after a few years of autonomy, and after the establishment of a Palestinian state, the Palestinians within Israel nevertheless ask to secede from Israel. How will Israel respond to this threatening challenge? This is, really, the decisive question, the one that keeps many of us from dispensing with the burden of suspicion and animosity, even if we want to do so.

It seems to me that part of the division in Israel over the question of the occupied territories derives from the fact that in the consciousness of most Jews in Israel the "territories" do not coincide—neither psychologically nor emotionally—with the borders of Israeli identity. One could say that the heat of the Israeli identity's "internal combustion" reaches, among most Jews in Israel, as far as the Green Line. Beyond it, the nature of this heat changes. Either it cools and diffuses or it becomes a conflagration. The fact is that to this day, twenty-five years after the Six-Day War, there is no Israeli consensus for annexing the territories. The people would prefer a peace agreement.

One can believe that giving up the territories will bring the Israelis back into the authentic sphere of experiencing their identity, to a true, current sense of Israeliness. Once again, for the first time in years, the borders of the country and the borders of Israeli identity will coincide. It is impossible to say that these will be the "borders of the national consensus," because there will be many who will be outraged by the retreat, but within these new-old borders the Jewish majority's sense of internal justice will without a doubt grow stronger, as will its determination to defend those borders—not out of fear, out of the reduction of its territory, but because the people's identity with its state, as an organic body maintaining an equally emotional and neuronic link with all its parts, will become clearer and more concrete.

The Palestinians in the territories can make a determined challenge to our right to rule them, partly because we ourselves, deep within, lack confidence in this right. But our identities fill the Green Line borders of the State of Israel with full force. There we also have moral force; and there the collective message we broadcast is unambiguous.

If, in addition to the geographical-external change there also occurs a cognitive change with regard to the Palestinian citizens' place in society—if we internalize the fact that they are equal partners, if we give the Palestinians the greatest measure of autonomy in areas that present no challenge to the country's sovereignty (education and culture, religion, community services, independent radio and television, etc.), if bicultural fluency develops in Israel, if it becomes possible to find Arab citizens in every ministry, in every institution, on every newspaper staff, in every school—if all this happens, then the majority in Israel (and I include both Jews and Arabs in this) will be steadfast, as well as correct, in their opposition to separatism. That same majority will also be a counterweight to passive tendencies of isolation, that "absent presence" which is also, in the final account, destructive to the country.

A true state of equal opportunity will put not only the Jews but also the Palestinians in Israel to the test. How willing are they really to be fully and equally integrated into Israeli culture? To what extent have they internalized life in Israel? How much are they willing to step out of the meantime and go into the present and future? To what extent will they be willing to sense a connection with, a sense of belonging to, the country, if it gives them maximum rights and treats them with respect?

The Palestinians in the occupied territories have reached a kind of national and political maturation through breaking the eternal framework, and through bloody struggle. Their brothers in Israel have achieved the same maturation without having to undergo such an intense crisis. For them it has been a long and painful process that has taught them many things and made them forget many others. Now they will once more have to connect themselves with parts of themselves that were suspended and put to sleep. Now they will have to rewrite themselves as citizens with equal rights and responsibilities, to redeem themselves from apathy and foreignness, to learn to breathe with both lungs.

A solution to the problem of the Palestinians in the occupied territories will certainly mitigate the dilemma of identity of the Palestinians in Israel. But it would be an error to wait until the peace process is completed. The final end of the occupation is liable to be put off for many long years, and precisely for this reason, the peace talks should consider the special circumstances of the Palestinians in Israel. Any agreement made with the Arabs should be complete and final, ending absolutely all border and land disputes, all claims and ambiguities between the two peoples.

There will be those who will be alarmed by this proposal —why are you giving them ideas, at the height of the negotiations! What is open to question here—after all, we're talking about Israeli citizens! Are you proposing to concede the power you achieved years ago? Nevertheless, hundreds of hours of talks strengthen my sense that now is the time to open discussion on the question of the Palestinians in Israel, and that it is in Israel's manifest interest to do this now, when we still have all our cards in hand. We should not give in to the urge for denial, to the faith that things will solve themselves—they won't.

Many Palestinians in Israel, including those who have come to terms with their Israeli citizenship, see Yassir Arafat as their representative. Toufiq Ziad, a member of the Knesset and mayor of Nazareth, said at a gathering in his city on November 15, 1991: "Shamir did not represent us at the Madrid conference and he will not represent us in the future. We say with all sincerity"—and here Ziad turned to the head of the Palestinian delegation to Madrid—"that we, the Palestinian Arab public in Israel, are represented by you." There are also reports that the Arab delegations to the peace conference prepared a special file on the Arab citizens of Israel, and they may bring it up at a later date.

If peace comes to the region, the ties between the two parts of the Palestinian people will become stronger. It may well be that those who live in Israel will carry—at the end of the process—Palestinian passports, and will vote for the Palestinian parliament. The situation then will be no less complex than the present one, and only truly daring thinking—not that of a people besieged, not defensive, Diaspora, minority thinking—can create a dynamic system of relations that will gradually release the partners in Israeliness from the mentality of conflict.

It is evident to everyone that Israel, which cannot raise the money necessary to absorb mass immigration, cannot—and apparently does not want to—set aside the necessary funds for improving the lot of the Palestinians within it. It is not hard to imagine the results of this discrimination. An explosion by the Palestinians in Israel over ongoing discrimination and humiliation will be complex and dangerous when an independent Palestinian entity exists. But if the issue of the Palestinians in Israel is raised in the framework of the peace talks, and Israel's objective difficulties in solving this problem are presented, one may certainly hope that the peace treaty will also include economic support from the United States, Europe, and the Middle East that will vault Israel's Arab society into a position of equal opportunity with the Jewish community, and will magnify the chances that all Israeli citizens can live a life of peace and satisfaction—a fully realized life, not only teeth-gritting defense of the boundaries of its existence.

It is not necessary to be a political or psychological genius to know that the continually constricting helplessness of the Palestinians in Israel will take its toll. The cost will be insult and discrimination, Israel's use of its superior force, its military guile, against Arabs in the territories. In particular, Israel will have to pay eventually for its ability to ignore the Palestinians' private and collective pain, for the selective blindness it has assumed. It will all be tallied up. Were we to read of the accumulation of these facts in a different context, in a country far from us, we would all be oracles—sometimes a person, or an entire nation, understands what he needs and what was hard for him to bear only when he suddenly breaks his bonds with hideous force.

Can we believe, may we demand of the Israeli Jew, whose life is surviving from one war to the next, that he act in opposition to what seem to be his basic survival instincts, instincts that have proven themselves in so many battles? That he try to formulate a common identity with those who are part of the family of his enemies? Such a resolute reversal requires enormous, almost superhuman strength (and perhaps this is the source of the despair and the doubts—that sometimes, in order to be a human being, one needs to counteract human nature). Will Israel succeed in mobilizing that strength? Or better said, do we clearly understand the significance of failure?

We are certainly not guests in the Middle East. Neither do we need—nor have we received—the explicit permission or agreement of the Arab countries to be here. But in the things I have heard and have quoted in these pages, in the lowered gazes, one may clearly make out some of the invisible webs we are liable to tear in our haste, or indelicacy, or apathy. The wisdom demanded to improve our situation, to improve our relations in the region, and, finally, to be part of it is very great. Not the wisdom of the engineer who builds the fighter jet, or that of the computer whiz—we have those in abundance. Instead, we need wisdom of the heart, the wisdom to know how to behave toward these people, even if they are still our enemies.

Once, when we were weak and dependent on the capriciousness of forceful others, we had no choice but to learn this lesson, and because we had no choice, it had the sour aftertaste of humiliation. Afterward, in the years of our independence, we threw it off, along with other signs of humiliation. But (shouting): "then" is over now.

I cannot conclude without relating something that many Israeli Jews might not know, something that to my mind illuminates in a painful and cruel way the relations this book describes.

"There is not one Arab who does not think to himself about how they will transfer him, nor am I free of that fear," Dr. Nazir Yunes, the surgeon from the Hillel Yafeh Hospital, told me, and added, "It's always on my mind. Either they'll passively press us to the wall and I'll have nothing to do here, or they'll do it physically: bring me to the border, on foot, in a truck, and say, Go! Why are you so surprised?"

"What are you talking about?" I said in anger and shock. "How can you believe that such a thing is at all possible? Who will allow such a thing to happen? Both outside and inside Israel people will fight any such attempt!"

Yunes smiled sorrowfully, nodding his head. "The people who advocate it have enough experience . . . They've already tried such methods on us, and they've succeeded."

I thought he was exaggerating, that he was expressing a totally personal and private fear; I was even insulted to hear such things from Yunes, who is in my eyes living proof that it is possible to realize the idea of a common Israeli citizenship. But afterward, in many other meetings I had, with common people and educated people, with old people and children, the threat of transfer continued to echo, and I felt the living fear. It was amazing and depressing to realize how familiar my interlocutors were with the technical terms and practical details—how they would be taken, where they would be led, in what they would be transported. Many were convinced, for instance, that a peace agreement would include an exchange—the Arabs would be expelled from Israel to the Palestinian state that would be established, and their villages and homes in the Galilee and Wadi Ara and the Negev would be inhabited by the Jewish settlers who would be evacuated from the "territories." One man, who asked to remain anonymous, an astute and impressive person, told me that for years, in a compulsive way, he has examined a certain kind of military truck on Israel's roads in order to estimate "how many of them there are already in Israel, and if there are enough."

I have been thinking about it ever since. People I know, citizens like me, live in the terror of that nightmare. Today, after the fact, I am no longer sure whether the anger I expressed at Dr. Nazir Yunes when he spoke to me about his fear of transfer was not a little overstated and meant to hide (from myself) the fact that somewhere, deep inside me, I knew that his fear was not unreasonable. Who knows what warped use many of us make of this fear to ensure that the problem of the Palestinians in Israel will never be the subject of an open and critical discussion.

When that anonymous man told me about the trucks he counts, I thought to myself, In the book I am now writing, there is the desire, which I do not always know how to realize (but which now, at least, I am confident of), to make room for you here. I sense that this is the opposite of the idea of transfer; that is, an attempt to internalize, finally, the Arabs in Israel, into Israeli life. To bring you to the place set aside for you with us, the Jews in Israel, the place imposed on all of us forty-four years ago and which has remained since then hard and twisted, like scar tissue on a bone that was broken and badly set and every careless movement threatens to break it again, and the entire body learns to move without using it. The place in which, only when we reside there together, we will be able to have our first conversation about all we have distorted and hidden for more than forty years. This, in my eyes, is the reason for this book: it is an invitation, in Hebrew, to enter and begin.

ACKNOWLEDGMENTS

During the process of writing this book I met the few who fight the war for integration. Organizations like Sikui, Forum, the New Israel Fund, and the Institute for Arab Studies of the Givat Haviva—Hakibbutz Ha'artzi College, where I stayed for a number of days and where I could appreciate and wonder at the great amount of work done there. Jews and Arabs work together in all these organizations. Their work and their daily lives demonstrate how possible that goal is.

It is a special pleasure for me to thank Mrs. Sarah Ozacky-Lazar, the research coordinator at Givat Haviva, who guided me during the writing of this book by giving advice, making contacts, setting up meetings, and, especially, by her dedication to relations between the nations. She has for years woven a dialogue with the Arabs in Israel—not out of paternalism, not out of sanctimoniousness, but with internal honesty, enlightenment, and a critical and sober outlook. I would like to dedicate this book to her and to all those who fight for all of us and persist in their dream. May their dream become reality.